PERFORMING THE FAITH

BONHOEFFER *and the* PRACTICE OF NONVIOLENCE

STANLEY HAUERWAS

Brazos Press

A Division of Baker Book House Co
Grand Rapids, Michigan 49516

© 2004 by Stanley Hauerwas

Published by Brazos Press
a division of Baker Book House Company
P.O. Box 6287, Grand Rapids, MI 49516-6287
www.brazospress.com

Printed in the United States of America

Scripture is taken from the New Revised Standard Version of the Bible, copyright 1989 by the Division of Christian Education of the National Council of the Churches of Christ in the USA. Used by permission.

Library of Congress Cataloging-in-Publication Data
Hauerwas, Stanley, 1940–
    Performing the faith : Bonhoeffer and the practice of nonviolence / Stanley Hauerwas.
      p.   cm.
    Includes bibliographical references and index.
    ISBN 1-58743-076-2 (pbk.)
    1. Bonhoeffer, Dietrich, 1906–1945. 2. Church and state—Germany—History—20th century. I. Title.
BX4827.B57H35 2004
261.7′092—dc22   2003020990

To
Louise and Bruce Kaye
Jo and Sam Wells
Darlene and Timothy Kimbrough
Patricia and Keith Meador
Jane and Rowan Williams

Contents

PREFACE

We live in dark times. September 11, 2001, decisively changed American politics for God knows how long. The change, moreover, cannot help but make Americans even more determined by what John Paul II calls the "culture of death" than we were before that fateful day. For American politics to be changed means, given American power, that the politics of the world is changed. I would wish it otherwise, but that is the way things are. To publish a book, even a book that tries to defend nonviolence, in the hope to make things better may be the ultimate foolishness. But writing is what I do. I wish I had some useful suggestions that might make the world after September 11, 2001, better, but I do not. Christians, however, have been given gifts that make it possible to go on when it is not clear how to go on—gifts as simple as being willing to tell one another the truth.

John Howard Yoder and James McClendon were not only my teachers but friends. Few days go by that I do not think of them and give God thanks for their lives and their work. September 11, 2001, has made their absence particularly poignant. I keep thinking they would have known what needs to be said. Many people now expect me to say what John and Jim would have said. I do not feel equal to that task. Thank God there are now many younger folk coming forward who have been shaped by John's and Jim's work who know better what needs to be said and done than I am able to say or to do. I hope that what I have tried to do in *Performing the Faith*, however, will be of some use for those so committed.

As usual I am beholden to many people who make my life possible as well as put up with my refusal not to work. Sarah Freedman continues to do the hard work that brings what I do to print. The Graduate Program in Religion at Duke attracts extraordinary students who make me think harder than I would otherwise wish. What a privilege it is to teach and to be taught by them. I am particularly grateful to Alex Sider and Charlie Collier for reading these essays and helping me prepare them for inclusion in this book. I am also fortunate to be a member of the faculty of the Divinity School at Duke University when many new appointments have been and continue to be made to an already strong faculty. It is a privilege to serve on a faculty with such colleagues. We are in debt to Greg Jones, the Dean of the Divinity School, for the work he has done to make Divinity School a reality.

Rodney Clapp first suggested the possibility of this book. That is not strictly true. Rodney thought the Bonhoeffer essays might make a good small book. I thought about that, but the more I thought about his suggestion the more I saw connections between the Bonhoeffer essays and other essays I had written and and some I was still to write. So Rodney got stuck with a bigger book than the one he first suggested. Thank God Rodney has a sense of humor. Bobbi Jo Heyboer, Rebecca Cooper, and Steve Ayers are tireless workers at Brazos Press. They care deeply about the books they publish because they care deeply about the church. I could not wish for better people to work with in the preparation and distribution of my books.

Paula makes my life possible. I am a gregarious person, which means I forget that I need to know how to be quietly at rest. With great patience Paula has slowly taught me how to be at rest, particularly the rest prayerful worship names. Going to church with Paula is a great joy. Her love of the church, the care with which she celebrates the Eucharist, is an inspiration for me.

Paula and I now worship at the Church of the Holy Family (Episcopal). No one will be well served by trying to explain how we found our way to Holy Family. However, our being at Holy Family helps explain why I have dedicated this book to our Anglican friends Darlene and Timothy Kimbrough, Patricia and Keith Meador, Louise and Bruce Kaye, Jo and Sam Wells, and Jane and Rowan Williams. Darlene, Timothy, Keith, and Patricia are friends from Holy Family. Bruce and Louise are Australians. Jo, Sam, Jane, and Rowan are English (though Rowan is Welsh). Paula and I have many Anglican friends, but these friends have reached out to us from near and far helping us remember that the Christian family makes possible friendship across time and space.

After all the jokes I have told about Anglicans, I suspect it is God's little joke on me that I now worship with Anglicans. Paula and I are well aware that Anglicanism, like all the mainstream Protestant denominations, lacks coherence. But that same incoherent church continues to produce people like Louise, Bruce, Sam, Jo, Timothy, Darlene, Patricia, Keith, Jane, and Rowan who help Paula and me have some intimation of what it might be like to live our lives as Christians. We live in dark times, but God gives us friends who make it possible to see through the darkness. Thank God for friends like these.

INTRODUCTION

*There can only be a community of peace when it does not rest
on lies and injustice. Where a community of peace endangers or
chokes truth and justice, the community of peace must be broken
and battle joined. If the battle is then on both sides really waged for
truth and for justice, the community of peace, though outwardly
destroyed, is made all the deeper and stronger in the battle over this
same cause. But should it become clear that one of the combatants
is only fighting for his own selfish ends, should even this form of the
community of peace be broken, there is revealed that reality which is
the ultimate and only tolerable ground of any community of peace,
the forgiveness of sins. There is a community of peace for Christians
only because one will forgive the other for his sins. The forgiveness
of sins still remains the sole ground of all peace, even where the
order of external peace remains preserved in truth and justice. It is
therefore also the ultimate ground on which all ecumenical work
rests, precisely where the cleavage appears hopeless. For Anglo-
Saxon thought, truth and justice remain constantly subordinate to
the ideal of peace. Indeed, the existence of peace is virtually itself the
proof that peace and justice have been preserved; because the order
of peace is a reality of the Gospel, of the kingdom of God, truth and
justice can never be contrary to it. But it has become clear that precisely this conception is illusory. The reality of the Gospel is not the
external order of peace, not even the peace of the battle for the same
cause, but only the peace of God, which brings about forgiveness of
sins, the reality in which truth and justice are both preserved.*[1]

1. Dietrich Bonhoeffer, *No Rusty Swords*, trans. John Bowden, ed. and introduced by
Edwin Robertson (New York: Harper and Row, 1956), pp. 168–69.

Performing the Faith: Bonhoeffer and the Practice of Nonviolence is no more and hopefully no less than an ongoing commentary on Bonhoeffer's extraordinary claim that if our common life rests on lies and injustice, then we cannot hope to be a community of peace. Accordingly this book is my attempt to display how the church by being the church serves the world. My oft-made claim that the first task of the church is not to make the world more just but to make the world the world has never been a call for the church to retreat from the world. The church can and should only exist in the world. Indeed the church needs the world as much as the world needs the church. What the church owes the world is what the church has been given, that is, the privilege to be a community capable of confessing our sins before God and one another. As Bonhoeffer suggests, our stumbling toward the truth begins with such confession making possible a politics that does not need to justify the evils we have perpetrated on one another, too often legitimated as "necessities."

Contrary to critics who accuse me of tempting Christians to withdraw from the world, my concern has always been to help Christians understand we cannot and should not avoid engagement with the world. I, of course, have tried to remind Christians that there is no reason to privilege the terms the world tries to set for such an engagement. That the church will often have a critical word to say to the world is not to abandon the world but rather to witness to our conviction as Christians that the world, as hard as it may try, cannot abandon being God's good creature. Moreover, Christians can never forget that it is not a matter of "us" against "them," because the line between church and world runs through the life of every Christian.

I assume, moreover, that the "terms" the world sets will be different in one time and place from another time and place. To maintain the distinction between church and world is the necessary ground for the work that needs to be done if the church is to discern what needs to be said to this time and this place. Too often Christians are tempted to rely on past achievements to avoid new challenges. For example, the good work often done in the name of "Christian social ethics" over the last century continued to assume a socially established Christianity. Whether you think such an establishment was a "good thing" or not (and I have argued that, at the very least, such an establishment was ambiguous for the church's mission to the world), such an arrangement no longer exists. I have tried to help us see how the loss of the political and social power of the church in allegedly advanced social orders like America offers Christians a new found freedom for discerning how the church can serve the world in which we now find ourselves.

Performing the Faith therefore represents my attempt to continue the stated purpose of *A Better Hope: Resources for a Church Confronting Capi-*

talism, Democracy, and Postmodernity.[2] In the "Introduction" to *A Better Hope,* I claimed the book was my attempt to provide a less polemical and more constructive engagement with the social order called America. Friends and enemies alike, however, pointed out that old habits are hard to break. Accordingly *A Better Hope* seemed more determined by my criticisms of "liberalism" than by any attempt to provide a constructive alternative. Since I believe that we are more likely to learn who we are or what we think from our friends and even more from our enemies, I grudgingly acknowledge that I did not find the means in *A Better Hope* to express my love or sense of responsibility to serve that part of the world called "America." That my acknowledgement is "grudging" is not only because I think, as I suggested above, that criticism can be an expression of love, but because I do not want essays like "Enduring" and "Captured in Time: Friendship and Aging" (written with Laura Yordy) that appeared in *A Better Hope* overlooked for their constructive implications. What could be more important in our time than for Christians to help us see that we, Christian and non-Christian alike, have all the time in the world to befriend and be befriended by those called "old"? I believe, moreover, that the discovery of such "timefulness" is crucial for any politics that would desire to be just.

In *Performing the Faith* I argue that the church gives no gift to the worlds in which it finds itself more politically important than the formation of a people constituted by the virtues necessary to endure the struggle to hear and speak truthfully to one another. Note: I do not assume that Christians are in some peculiar possession of the truth that legitimates their imposition of that truth on others. Christians qua Christians have no corner on the truth because, as Bonhoeffer argued, to speak truthfully requires the recognition that the One who is the Truth is the living God who often meets us in the face of the stranger. Christians understand that they are the people who have been claimed by the ultimate stranger, that is, the God who would be known through the Jews. Christians cannot, therefore, ever presume that they will not have to learn from those who are not Christians.

That the church exists and must exist if there is to be a world is constitutive of Christian claims about the way things are. "No church, no world" is a robust claim that all that is is created and that creation rightly understood has an end. Which is what Christians have meant when they say that our lives as well as all that is must be understood eschatologically. We were created to enjoy God, to share in God's enjoyment of God's creation, to have the time in a world that too often believes there is not "enough" time to be timeful creatures. Such a time Christians believe

2. Grand Rapids: Brazos, 2000.

has been given to us through the life, death, and resurrection of Jesus. Creation and redemption name the great drama in which we become participants, performers, in God's care of all that is. In more formal theological terms this means that the distinction between church and world is more fundamental than the distinction between nature and grace. Elsewhere I have argued that an account of nature is unavoidable for Christian theology if we are to rightly acknowledge that God graciously desires that all that is exists even though existence was not required given the relation between the Father, Son, and Holy Spirit.[3] But the nature/grace distinction can and too often has become an invitation for Christians to forget that our created status means all that is is contingent "all the way down." The distinction between church and world is the theologically primitive distinction, just to the extent that Christian theology must insist that we can only know the truth about who we are by attending to a story. By "theologically primitive" I mean that even the difference between creation and redemption cannot be used to make considerations concerning the relation between church and world secondary.[4]

3. See, for example, the chapter entitled "The Truth about God: The Decalogue as Condition for Truthful Speech," in *Sanctify Them in the Truth: Holiness Exemplified* (Nashville: Abingdon, 1998), pp. 37–59.

4. This comment reflects one of my worries about how H. Richard Niebuhr reasoned in his famous book, *Christ and Culture*. "How H. Richard Niebuhr Reasoned" refers to the now-famous essay with the same name by John Howard Yoder that appears in *Authentic Transformation: A New Vision of Christ and Culture* (Nashville: Abingdon, 1996), pp. 31–89. Yoder's essay has been dismissed by James Gustafson in a "Preface" Gustafson wrote to the republication of *Christ and Culture* (San Francisco: Harper, 2001). Gustafson characterizes Yoder's critical essay as "laced with more *ad hominem* arguments and fortified with more gratuitous footnotes than anything I ever read by scholars in the field of Christian ethics" (p. xxiii). I obviously disagree with Gustafson's characterization of Yoder's essay, but one of the issues I wished Yoder might have developed more is the way Niebuhr uses the creation/redemption distinction to trump any attempt to think eschatologically (not to mention apocalyptically) in terms of the relation between church and world. Yoder observes that "the New Testament writers could not say with Niebuhr that nature or creation is the domain of the Father and history that of the Spirit, and therefore not subject to the Son. Nor could the New Testament writers agree in contrasting the will of the Father or of the Spirit with the teaching and example of the Son. Yet further: in a few New Testament texts Jesus is described as uniquely identified both with 'The Father' (John 14:6ff) and with 'The Spirit' (Chapters 14–16)" (p. 60). Yoder quite rightly calls attention to the implications concerning the Trinity given Niebuhr's analysis, but equally problematic is Niebuhr's use of the creation/redemption scheme to make the church invisible. I would, moreover, contend that the invisibility of the church in *Christ and Culture* is the result of Niebuhr's failure to take account of the eschatological character of the Christian faith. I realize this may appear an odd criticism of a man who wrote *The Kingdom of God in America*, but unfortunately I think anyone so determinatively influenced by Troeltsch as Niebuhr was would necessarily have difficulty with eschatology. You can be fairly sure that when transcendence, especially in the name of "radical monotheism," becomes the

To learn to tell the truth, in a world eschatologically constituted, requires the never-ending work to discover the connections between the contingencies that constitute existence. Such connections are displayed in narratives that at once constitute who we are but also hide from us who we are. For we desire to deny our contingency by living as if the way things are is the way things have to be. Violence lies in our attempt to show the "necessity" that the way we live is the way we must live. The quest for certainty is always an indication that we fear acknowledging that our lives always begin in the middle. If we are to live truthful lives we must recognize that any truth to be had in this life requires the ongoing, never-ending discoveries of the connections made possible by a truthful story. Christians call this way of life "faith."[5]

I began *In Good Company: The Church as Polis* with the claim that "Christianity is connections."[6] I thought such a claim particularly appropriate in a book that struggled with questions of Christian unity. Yet I think theology is always the attempt to make articulate the connections necessary if we are to understand what Christians believe and why they believe what they believe rightly shapes their lives and their understanding of the world in which we find ourselves. Accordingly theology is never finished, because new occasions force us to discover connections between what we say as Christians and what we do that we had not anticipated. Thus my attempt in *Performing the Faith* to develop the connections between truthfulness, nonviolence, and the process necessary for the discovery of goods in common rightly called politics.[7]

---

hallmark of a theologian's understanding of God, eschatology will disappear all together or, at the very best, have a secondary role.

5. Rowan Williams puts the matter this way: "Living in truth means living where Jesus lives. . . . When Jesus speaks of being 'consecrated in the truth,' the reader is immediately invited to connect this with Jesus' consecration of himself, which can only mean the death he is to endure. Truth and death are brought together with alarming closeness: truthful living is the full acceptance of the real and concrete danger of pursuing faithfulness in this world; it is an acceptance of risk and mortality. It is also a letting go of what denies such mortality, what deceives us into believing that faith will not put us at risk—literally at risk of persecution and death, and more widely at risk of losing those securities and defences which tame the God we worship in Christ." Rowan Williams, *Christ on Trial: How the Gospel Unsettles Our Judgement* (London: Fount, 2000), p. 78.

6. Stanley Hauerwas, *In Good Company: The Church as Polis* (Notre Dame, Ind.: University of Notre Dame Press, 1995), p. xiii.

7. I am aware that having written so much makes readers wary of even knowing where to begin to get a handle on what I am about. My hope is that a reader can begin anywhere because where anyone might begin hopefully will raise questions about how I can say "X" if I also say "Y," which will only require further reading. For example the claims made in this sentence concerning the common good can be found in my early essay, "Politics, Vision, and the Common Good," which appeared in *Vision and Virtue: Essays in Christian Ethical Reflection* (Notre Dame, Ind.: University of Notre Dame Press, 1981), pp. 222–40.

Large themes to be sure, that no book or a lifetime of books could hope to treat adequately, but you have to start somewhere.

Performing the Faith starts with Bonhoeffer. That I begin with Bonhoeffer is the result of contingencies—the most important that Bill Cavanaugh was one of my students when I taught at the University of Notre Dame. He says I saved him from becoming a lawyer. Instead he has become a theologian whose work is attracting the attention it deserves.[8] Bill and Peter Scott are editing the *Blackwell Companion to Political Theology*. Bill called me saying he and Peter would like me to do the article on Reinhold Niebuhr. I said "No way." If I do Niebuhr one more time, people will think I have a fetish. I said "Who do you have left?" Bill indicated Bonhoeffer, and I said "I would gladly take him." I did so, as I explain in the first essay on Bonhoeffer, because I owe him so much.

I took a summer and read and reread much that Bonhoeffer had written as well as some of the extremely good scholarly work about him. I expected to find myself in deep sympathy with Bonhoeffer, but I had not expected to discover how similar Bonhoeffer's ecclesial reflections were to lessons I have learned from John Howard Yoder. I am no Bonhoeffer scholar, which means I look forward to having those who are tell me where I may or may not have gotten Bonhoeffer wrong, but I think my account of Bonhoeffer offers a different perspective on his work. I acknowledge my presentation of Bonhoeffer makes Bonhoeffer sound very much like Yoder (and me), but I think I have made a good case for why that is not as crazy as it sounds. I confess I hope my account of Bonhoeffer makes life difficult for my critics who hold Bonhoeffer in high regard but dismiss me as a "sectarian." If I am right about Bonhoeffer, then they must equally dismiss Bonhoeffer.[9]

The book was originally published by Fides Press in 1974. Even in that early essay I was aware of the difference between a politics understood in terms of the common good and a politics that aspired to no more than "the common interest." Accordingly my criticisms of liberalism then and now draw on accounts of democratic process and speech that depend on a notion of goods that are not the product of choice. Christians rightly believe that the good in common, which gives order to the many goods of life, is God, but such a view does not necessarily entail, as is often assumed, theocracy. For if the God who is our good is the God found in Christ, then Christians can only exemplify through our worship of God what such a politics entails. Coercion is simply unthinkable for a politics constituted by worship of such a God.

8. See, for example, Cavanaugh's *Torture and Eucharist* (Oxford, U.K.: Oxford University Press, 1998).

9. In particular I hope such critics will attend to Bonhoeffer's criticisms of Troeltsch, to be found in his *Sanctorum Communio: A Theological Study of the Sociology of the Church*, trans. Reinhard Krauss and Nancy Lukens (Minneapolis: Fortress, 1998). For example, Bonhoeffer observes, "the sanctorum communio, the Christian community of love as a sociological type, is dependent upon the word of God, and it alone. According to the promise in Isaiah 55:11, it is present within every historical form in which

I hope, moreover, that I have established a case for Bonhoeffer's continuing relevance. I suspect some assume that Bonhoeffer's (and Barth's) work was peculiarly suited to a totalitarian context that makes his reflections less useful for us who live in democracies. As I try to show, however, such an understanding of Bonhoeffer's work fails to grapple with his understanding of why no regime, including democratic regimes, can hope to be just without also being truthful. But the truth necessary to sustain a nonviolent politics is not just "there," but requires the ongoing and often painful telling and retelling of the stories that constitute the legitimating narratives for the good governance of a people.[10] If "democracy" names those forms of social and political life committed to the ongoing testing of the stories that legitimate or at least make intelligible the cooperation necessary to discover the goods in common, then I certainly think Christians have a stake in sustaining forms of life so constituted. Yet I continue to share John Howard Yoder's concern that governments that claim to rule in the name of "the people" are adept at hiding not only from "the people" but themselves the violence inherent in the order they have learned to call "peace."[11]

One of the criticisms that some may make of the account of politics I provide through my presentation of Bonhoeffer's work is that I do not deal with the very *esse* of politics, that is, power. Nonviolence may be a correlative of truthfulness, but it may be objected that politics is

---

the word is preached. The distinction between church and sect suggested by Weber and Troeltsch is untenable both historically and sociologically. Based on the efficacy of the word, we must believe the sanctorum communio to be present even with the sociologically unique type of the Roman Catholic church. Striving to attain the true church and pure doctrine is inherently necessary" (pp. 270–71). It may be objected that Bonhoeffer misunderstands what Weber and Troeltsch meant by "ideal types," but I think it is clear Bonhoeffer understood them very well indeed. The problem for Bonhoeffer with Weber and Troeltsch was not their "method," but their assumption that the work of the Holy Spirit was not itself a "sociology."

10. This emphasis on the importance of narratives for truthful accounts of our individual as well as common lives has recently been explored by Bernard Williams in his *Truth and Truthfulness* (Princeton, N.J.: Princeton University Press, 2002), pp. 233–69. Williams commenting on Hayden White's alleged rejection of historical truth observes that White rightly recognizes that history is made up of truths. But that is only the start of the problem since the truths in any history are a selection, so issues of relevance never go away. But even more important is the issue of the story that is being told. As Williams puts it, "With history as with some everyday narrative, every statement in it can be true and it can still tell the wrong story" (p. 244).

11. See Yoder's essay "The Christian Case for Democracy," in his book *The Priestly Kingdom: Social Ethics as Gospel* (Notre Dame, Ind.: University of Notre Dame Press, 2001), pp. 151–71. I am grateful to the University of Notre Dame for keeping this book originally published in 1984 in print. They did so on the condition I would write a "Foreword" to the 2001 edition. I was pleased to do so but I worry that some may have the impression that by reading me they will have read Yoder. There is no substitute for the patient reading of Yoder's work.

not about truth or nonviolence but rather about the necessity of coercion for sustaining any cooperative work in the world as we know it. I acknowledge that these essays do not confront head-on the challenge that comes from those who pride themselves on being political realists, but I refuse to let such a view of politics, influential and pervasive as it is, determine the terms of the debate. At the very least I think that recent work about the diffuse character of power has helped us see that "realism's" realism about power at the very least lacks subtlety. There is no greater power than the power of a community of truth.

I noted at the beginning of this "Introduction" that this book is an ongoing commentary on Bonhoeffer's claim that a community of peace can only exist if it does not rest on lies and injustice. Astute readers will notice that Bonhoeffer claims that such a community is possible for Christians through the forgiveness of sins. I cannot pretend that *Performing the Faith* adequately explores why the forgiveness of sins is necessary if we are to discover the nonviolence truthfulness makes possible. The chapter "Punishing Christians" below certainly touches on the interrelation of forgiveness, truthfulness, and justice, but much more needs to be said.

The interrelation between forgiveness, truthfulness, and nonviolence has been a theme at the heart of my work for many years.[12] The essay "Why Time Cannot and Should Not Heal the Wounds of History, But Time Has Been and Can Be Redeemed," included in *A Better Hope*, is my most sustained attempt to develop the connection between the practices of forgiveness, nonviolence, and the formation of truthful memory.[13] In other essays I have suggested that the modern discipline of history too often is a form of forgetting just to the extent that a false objectivity is used to occlude whose story is being told and to what purpose.[14] If we are to tell our stories truthfully and, more importantly, live acknowledging the violence that comes with the gifts of our past, we can do so only if we have the skill to be forgiven. "Penance" names the search for

12. I should like to think that some of the work of my students has done better than anything I have done toward working out these themes. I am thinking in particular of Greg Jones, *Embodying Forgiveness: A Theological Analysis* (Grand Rapids: Eerdmans, 1995); William Cavanaugh, *Torture and Eucharist: Theology, Politics, and the Body of Christ* (Oxford, U.K.: Basil Blackwell, 1998); and Daniel Bell, *Liberation Theology after the End of History: The Refusal to Cease Suffering* (London: Routledge, 2001).

13. *A Better Hope*, pp. 139–54.

14. See, for example, my essay "Christians in the Hands of Flaccid Secularists: Theology and Moral Inquiry in the Modern University," in *Sanctify Them in the Truth*, pp. 201–18. Many of the chapters in my *Wilderness Wanderings: Probing Twentieth-Century Theology and Philosophy* (Boulder, Colo.: Westview, 1997) touch on this theme. For a wonderful counterhistory of America see Howard Zinn, *A People's History of America* (San Francisco: HarperCollins, 1999).

the skills through which we avoid the false stories that would justify the violence of the past, which cannot help but ensure an even more violent present and future.

Some may be puzzled why I have included in this book the chapters in the middle section, "Truthful Performances." I hope after having read chapters 3 through 6 the reader will understand why these chapters are crucial for the case I am trying to make about the relation between truthfulness and nonviolence. If, as I argue in "Connections Created and Contingent" (ch. 4), it is contingency all the way down, then the kind of performance James Fodor and I try to display in "Performing Faith" (ch. 3) is a necessary resource for Christians if we are in fact to be an alternative to the violent stories that grip our lives.[15] Such performances remind us that truth can never be guaranteed by a theory, but rather is the ongoing struggle to locate the lies that lay in our speech. Indeed few temptations are more inimical for our ability to speak truthfully to one another than the attempt to secure truth against the contingency of our existence.

The chapters in "Truthful Performances," moreover, develop some of the suggestions begun in the first chapter on Bonhoeffer and in particular the understanding of God that Bonhoeffer thought necessary if we are to make sense of the kind of life to which Christians are called. The chapters in the middle section make candid the connections—indeed, the metaphysical connections—that the Christian worship of God makes possible. Through having our bodies bent toward God through praise, we are enabled to see that all that is is "charged with the grandeur of God."[16] Accordingly these chapters reprise motifs of my early work. The

15. For an extraordinary account of the kind of work we so desperately need if we are to understand the significance of performance for the formation of the Christian imagination, see Sarah Beckwith, *Signifying God: Social Relation and Symbolic Act in the York Corpus Christi Plays* (Chicago: University of Chicago Press, 2001). Beckwith argues that the "Corpus Christi theater in York had as its primary premise that the 'token of the body of Christ is not the thing tokened.' The pageants assume at once a noncoincidence of token and thing tokened and the radically ambiguous force of the demonstrative pronoun at the heart of the mass. That is the force at once of their symbolic energy and their liturgical power. As such they constitute a complex kind of para-liturgy; the very gap between an amateur (known) local actor and sacred role, and the juxtaposition of word and thing onstage help to make the Corpus Christi theater a commentary upon and an interaction with the liturgy of the mass and offices. In that they seek both to embody and to show the limits of the presence of Christ in the body of the faithful, they are also an emphatic extenuation as well as a diagnosis of the interrelationship between eucharist and ecclesiology. They are a complex metaphorical predication of the body of Christ, and as such are not reducible to orthodox doctrines that defend consecration and spectacle as the central moment and meaning of the mass as a priestly sacrifice" (p. 135).

16. Gerard Manley Hopkins, "God's Grandeur," in *Modern American and Modern British Poetry*, edited by Louis Untermeyer (New York: Harcourt, Brace, and World, 1953), p. 429.

title (as well as the content) of my first book, *Vision and Virtue: Essays in Christian Ethical Reflection*, still names a set of essential connections for me.[17] I still believe you can only act in a world you can see, but you can only see by learning to say.[18] Just as important, however, is my attempt in these chapters to suggest why no account of the Christian life is adequate that ignores the beauty of God's creation as well as the beauty created in response to that creation we sometimes call art.

In "The Narrative Turn: Thirty Years Later" (ch. 5) I explore the importance of narrative for how moral rationality should be understood. But just as important, I try to show why the significance of narrative is a correlate of the Christian contention that only God can act without loss. To call attention to narrative is, therefore, not an attempt to avoid claims about the truthfulness of Christian convictions, but rather is constitutive of the claim that all that is is created. That claim has everything to do with our ability to see the beauty of God's creation—a beauty that refuses to submit to our prideful desire to control what we fear we cannot subject to our wills. To be a Christian is to undergo continual training necessary in learning how to be "out of control." That is why "good art," even as it attracts us, often frightens.

There is also something "new" in this section, that is, I actually write about Wittgenstein. I hope that the work I have done in the past manifests how deeply I have tried to absorb the lessons one should learn from Wittgenstein, but those lessons are not easily learned because they require such a profound transformation of the intellectual and moral habits so characteristic of modernity. It is my hope, however, that the chapter "Connections Created and Contingent" (ch. 4) will not only make more explicit the connections between contingency, narrative, and the necessity of witness, but may help some better understand why "my work," as I suggested above, can only be investigative and occasional. That the way I work is occasional, however, makes it all the more important that there are in fact connections between my essays that my readers can discover.[19] In particular the chapters in the middle section

17. See n. 7 above.

18. I confess, however, I am embarrassed by early formulations of this claim. For example, in the "Introduction" to *Vision and Virtue* I observe that "we do not come to see just by looking but by training our vision through the metaphors and symbols that constitute our central convictions" (p. 2). I am not sure why I used the language of symbols, but it is clearly a mistake. "Metaphors" maybe, but certainly not "symbols." Moreover the claim that we "train our vision" still suggests I remained captured by stronger notions of agency than I now think warranted.

19. John Webster helpfully distinguishes between the occasional and contextual nature of theology. He observes, "all theology is occasional: bound up in its conception of its own calling is a certain reading of the circumstances into which it speaks. The term 'occasional' is much to be preferred to the more familiar 'contextual.' Talk of theology

of this book should help the reader understand better why I have long contended that considerations of the truthfulness of Christian claims about the world cannot be separated from lives lived truthfully.[20]

I have written the chapters in the middle section keeping in mind the claims I make in *With the Grain of the Universe: The Church's Witness and Natural Theology* about "witness."[21] In a recent letter to me in response to the "Book Symposium" on *With the Grain of the Universe* in *Modern Theology*, Dennis O'Brien, a good Wittgensteinian, spells out how he understands the relation of conviction, witness, and evidence, and I find that very helpful.[22] He suggests that it is very interesting to watch what happens when you transpose questions of faith into those of artistic creation.

> Cézanne looks at his contemporary impressionists and adopts the *conviction* that one should introduce a certain rigor and order into landscape painting. "Redoing Poussin in nature" as he put it. If he actually creates a new painting that is a *revelation*. It was not enough for Cezanne to have the slogan or the intent, he had to actually create a vision which

---

as 'contextual' readily suggests that contexts are given, transparent and self-evident to those who operate in them, and that they require no theology for their elucidation; and it can also, more alarmingly, make context into a fate before which theological reflection is passive, to which it must adapt or reconcile itself if it wants to survive. At its best, of course, attention to 'context' can remind theology that there is no pure language of Zion, and that theology's conceptual equipment is borrowed from elsewhere. But at its worst it is a form of mental and spiritual laziness, an unwillingness to admit that theology must go about its own business if it is to speak prophetically and compassionately about the gospel to its neighbors. Much better, therefore, simply to speak of the 'occasions' towards which theology directs itself. Theology is responsible for articulating a theological reading of these occasions. It needs to learn to interpret its present situation, not merely as a set of cultural norms or constraints or opportunities, but as an episode in the history of the gospel's dealing with humanity, as one further chapter in the history of holiness and its overcoming of disorder, wickedness and unbelief." John Webster, *Word and Church: Essays in Christian Dogmatic* (Edinburgh, U.K.: T & T Clark, 2001), pp. 4–5.

20. In *Christ on Trial* Rowan Williams suggests that the "historic language of faith," that is, the language often called "doctrine," is meant "to hold us still before Jesus" (p. 37). He explains, "what we most need is a certain distance from the underlying attitude which assumes that doctrinal statements are there first and foremost to assert a *position* which may be accepted or contested, like other positions—rather than being there to place us in a certain kind of relationship to truth, such that we can be changed by it" (p. 39). Williams later suggests that "God is in the connections we cannot make," which I take to be a reminder that Christians of all people can never forget that God is incomprehensible. Christians need to recover the confident speech of praise of God, and we will be able to do so if we do not forget that all our speech is inadequate.

21. Grand Rapids: Brazos, 2001.

22. Paul Griffiths and Peter Ochs kindly wrote essays responding to *With the Grain of the Universe* to which I responded. Their essays and my response are to be found in *Modern Theology* 19/1 (January 2003): 67–102.

instantiated the slogan *and* was judged to be artistically significant. Cezanne was, I suppose, someone who was not only *convinced* that order should be inscribed in landscape, he was also a *witness* in his *works* to that conviction. His actual *oeuvre* is, in turn, *evidence* of the value of his conviction.

O'Brien observes that he thinks that the artistic case puts the connection between conviction–witness–evidence in a quite different framework than those often associated with some "scientific" epistemology. The artistic case does so because art relates to the singular, what O'Brien calls "signatured truth," and therefore depends on "revelation."[23] We simply do not know if there can be landscape painting until it is actually done. Moreover we must remember that for many centuries it was not done, just as sculpture is rare in Byzantine art. According to O'Brien, one might believe that landscape art would be possible or that one could move "beyond" impressionism as Cézanne intended,

> but one would not be able to validate that conviction until a named artist actually impressed a signatured high value into his work. The proof of Cezanne's conviction is not some abstract idea that has been validated, it just is Cezanne's work. If I am Picasso and I see for the first time the work of Cezanne, I am *convinced* that this direction in art is of great importance. What is odd, however, is that I do not copy Cezanne, I create my own signatured work. In that way, I witness to the value of Cezanne's turn in landscape painting but in a manner which is itself singular, another sort of revelation—but also within a specifiable tradition of art.

23. For O'Brien's understanding of "signatured truth," see his *The Idea of a Catholic University* (Chicago: University of Chicago Press, 2002), pp. 33–46. I am extremely grateful to Dennis O'Brien for his permission to quote from his letter. I should say O'Brien's remarks are primarily in response to Paul Griffiths's essay "Witness and Conviction in *With the Grain of the Universe*" (see n. 19). I will have to leave it to others to assess O'Brien's claim that the connection between conviction-witness-evidence is quite different in science than in art. I am not at all sure that science is not also "signatured." The assumption that science is not signatured I suspect is thought to be an adequate account of science because of the widespread assumption that a science is intelligible in and of itself. So to understand a science, you do not need to know the history of that science. That assumption is one I would certainly want to challenge. I suspect, however, that the attempt to explore the manner in which science and art may be similar or different cannot be fruitfully undertaken by using general categories such as "science" and "art."

Some familiar with my work may worry that my use of O'Brien's account of art, and in particular the use of the general notion of "revelation," may suggest I think the Christian understanding of revelation is an example of a more general account of revelation. Such an interpretation, however, would be a mistake. O'Brien's use of revelation in an artistic context is meant no more than to provide an illuminating analogy. In short, O'Brien is not trying to offer some general account of "revelation."

O'Brien observes that the close linkage of conviction–witness (works)–evidence he thinks characteristic of the artistic case does not make the relation between convictions, witness, and evidence analytic in a logical sense. Rather we can ask questions about what the artist's convictions were (to redo Poussin), what the works are actually like, and how the works give evidence that the conviction makes sense in art. "Linking the three is a matter of perception and judgment—'Yes, I see what he wanted to do, but he failed to bring it off, and frankly, I doubt that it is a possible direction for art at all.'"

Though O'Brien thinks Wittgenstein's notion of "language use" is quite different than a pragmatist's sense of "use," I think the account he has given of the relation between conviction, witness, and evidence is quite similar to the account I provide of James's understanding of the "will to believe" in *With the Grain of the Universe*.[24] That account, moreover, is crucial for understanding the way I display Barth's *Dogmatics* in *With the Grain of the Universe*. Barth's *Dogmatics* is a performance, a witness, through which we learn the skills to go on in a way no doubt different from Barth. For there is no way to be faithful to Barth without being different from Barth. That is why Dietrich Bonhoeffer, exactly because he followed Barth in his own way, witnesses to the power of Barth's performance.

I think O'Brien's use of the work of artists to clarify the relation between convictions, witness, and evidence is extremely illuminating, but art is art and not the gospel.[25] The kind of witness that is the church is different from the witness of the artist. It is possible to distinguish the artists from their art, but the witness of the church cannot be distinguished from that to which the church witnesses.[26] That the church is often less than it is meant to be is but part of the witness the church must make to the world on behalf of the world; for nothing is more important for the world than for Christians to learn to confess our sins. Accordingly, Christians can never assume we have "finally gotten it right," exactly because we worship the One who comes often into our lives as

24. See Dennis O'Brien, "The Unity of Wittgenstein's Thought," *International Philosophical Quarterly* 6/1 (March 1966): 45–70. In his essay in *Modern Theology* Ochs suggests I have a "pragmatic theory of truth." I have no reason to deny that may be the case, but I worry a bit about such a characterization because I prefer to remain agnostic about the need for a theory, even a pragmatic theory. See Ochs, "On Hauerwas' *With the Grain of the Universe*," p. 78 (see n. 19).

25. Though I think if the gospel did not produce art, it would not be the gospel. A strong claim to be sure, but one I begin to explore in "Suffering Beauty: The Liturgical Formation of Christ's Body" (ch. 6).

26. See, for example, the chapter "The Church as God's New Language," in *Christian Existence Today* (Grand Rapids: Brazos, 2001), pp. 47–66. I am extremely grateful to Brazos Press for keeping this book in print.

the stranger we had not anticipated. For Christians, truth can never be a possession but rather must be received as a gift. Christian tradition rightly understood is one long investigation provoked by the questions that must be asked by a people who worship the Father, Son, and Holy Spirit. As O'Brien suggests, the relationship between conviction, witness, and evidence is not analytic in art nor is it analytic for the Christian faith. Both art and Christianity require skills hard won, but the skills to be a Christian are finally matters of life and death.

The Christian practice of nonviolence is one of those sets of skills required by the Christian conviction that the powers that draw on our fear of death have been defeated. If the chapters in "Truthful Performances" are meant as a commentary on the first chapter of this book, "Dietrich Bonhoeffer's Political Theology," the chapters in "Performing Nonviolence" are meant as commentary on "Bonhoeffer Performing the Faith." It is my hope, moreover, that this group of chapters on nonviolence makes clear that the church's practice of nonviolence does not require the church to withdraw from the world but rather provides the condition necessary for the church's service to the world. What the church has to give to the world is a politics of nonviolence made possible by a people who have learned through worship to speak truthfully to one another. Such a politics can never presume it knows what counts and does not count as "violence." Pacifism and nonviolence are inadequate to describe the kind of peace that should be characteristic of Christian worship. Pacifism is just too "passive" and nonviolence too dependent on being "not violence." We can only begin to understand the violence that grips our lives by being embedded in more determinative practices of peace—practices as common and as extraordinary as prayer and the singing of hymns.

Christian pacifism is not a heroic ethic for the few. That is why it is so important for those committed to Christian nonviolence to help ourselves and those not so committed to see that our lives in fact are constituted by nonviolent practices we often fail to acknowledge. Pacifists do not, or at least should not, think their lives are less compromised than those who defend the use of violence in support of the neighbor. There is no "safe harbor" for pacifist or just warriors. It is crucial to remember, as I suggest in "Explaining Christian Nonviolence" (ch. 7), that Christians are never pacifists or just warriors, but rather first and foremost we are disciples of Jesus Christ.[27] "Pacifism" names the ongoing form of

---

27. I was reminded of the importance of this way of putting the matter by Enda Mc-Donagh. Enda and I have collaborated on drafting an "Appeal" that calls for the end of war. We do not think such an appeal to be utopian. We know that war will continue. We simply want people to begin to remember when they say "war," they are describing a way of life that Christ has ended. At a conference at Notre Dame in which Enda and I presented

habituation necessary to force our imaginations to discover forms of life otherwise unknown or, if imagined, too often described by those who think there is no alternative to violence as "unrealistic."

The chapter on punishment ("Punishing Christians") is my attempt to force myself to think through the challenge of punishment for those committed to nonviolence. Punishment cannot and should not be avoided. Moreover, it cannot be denied that punishment may be more or less violent. By calling attention to how the church should (and has) punished, I hope to suggest that there are alternatives to the violent and ineffective forms of punishment so characteristic of our times. At the very least what the church owes the world is examples. If the church does not know how to punish through excommunication, a form of punishment shaped by the hope of reconciliation, then we have nothing to offer the world.

The essay on punishment is also my attempt to provide an apologetic for Christian nonviolence. I suspect that one of the reasons many Christians cannot say they are pacifists is that they think pacifism is simply assumed to be "unrealistic," e.g., someone needs to stand in the way of violent people in order to protect the innocent. Christians can acknowledge that those who feel called to be police do so in good faith hoping to make the world less violent, but we also think we can never accept the world's violence as a given. There is, therefore, no reason pacifists cannot join with those committed to just policing to try to find less violent ways for the police to perform their duties.[28] Such an exploration I suspect would force not only a more critical focus on who should be a policeman or how police work should be done, but also raise fundamental issues about what kind of societal practices need to be in place if those called to the police function are to avoid becoming cynical or indifferent.

Rowan Williams, Archbishop of Canterbury, in his Dimbleby Lecture (2002) interestingly calls attention to the challenge punishment presents for those living in societies like modern England. His observations about punishment follow his account of the loss of politics in what he calls the emerging "market states." According to Williams, such states are now servants of global capitalism, which means that they are unable to

---

our "Appeal," Enda rightly reminded the conference that Christians are not first pacifist or just warriors, but disciples of Christ. In that reminder, Enda McDonagh, a priest of the Roman Catholic Church, and John Howard Yoder are in fundamental agreement. The text of the "appeal" has been published in *Quaker Theology* 2 (fall 2002): 71–79.

28. See, for example, Tobias Wainwright's "From Police Officers to Peace Officers," in *The Wisdom of the Cross: Essays in Honor of John Howard Yoder*, ed. Stanley Hauerwas, Chris Huebner, Harry Huebner, and Mark Thiessen Nation (Grand Rapids: Eerdmans, 1999), pp. 84–114.

be the focus for conversations necessary to discover goods in common. Rather, market states derive their legitimacy by trying to provide insurance to voters who seek the maximum possible freedom without the corresponding risks. Such states push "politics towards a consumerist model, with the state as the guarantor of 'purchasing power', it raises short-term expectations. By raising short-term expectations, it invites instability, reactive administration, rule by opinion poll and pressure."[29]

The problem with such states, according to Williams, is the loss of any account to legitimate, much less make coherent, activities as basic as the education of the youth. To educate well requires a confidence in a tradition necessary for children to become adults who are able to make critical judgments about the common life. The archbishop argues that to meet the challenge of education in such traditions requires some account of our existence that shows how each of us exists first in relation to something other than ourselves, our needs, our instincts. For to "see or know anything adequately is to be aware of its relation to the eternal. So that we care—say—about the environment not simply because of concern for the human future of our descendants (since we see them in potential relation to God and therefore as people having a claim to live in an environment that is not ruined), but also because of the prior relation that the material world to itself, has to its maker."

Accordingly our immediate agenda cannot exhaust what can be said about the world. This is particularly important, according to Archbishop Williams, when considering long-term moral and social issues such as penal policy. For there are things

> that must be said about penal policy if you want to see both criminal and victim in the light of their prior relation to God, not just in relation to each other or to "society." Penal policy should, in a religious perspective, be asking about how everyone involved grows in human maturity. Without that, there is no mending of the relations broken by crime; but it can't happen unless there is some radical awareness of a person's distinctiveness in relation to God. And I'm not talking about a sentimental belief in the innate capacities of the criminal, let alone seeing the criminal as victim; it's simply a recognition that some presence, some other relationship is at work in the offender, over and above what is involved in dealing with the offence itself.

"Punishing Christians" is my attempt to at least begin to think through not only how Christians should think about punishment, but how we should practice punishment. If Christians are to have anything to say

29. Rowan Williams's "The Dimbleby Lecture, 2002" can be found on the Archbishop's Web site at http://www.archbishopofcanterbury.org/sermons_speeches/021219.html.

about punishment to social orders like America or England, we will do so only if we are freed from the sentimental humanism that too often shapes the speech and imagination of those who call for prison reform or the end of the death penalty. The church owes the world exemplification of the way of life made possible by the death and resurrection of Jesus. Christians should never assume that societies like America or England are unable to respond to the witness of the church even on matters like punishment. The God we worship is after all the Lord of life and death making impossible the loss of hope.

Performing the Faith ends with my reflections on September 11, 2001. That it does so is not only appropriate but necessary. Pacifists do have something to say about September 11, 2001. Too often it is assumed that all pacifists can say when faced by events like September 11, 2001, are platitudes such as "Give peace a chance." Of course we should want to give peace a chance, but we cannot confuse the reigning order with peace. If what I have argued in *Performing the Faith* is right, pacifists must begin with the refusal to accept the lies that make "war" the only response to September 11, 2001.[30] If "peace is to have a chance," it must be a peace that refuses to underwrite the culture of death that has determined the American reactions to September 11, 2001.

I have followed my chapter on September 11, 2001, with the sermon I preached in the Divinity School Chapel on the first anniversary of the destruction of the World Trade Center and the attack on the Pentagon. The sermon, I hope, suggests that Christians who are Americans (and I count myself as belonging to that species) are caught between two quite different stories. There is no way that the stories can both be true requiring, as they do, two quite different kinds of people with equally incompatible understandings of reality. Christians cannot nor should we deny that the stories we associate with being American deeply grip our lives. We also have to be truthful about that. But at the very least by being forced to confess our complicity with the death-avoidance practices of America, we can at least begin to offer an alternative to our neighbors.

The prayer in the *Book of Common Prayer* we are given to pray after we have received the body and blood of Christ is this:

> Eternal God, heavenly Father,
> you have graciously accepted us as living members
> of your Son our Savior Jesus Christ,

---

30. For my response to those who try to justify the war against terrorism on just war grounds, see my "In Time of War," *First Things* 120 (February 2002): 11–15. Alex Sider and I have also written a response to Darrell Cole's "Listening to Pacifists" (*First Things* 125 [August/September 2003: 22–25]) called "Pacifism Redux" (*First Things* 128 [December 2002]: 2–3).

and you have fed us with spiritual food
in the Sacrament of his Body and Blood.
Send us now into the world in peace,
and grant us strength and courage
to love and serve you
with gladness and singleness of heart;
through Christ our Lord. Amen.

To pray that prayer is what the church owes the world. If this book in some small way helps Christians regain the significance of such prayers I will be deeply grateful.

I

BONHOEFFER ON POLITICS AND TRUTH

1

DIETRICH BONHOEFFER'S
POLITICAL THEOLOGY

1. THE FRAGMENTS THAT WERE BONHOEFFER'S LIFE AND WORK

The primary confession of the Christian before the world is the deed which interprets itself. If the deed is to have become a force, then the world itself will long to confess the Word. This is not the same as loudly shrieking out propaganda. This Word must be preserved as the most sacred possession of the community. This is a matter between God and the community, not between the community and the world. It is the Word of recognition between friends, not a word to use against enemies. This attitude was first learned at baptism. The deed alone is our confession of faith before the world.[1]

So wrote Bonhoeffer in 1932 just before the German church struggle with Hitler began. This may seem an odd passage to begin an essay on Bonhoeffer's political theology, but it is so only if one assumes a distinction can be made between Bonhoeffer's theology, at least his early

1. Dietrich Bonhoeffer, "The Nature of the Church," in *A Testament to Freedom: The Essential Writings of Dietrich Bonhoeffer*, ed. Geoffrey Kelly and F. Burton Nelson, trans. John Bowden (San Francisco: HarperCollins, 1990), p. 91.

theology found in *Sanctorum Communio*[2] and *Act and Being*,[3] and his later involvement with the *Abwehr* plot against Hitler. Indeed it will be the burden of my account of Bonhoeffer's life and theology to show that from the very beginning Bonhoeffer was attempting to develop a theological politics from which we still have much to learn.[4] Bonhoeffer may have even regarded *Sanctorum Communio* and *Act and Being* as his "academic theology," which no doubt they were, but I will argue that the theological position Bonhoeffer took in those books made the subsequent politics of his life and work inevitable.

Anyone who has read Eberhard Bethge's *Dietrich Bonhoeffer: A Biography* knows it is impossible to distinguish between Bonhoeffer's life and work.[5] Indeed Marilynne Robinson uses the passage with which I began to challenge those who think the consistency as well as significance of Bonhoeffer's theology is given a prominence it might not have due to his courageous political activity and death.[6] It is no doubt true that Bonhoeffer's fame as well as his theological significance were attributed to his unfinished *Ethics*[7] and his *Letters and Papers from Prison*.[8] Many, quite understandably, interpreted some of Bonhoeffer's own remarks in his prison correspondence to suggest his political opposition to the Nazis had occasioned a fundamental shift in his theology.[9] I will try to show, however, that Bonhoeffer's work from beginning to end was the attempt to reclaim the visibility of the church as the necessary condition for the proclamation of the gospel in a world that no longer privileged Christianity. That he was hanged by the personal order of Himmler on April 9, 1945, at Flossenburg Concentration Camp means he has now become for those of us who come after him part of God's visibility.

2. Dietrich Bonhoeffer, *Sanctorum Communio: A Theological Study of the Sociology of the Church*, trans. Reinhard Krauss and Nancy Lukens (Minneapolis: Fortress, 1998).

3. Dietrich Bonhoeffer, *Act and Being*, trans. H. Martin Rumscheidt (Minneapolis: Fortress, 1996).

4. For the distinction between political theology and theological politics see Arne Rasmusson, *The Church as Polis: From Political Theology to Theological Politics as Exemplified by Jurgen Moltmann and Stanley Hauerwas* (Notre Dame, Ind.: University of Notre Dame Press, 1995).

5. Eberhard Bethge, *Dietrich Bonhoeffer: A Biography* (rev. ed.; Minneapolis: Fortress, 2000).

6. Marilynne Robinson, *The Death of Adam: Essays on Modern Thought* (Boston: Houghton Mifflin, 1998), pp. 110–11.

7. Dietrich Bonhoeffer, *Ethics* (New York: Macmillan, 1962).

8. Dietrich Bonhoeffer, *Letters and Papers from Prison*, ed. Eberhard Bethge, trans. Reginald Fuller, Frank Clark, and John Bowden (enlarged ed.; New York: Touchstone, 1997).

9. I am referring to Bonhoeffer's remarks about Barth's "positivism of revelation" and his infamous suggestion that Christians must now live in the world as if *"et si deus non daretur"* (as if God does not exist). See *Letters and Papers from Prison*, pp. 328 and 360.

I am, of course, aware that my account of Bonhoeffer and, in particular, my emphasis on his ecclesiology for rightly interpreting his life and work, will lead some to suspect that my account of Bonhoeffer sounds far too much like positions that have become associated with my own work. I have no reason to deny that to be the case, but if it is true it is only because I first learned what I think from reading Bonhoeffer (and Barth). This is the first essay I have ever written on Bonhoeffer, but it is certainly not the first time I have read him. I am sure Bonhoeffer's *Discipleship*, which I read as a student in seminary, was the reason some years later John Howard Yoder's *The Politics of Jesus* had such a profound influence on me.[10] Both books convinced me that Christology cannot be abstracted from accounts of discipleship or, put more systematically, we must say, as Bonhoeffer puts it in *Sanctorum Communio*, that "the church of Jesus Christ that is actualized by the Holy Spirit is really the church here and now."[11] The reason I have not written on Bonhoeffer has everything to do with the reception of his work when it was translated into English. The first book by Bonhoeffer usually read by English readers was *Letters and Papers from Prison*. As a result Bonhoeffer was hailed as champion of the "death of God" movement and/or one of the first to anticipate the Christian celebration of the "secular city."[12] On the basis of Bonhoeffer's *Ethics*, Joseph Fletcher went so far as to claim him as an advocate of situation ethics.[13] As a result I simply decided not to claim Bonhoeffer in support of the position I was trying to develop, though in fact he was one of my most important teachers. That I write now about Bonhoeffer is my way of trying to acknowledge a debt long overdue.

Of course one other difficulty stood in the way of acknowledging the significance of Bonhoeffer for my work: namely, that Bonhoeffer's decision to participate in the plot to kill Hitler seemed to make him an unlikely candidate to support a pacifist position. How to understand Bonhoeffer's involvement with the conspiracy associated with Admiral Canaris and Bonhoeffer's brother-in-law, Hans von Dohnanyi, I think can never be determined with certainty. Bonhoeffer gratefully accepted von Dohnanyi's offer to become a member of the *Abwehr* because it gave him the means to avoid conscription and the dreaded necessity to take the oath of loyalty to Hitler. Many assume Bonhoeffer knew

---

10. Dietrich Bonhoeffer, *Discipleship* (Minneapolis: Fortress, 2001). This book was originally published in English as *The Cost of Discipleship* (New York: Macmillan, 1949). John Howard Yoder, *The Politics of Jesus* (2d ed.; Grand Rapids: Eerdmans, 1994).

11. Bonhoeffer, *Sanctorum Communio*, p. 208.

12. It is extremely instructive, for example, to reread Harvey Cox's use of Bonhoeffer in *The Secular City* (New York: Macmillan, 1965).

13. Joseph Fletcher, *Situation Ethics* (Philadelphia: Westminster, 1966), pp. 28, 33.

the conspiracy involved an attempt to kill Hitler, but that remains in doubt. In spite of his complete lack of knowledge of guns or bombs, he offered to be the one to assassinate Hitler. Yet the secrecy required by the conspiracy means that we do not have available any texts that could help us know how Bonhoeffer understood how this part of his life fit or did not fit with his theological convictions or his earlier commitment to pacifism.[14]

That we cannot know how Bonhoeffer understood his participation in the attempt to kill Hitler and thus how his whole life "makes sense" is not a peculiarity Bonhoeffer would think unique to his life. The primary confession of the Christian may be the deed that interprets itself, but according to Bonhoeffer our lives cannot be seen as such a deed. Only "Jesus' testimony to himself stands by itself, self-authenticating."[15] In contrast, our lives, no matter how earnestly or faithfully lived, can be no more than fragments. In a letter to Bethge in 1944 Bonhoeffer wrote:

> The important thing today is that we should be able to discern from the fragments of our life how the whole was arranged and planned, and what material it consists of. For really, there are some fragments that are only worth throwing into the dustbin (even a decent "hell" is too good for them), and others whose importance lasts for centuries, because their completion can only be a matter for God, and so they are fragments and must be fragments—I'm thinking, e.g., of the *Art of Fugue*. If our life is but the remotest reflection of such a fragment, if we accumulate, at least for a short time, a wealth of themes and weld them into a harmony in which the great counterpoint is maintained from start to finish, so that at last, when it breaks off abruptly, we can sing no more than the chorale, "I come before thy throne," we will not bemoan the fragmentariness of our life, but rather rejoice in it. I can never get away from Jeremiah 45. Do you still remember that Saturday evening in Finkenwalde when I expounded

14. Larry Rasmussen's *Dietrich Bonhoeffer: Reality and Resistance* (Nashville: Abingdon, 1972) remains one of the best attempts to understand Bonhoeffer's involvement in the plot to kill Hitler. I remain unconvinced, however, that Bonhoeffer thought this aspect of his life could be justified even if he did, as Rasmussen suggests, think in terms of just war considerations. For quite different accounts see Greg Jones, *Embodying Forgiveness: A Theological Analysis* (Grand Rapids: Eerdmans, 1995), pp. 3–33; and James McClendon's *Systematic Theology: Ethics* (Nashville: Abingdon, 1986), pp. 188–211. Geffrey Kelly and Burton Nelson's fine book, *The Cost of Moral Leadership: The Spirituality of Dietrich Bonhoeffer* (Grand Rapids: Eerdmans, 2003) was published after I had written this and the next chapter on Bonhoeffer. I am happy to say that the main outline of their view of Bonhoeffer accords with the account I provide, but they are closer to Rasmussen's view concerning the change that Bonhoeffer's participation in the plot to kill Hitler may have had on his position. Their account certainly can be defended, but I think it is a mistake to think Bonhoeffer "adjusted" his theology to accommodate his participation in the plot.

15. Dietrich Bonhoeffer, *Christ the Center* (New York: Harper Collins, 1966), p. 32.

it? Here, too, is a necessary fragment of life—"but I will you your life as a prize of war."[16]

However, thanks to Eberhard Bethge's great biography of Bonhoeffer, we know the main outlines of Bonhoeffer's life. Bethge's biography makes it impossible to treat Bonhoeffer's theology apart from his life. Therefore I must give some brief overview of his life no matter how inadequate. I have chosen, however, to highlight those aspects of Bonhoeffer's life that suggest his passion for the church. Yet I must be careful not to make Bonhoeffer's life appear too singular. In a letter to Bethge in 1944, Bonhoeffer observed that there is always a danger that intense and erotic love may destroy what he calls "the polyphony of life." He continues: "what I mean is that God wants us to love him eternally with our whole hearts—not in such a way as to injure or weaken our earthly love, but to provide a kind of *cantus firmus* to which the other melodies of life provide the counterpoint."[17] Bonhoeffer's life was a polyphony, which his commitment to the church only enriched.

It is by no means clear where Bonhoeffer's passion for God and God's church came from. In a wonderful letter to Bethge in 1942 he confesses that "my resistance against everything 'religious' grows. Often it amounts to an instinctive revulsion, which is certainly not good. I am not religious by nature. But I have to think continually of God and Christ; authenticity, life, freedom, and compassion mean a great deal to me. It is just their religious manifestations which are so unattractive."[18] Prison only served to confirm his views about religion. He writes to Bethge in 1943, "Don't worry, I shan't come out of here a *homo religiosus!* On the contrary my suspicion and horror of religiosity are greater than ever."[19]

The source of Bonhoeffer's faith is even more mysterious given his family background. He was born, along with his twin sister Sabine, on February 4, 1906. His father, Karl Bonhoeffer, was from a distinguished German family as was his mother, Paula von Hase. The Bonhoeffers

16. Bonhoeffer, *Letters and Papers from Prison*, p. 219. Bonhoeffer's brother-in-law, G. Leibholz, uses this quote in his wonderful "Memoir" in *The Cost of Discipleship*, p. 26. In *Life Together* (Minneapolis: Fortress, 1996) Bonhoeffer observes, "only in the Holy Scriptures do we get to know our own story. The God of Abraham, Isaac, and Jacob is the God and Father of Jesus Christ and our God" (p. 62).

17. Bonhoeffer, *Letters and Papers from Prison*, p. 303.

18. Quoted in Bethge, *Dietrich Bonhoeffer*, p. 722. At least one of the reasons Bonhoeffer was attracted to Barth is that he shared Barth's distaste for pietism in any form. For example, Bonhoeffer complains that any definition of faith as "personal faith," "personal decision for Jesus," or "free decision of the individual" cannot help but distort the biblical understanding of faith. Bonhoeffer, *True Patriotism*, ed. Edwin Robertson (New York: Harper and Row, 1973), pp. 149–50.

19. Bonhoeffer, *Letters and Papers from Prison*, p. 135.

had five children, three boys and two girls, before Bonhoeffer and his sister were born. One daughter was born after Dietrich and Sabine. Bonhoeffer's father was the leading psychiatrist in Germany, holding a chair at the University of Berlin. His father was not openly hostile to Christianity: he was willing for his wife to use familiar Christian celebrations as family events. In Bonhoeffer's family Christianity simply seems to have been part of the furniture that upper-class Germans assumed came with their privileges.

There is no question that Bonhoeffer's bearing and personality were shaped by his class. He took full advantage of the cultural and academic resources available to him. He became a talented pianist, and music was a wellspring on which he drew for support in the darkest times of his life. That he existed in such a culturally rich family is one of the reasons no one could understand his quite early decision to be a theologian. There had been theologians on both sides of Bonhoeffer's family, but given the opportunities before Bonhoeffer it was not clear why of all the ways he might have taken his life he decided to be a theologian.

Yet at seventeen he began his theological studies at Tübingen. But Tübingen was but preparation for his coming back to Berlin to study with the great Protestant liberals—Adolf von Harnack, Reinhold Seeberg, and Karl Holl.[20] He was soon recognized as someone with extraordinary intellectual power, completing his first dissertation, *Sanctorum Communio*, under Seeberg's direction in 1927. In spite of being at the center of Protestant liberalism, Bonhoeffer had come under the influence of Karl Barth. In *Sanctorum Communio* Bonhoeffer displayed the creative synthesis that would mark all his subsequent work—i.e., the firm conviction that Christian theology must insist that "only the concept of revelation can lead to the Christian concept of the church" coupled with the Lutheran stress on the absolute necessity that the same church that is known by revelation is also the concrete historical community that in spite of all its imperfections and modest appearances "is the body of Christ, Christ's presence on earth."[21]

Bonhoeffer was clearly on the path to becoming the paradigmatic German academic theologian. However, for some reason Bonhoeffer

20. Arne Rasmussen reminds me that Seeberg was not clearly indentified as a liberal Protestant when Bonhoeffer studied with him. That his work now strikes us as "liberal" is the result of the turn Barth and Bonhoeffer represent.

21. Bonhoeffer, *Sanctorum Communio*, pp. 134, 209. Barth many years later regarded *Sanctorum Communio* as a theological miracle, finding it hard to believe such an extraordinary book could be written by someone who was only twenty-one, but, even more startling, could have been written at Berlin. Barth observes that if any vindication of the school of Seeberg is possible, it is so because this book exists. Karl Barth, *Church Dogmatics* III/4 (Edinburgh, U.K.: T & T Clark, 1958), p. 641.

felt drawn to the ministry and took the examinations necessary to be ordained and appointed to a church. Bethge observes that Bonhoeffer's family continued to assume Bonhoeffer would ultimately become an academic, but Bonhoeffer thought his problem "was not how to enter the academic world, it was how to escape it."[22] Yet he returned to Berlin, finishing his second dissertation, *Act and Being,* in 1930. In *Act and Being* Bonhoeffer develops the Barthian insistence that God's being is act, but he worries that though Barth readily uses "temporal categories (instant, not beforehand, afterward, etc.), his concept of act still should not be regarded as temporal."[23]

Before assuming the position of lecturer at the University of Berlin, Bonhoeffer spent a year at Union Seminary in New York. Bonhoeffer was not the least attracted to American theology, finding it superficial, but he was drawn deeply to the life of the African-American church. Bethge tells us that almost every Sunday Bonhoeffer accompanied his African-American friend, Frank Fisher, to the Abyssinian Baptist Church in Harlem.[24] Though Bonhoeffer's characterization of the American church as "Protestantism without Reformation" is often quoted, I suspect more important for understanding Bonhoeffer is his observation that the fundamental characteristic of American thought is that "they do not see the radical claim of truth on the shaping of their lives. Community is therefore founded less on truth than on the spirit of 'fairness.' "[25] According to Bonhoeffer the result is "a certain levelling" in intellectual demands and accomplishments.

That truth mattered so deeply for Bonhoeffer may account for an extraordinary letter he wrote to a friend in 1936. The letter begins, "Then something happened." He does not tell us what happened but he says it transformed his life. Before "something happened," he confesses he plunged into work in a very unchristian way, but then for the first time

22. Bethge, *Dietrich Bonhoeffer,* p. 96.

23. Bonhoeffer, *Act and Being,* p. 84. Charles Marsh has best demonstrated the influence of Barth on Bonhoeffer in his *Reclaiming Dietrich Bonhoeffer* (New York: Oxford University Press, 1994). Bonhoeffer may have revised his criticism of Barth after he had the opportunity to read the early volumes of the *Dogmatics.* For example in an essay, "The Visible Church in the New Testament," written in 1936, Bonhoeffer notes that there are two dangers that must be avoided in response to the question of the place of the church in the world: (1) a docetic eschatology in which the church by its very nature is assumed to be an incorporeal concept, and (2) a secular ecclesiology with a magical view of the sacraments. Bonhoeffer, displaying a sense of humor that is often present in his work, says, "The former danger arises from the theology of Barth, understood wrongly; the latter from the theology of Dibelius, understood correctly." *A Testament to Freedom,* pp. 160–61.

24. Bethge, *Dietrich Bonhoeffer,* p. 150.

25. Bonhoeffer, *No Rusty Swords,* ed. Edwin Robertson (New York: Harper and Row, 1965), p. 87.

"I discovered the Bible. . . . I had often preached, I had seen a great deal of the church, spoken and preached about it—but I had not yet become a Christian."[26] Bonhoeffer continues, confessing that he had turned the doctrine of Jesus Christ into something of a personal advantage for himself, but the Bible, and in particular the Sermon on the Mount, freed him from his self-preoccupation. It became clear that "the life of a servant of Jesus Christ must belong to the church, and step by step it became clearer to me how far that must go. Then came the crisis of 1933. This strengthened me in it. The revival of the church and of the ministry became my supreme concern."[27]

This letter is remarkable not only because of what it tells us about Bonhoeffer, but because in the same letter this change is also linked with his becoming a pacifist. "I suddenly saw the Christian pacifism that I had recently passionately opposed to be self-evident."[28] No doubt coming into contact with Jean Lasserre at Union accounts for Bonhoeffer at least becoming sympathetic to pacifism, but I suspect equally important was Bonhoeffer's passion for the truth. In an address to the Youth Peace Conference in Czechoslovakia in 1932, Bonhoeffer says,

> There can only be a community of peace when it does not rest on *lies* and *injustice*. There is a community of peace for Christians only because one will forgive the other for his sins. The forgiveness of sins still remains the sole ground of all peace, even where the order of external peace remains preserved in truth and justice. It is therefore also the ultimate ground on which all ecumenical work rests, precisely where the cleavage appears hopeless.[29]

Bonhoeffer's life becomes an unfolding of his complete commitment to the church. Until he joined the *Abwehr*, his opposition to the Nazis would be fought through the church in and, perhaps as important, outside Germany. In 1933 he was appointed as pastor to the German church in London in hopes that such an appointment would allow him to make contacts in order to help the world understand the danger the

26. Bethge, *Dietrich Bonhoeffer*, p. 205.
27. Ibid.
28. Ibid.
29. Bonhoeffer, *No Rusty Swords*, pp. 168–69. It simply is not clear what kind of pacifism Bonhoeffer represented. He clearly has no time for humanistic justifications of pacifism because they confuse safety with peace. Yet it is not clear to me that Bonhoeffer assumed that his christological pacifism required the disavowal of violence in every circumstance. In his famous Fano conference address in 1934 he does say, "brothers in Christ obey his word; they do not doubt or question, but keep his commandment of peace. They cannot take up arms against Christ himself—yet this is what they do if they take up arms against one another!" *No Rusty Swords*, p. 290.

Nazis represented. That danger he understood to be nothing less than the "brutal attempt to make history without God and to found it on the strength of man alone."[30] While in England Bonhoeffer developed a close and lasting friendship with George Bell, Bishop of Chichester, who worked tirelessly on Bonhoeffer's behalf.

Before leaving Germany, Bonhoeffer with Martin Niemoller had drafted the *Bethel Confession* for the Pastors' Emergency League, which in the strongest language possible challenged the anti-Semitism of the German church. The *Bethel Confession* and the *Barmen Declaration* became the crucial documents that gave Bonhoeffer hope that the church of Jesus Christ not only existed but was sufficient to provide resistance to the Nazis. He could, therefore, declare in 1936 that "the government of the national church has cut itself off from the Christian church. The Confessing Church is the true church of Jesus Christ in Germany."[31] He was unafraid to draw the implication: "The question of church membership is the question of salvation. The boundaries of the church are the boundaries of salvation. Whoever knowingly cuts himself off from the Confessing Church in Germany cuts himself off from salvation."[32]

Bonhoeffer returned to Germany in 1935 in answer to a call from the Confessing Church to direct a preacher's seminary at Finkenwald. Bonhoeffer's passion for Christian community seems to have found its most intense expression at Finkenwald. During his time there he not only finished *Discipleship* but also his extraordinary account of Christian community, *Life Together*.[33] At Finkenwald Bonhoeffer encouraged the seminarians to confess their sins to another member of the community, but he also established with a core group the House of Brethren committed to leading "a communal life in daily and strict obedience to the will of Christ Jesus, in the exercise of the humblest and highest service one Christian can perform for another; they must learn to recognize the strength and liberation to be found in service to one another and communal life in a Christian community. . . . They have to learn to serve the truth alone in the study of the Bible and its interpretation in their sermons and teaching."[34]

30. Gerhard Leibholz, "Memoir," in Dietrich Bonhoeffer, *The Cost of Discipleship* (New York: Fortress, 1961), p. 11. Leibholz was Bonhoeffer's twin sister's husband who was also Jewish. The Bonhoeffer family desperately made arrangements for the Leibholz family to escape to England.

31. Bonhoeffer, *A Testament to Freedom*, p. 169.

32. Ibid., p. 173.

33. Dietrich Bonhoeffer, *Life Together* and *The Prayerbook of the Bible* (Minneapolis: Fortress, 1996).

34. Quoted by Bethge in *Dietrich Bonhoeffer*, p. 467.

During his time at Finkenwald Bonhoeffer continued to be engaged in the ecumenical movement as well as the work of the Confessing Church. Developments in the latter could not help but be a continuing disappointment to Bonhoeffer. No doubt equally troubling was the conscription and death of many of the students he taught at Finkenwald. Finally in 1940 the Gestapo closed the seminary, which meant Bonhoeffer was without an ecclesial appointment. He was now vulnerable to conscription. Because of his international connections, von Dohnanyi justified Bonhoeffer's appointment to the *Abwehr* on grounds that through his ecumenical connections he could discover valuable information on the Reich. In effect Bonhoeffer became a double agent, often making trips to Switzerland and Sweden to meet Bell and other ecumenical representatives in the hope that Bell might be able to convince the Allies to state their war aims in a manner that would not make it more difficult for those committed to Hitler's overthrow.

Without a church connection Bonhoeffer turned again to his passion for theology, beginning work on the book we now know as his *Ethics*. Much of that book was written at the Benedictine monastery at Ettal, which served as Bonhoeffer's retreat from the world. But Bonhoeffer knew no retreat was possible, and he was finally arrested for "subversion of the armed forces" on April 5, 1943. Imprisoned in Tegel prison, he was under interrogation in preparation for being tried. There he wrote most of the material we now know as *Letters and Papers from Prison*. On July 20, 1944, von Stauffenberg's attempt on Hitler's life failed with the subsequent discovery of Canaris's files in the Zossen bunker. Those files clearly implicated Bonhoeffer and von Dohnanyi in the conspiracy. Bonhoeffer was moved to Buchenwald and finally to Flossenburg, where he was hanged on April 9th. His fellow prisoners and guards testify that throughout his imprisonment he not only functioned as their pastor but died as well as he had lived.

His was a life that was at once theological and political. It was so, however, not because he died at the hands of the Nazis. Bonhoeffer's life and work would have been political if the Nazis had never existed; for Bonhoeffer saw clearly that the failure of the church when confronted with Hitler began long before the Nazi challenge. Hitler forced a church long accustomed to privileges dependent on its invisibility to become visible. The church in Germany, however, had simply lost the resources to reclaim its space in the world. How that space can be reclaimed not only in the face of the Nazis but when time seems "normal" is the heart of Bonhoeffer's theological politics.

2. BONHOEFFER'S RECOVERY OF THE POLITICAL SIGNIFICANCE OF THE VISIBLE CHURCH

In an essay entitled "The Constantinian Sources of Western Social Ethics,"[35] John Howard Yoder makes the striking observation that after the Constantinian shift the meaning of the word "Christian" changes. Prior to Constantine it took exceptional conviction to be a Christian. After Constantine it takes exceptional courage not to be counted as a Christian. This development, according to Yoder, called forth a new doctrinal development, "namely the doctrine of the invisibility of the church." Before Constantine, one knew as a fact of everyday experience that there was a church, but one had to have faith that God was governing history. After Constantine, people assumed as a fact God was governing history through the emperor, but one had to take it on faith that within the nominally Christian mass there was a community of true believers. No longer could being a Christian be identified with church membership, since many "Christians" in the church clearly had not chosen to follow Christ. Now to be a Christian is transmuted to "inwardness."[36]

Bonhoeffer is obviously a Lutheran and Lutherans are seldom confused with Anabaptists, but Bonhoeffer's account of the challenge facing the church closely parallels Yoder's account above.[37] For example, in notes for a lecture at Finkenwald, Bonhoeffer observes that the consequence of Luther's doctrine of grace is that the church should live in the world and, according to Romans 13, in its ordinances. "Thus in his own way Luther confirms Constantine's covenant with the church. As a result, a minimal ethic prevailed. Luther of course wanted a complete ethic for everyone, not only for monastic orders. Thus the existence of the Christian became the existence of the citizen. The nature of the church vanished into the invisible realm. But in this way the New Testament message was fundamentally misunderstood, inner-worldliness became a principle."[38]

35. John Howard Yoder, *The Priestly Kingdom: Social Ethics as Gospel* (Notre Dame, Ind.: University of Notre Dame Press, 2001), pp. 135–49.

36. Ibid., pp. 136–37.

37. I think it is not accidental that those who have been schooled by Yoder's work have noticed Bonhoeffer's insistence on the visibility of the church. See, for example, Mark Thiessen Nation, "Discipleship in a World Full of Nazis," in *The Wisdom of the Cross: Essays in Honor of John Howard Yoder*, ed. Stanley Hauerwas, Chris Huebner, Harry Huebner, and Mark Thiessen Nation (Grand Rapids: Eerdmans, 1999), pp. 249–77; and Barry Harvey, "A Post-Critical Approach to a 'Religionless Christianity,'" in *Theology and the Practice of Responsibility* (Valley Forge, Pa.: Trinity Press, 1994), pp. 39–58.

38. Bonhoeffer, *No Rusty Swords*, p. 324. In *True Patriotism* Bonhoeffer notes that the defining mark of the Constantinian age was not that Christians began to baptize their

Faced with this result, Bonhoeffer argues that the church must define its limits by severing heresy from its body. "It has to make itself distinct and to be a community which hears the Apocalypse. It has to testify to its alien nature and to resist the false principle of inner-worldliness. Friendship between the church and the world is not normal, but abnormal. The community *must* suffer like Christ, without wonderment. The cross stands *visibly* over the community."[39] It is not hard to see how his stress on the necessity of visibility led him to write a book like *Discipleship*. Holiness but names God's way of making his will for his people visible. "To flee into invisibility is to deny the call. Any community of Jesus which wants to be invisible is no longer a community that follows him."[40]

According to Bonhoeffer, sanctification, properly understood, is the church's politics. For sanctification is only possible within the visible church community. "That is the 'political' character of the church community. A merely personal sanctification which seeks to bypass this openly visible separation of the church-community from the world confuses the pious desires to the religious flesh with the sanctification of the church-community, which has been accomplished in Christ's death and is being actualized by the seal of God. . . . Sanctification through the seal of the Holy Spirit always places the church in the midst of struggle."[41] Put as starkly as possible, Bonhoeffer clearly saw that the holiness of the church is necessary for the redemption of the world.[42]

I am not suggesting that when Bonhoeffer wrote *Sanctorum Communio*, he did so with the clarity that can be found in the lectures he gave at Finkenwald or in his *Discipleship*. In *Sanctorum Communio* his concerns may be described as more strictly theological, but the "strictly theological" even that early was against the background of Protestant liberal mistakes, and in particular Troeltsch, that made inevitable his disease with the stance of the German churches toward the world. According to Bonhoeffer, "The church is God's new will and purpose for humanity. God's will is always directed toward the concrete, historical human being. But this means that it begins to be implemented *in his-*

---

children, but "that baptism became a qualification for civic life. The false development lies not in infant baptism but in the secular qualification of baptism. The two should clearly be distinguished" (p. 160).

39. Ibid., p. 324.

40. Ibid., p. 113.

41. Ibid., pp. 261–62.

42. For example, Bonhoeffer in his *Ethics* claims that the justification of the Western world lies in the divine justification of the church. The latter is possible only if the church is led to a full confession of her guilt through the cross (p. 52).

tory. God's will must become visible and comprehensible at some point in history."[43]

From the beginning to the end of his work Bonhoeffer relentlessly explores and searches for what it means for the church to faithfully manifest God's visibility. For example, in his *Ethics* he notes that the church occupies a space in the world through her public worship, her parish life, and her organization. That the church takes up space is but a correlative that God in Jesus Christ occupies space in the world. "And so, too, the Church of Jesus Christ is the place, in other words the space in the world, at which the reign of Jesus Christ over the whole world is evidenced and proclaimed."[44] Bonhoeffer's ecclesiology is but the expression of his Christology, in which the reality of Christ determines all that is.

For Bonhoeffer it is in Jesus Christ that the whole of reality is taken up, that reality has an origin and end.

> For that reason it is only in Him, and with Him as the point of departure, that there can be an action which is in accordance with reality. The origin of action which accords with reality is not the pseudo-Lutheran Christ who exists solely for the purpose of sanctioning the facts as they are, nor the Christ of radical enthusiasm whose function is to bless every revolution, but it is the incarnate God Jesus who has accepted man and who has loved, condemned and reconciled man and with him the world.[45]

As Christ was in the world so the church is in the world. These are not pious sentiments, but reality-making claims that challenge the way things are. They are the very heart of Bonhoeffer's theological politics, a politics that requires the church to be the church in order that the world can be the world. Bonhoeffer's call for the world to be the world is but the outworking of his Christology and ecclesiology. For the church to let the world be the world means the church refuses to live by the privileges granted on the world's terms. "Real secularity consists in the church's being able to renounce all privileges and all its property but never Christ's Word and the forgiveness of sins. With Christ and the forgiveness of sins to fall back on, the church is free to give up everything else."[46] Such freedom, moreover, is the necessary condition for the church to be the zone of truth in a world of mendacity.[47]

43. Bonhoeffer, *Sanctorum Communio*, p. 141.
44. Bonhoeffer, *Ethics*, p. 68.
45. Ibid., p. 199.
46. Bonhoeffer, *A Testament to Freedom*, p. 92.
47. Bonhoeffer, *No Rusty Swords*, p. 160. One of the constructive ways one might represent Bonhoeffer's politics is, and I will do this in the next chapter, to look closely at

Sanctorum Communio was Bonhoeffer's attempt to develop a "specifically Christian sociology" as an alternative to Troeltsch.[48] Bonhoeffer argues that the very categories—church/sect/mysticism, *Gemeinschaft/ Gesellschaft*—must be rejected if the visibility of the church is to be reclaimed. Troeltsch confuses questions of origins with essences, with the result that the gospel is subjected to the world. The very choice between voluntary association and compulsory organization is rendered unacceptable by the "Protestant understanding of the Spirit and the church-community, in the former because it does not take the reality of the Spirit into account at all, and in the latter in that it severs the essential relation between Spirit and church-community, thereby completely losing any sociological interest."[49]

From Bonhoeffer's perspective Troeltsch is but one of the most powerful representatives of the Protestant liberal presumption that the gospel is purely religious, encompassing the outlook of the individual, but is indifferent and unconcerned with worldly institutions.[50] The sociology of Protestant liberalism, therefore, is but the other side of liberal separation of Jesus from the Christ. Protestant liberalism continues the docetic christological heresy that results in an equally pernicious docetic ecclesiology.[51] Protestant liberalism is the theological expression of the sociology of the invisible church that "conceded to the world the right to determine Christ's place in the world; in the conflict between the church and the world it accepted the comparatively easy terms of peace that the world dictated. Its strength was that it did not try to put the clock back, and that it genuinely accepted the battle (Troeltsch), even though this ended with its defeat."[52]

Bonhoeffer's work was to provide a complete alternative to the liberal Protestant attempt to make peace with the world. In a lecture at the beginning of his Finkenwald period concerning the interpretation of Scripture, Bonhoeffer asserts that their intention "should be not to justify Christianity in this present age, but *to justify the present age before the Christian message.*"[53] Bonhoeffer's attack in *Letters and Papers from*

---

his understanding of lying. The demand of truthfulness runs from the beginning to the end of his work culminating, of course, with his discussion in the *Ethics*, pp. 326–34. For example, his remark that anyone who tells the truth cynically is lying is an invitation to extended reflection on the kind of politics necessary to produce people who can tell the truth without cynicism. *Letters and Papers from Prison*, p. 163.

48. Bonhoeffer, *Sanctorum Communio*, p. 277.

49. Ibid., p. 260.

50. Bonhoeffer, *Ethics*, p. 287.

51. Bonhoeffer, *Christ the Center* (New York: Harper & Row, 1966), pp. 71–85. Earlier in *Christ the Center* Bonhoeffer observes, "Ritschl and Herrmann put the resurrection on one side, Schleiermacher symbolizes it; in so doing they destroy the church" (p. 45).

52. Bonhoeffer, *Letters and Papers from Prison*, p. 327.

53. Bonhoeffer, *No Rusty Swords*, p. 310.

Prison on the liberal Protestant apologetics that tries to secure "faith" on the edges of life and the despair such edges allegedly create is but a continuation of his attack on Protestant pietism as well as his refusal to let the proclamation of the gospel be marginalized. For the same reasons he had little regard for existentialist philosophers or psychotherapists, whom he regarded as but a secularized "methodism."[54]

Unfortunately Bonhoeffer's suggestion about Barth's "positivism of revelation" and the correlative need for a nonreligious interpretation of theological concepts has led some to think Bonhoeffer wanted Christians to become "secular."[55] The exact opposite is the case. He is insisting that if in fact reality is redeemed by Christ, Christians must claim the center, refusing to use the "world's" weakness to make the gospel intelligible. He refuses all strategies that try "to make room for God on the borders," thinking it better to leave certain problems unsolved. The gospel is not an answer to questions produced by human anxiety, but a proclamation of a "fact." Thus Bonhoeffer's wonderful remark: "Belief in the Resurrection is not the solution to the problem of death. God's 'beyond' is not the beyond of our cognitive faculties. The transcendence of epistemological theory has nothing to do with the transcendence of God. God is beyond in the midst of life. The church stands, not at the boundaries where human powers give out, but in the middle of the village."[56]

Bonhoeffer's call for a Christian worldliness, moreover, is not his turning away from the kind of community discipline he so eloquently defended in *Discipleship* and *Life Together*. In his confession in *Letters and Papers from Prison* that at one time he mistakenly assumed he could acquire faith by living a holy life, he is not rejecting the form of life they lived at Finkenwald. When he says he now sees some of the dangers of *Discipleship*, though he still stands by the book, he is continuing to reject the false dualism inherited from Troeltsch. Rather he is making the christological point that the incarnation, the crucifixion, and the resurrection must be held in unity to rightly understand the church's relationship to the world. An emphasis on incarnation too often leads to compromise, while an ethic based on cross and resurrection too often leads to radicalism and enthusiasm.[57] The church names that community that lives in radical hope in a world without hope. To so live means the

54. Bonhoeffer, *Letters and Papers from Prison*, pp. 326–27. "Methodism" simply seems to have been Bonhoeffer's general characterization of pietistic traditions. Unfortunately his use of "methodism" as a term of derision the denomination bearing that name too often deserves.

55. Ibid., p. 328.

56. Ibid., p. 282.

57. Bonhoeffer, *Ethics*, pp. 88–89.

church cannot help but be different from the world, but such a difference is not an end in itself but represents rather "the fruits which automatically follow from an authentic proclamation of the gospel."[58]

This I believe to be Bonhoeffer's theological politics. He sought to recover the visibility of the church because "it is essential to the revelation of God in Jesus Christ that it occupies space within the world."[59] Put positively, in Jesus Christ God has occupied space in the world and continues to do so through the work of the Holy Spirit's calling the church to faithfulness. These were the convictions Bonhoeffer brought to his war with the Nazis. These were the convictions that made him the most insightful and powerful force shaping the church's witness against Hitler. Hitler was exactly the kind of enemy that makes Bonhoeffer's (and Barth's) theological politics so compelling. The question remains, however, whether Bonhoeffer (or Barth) provides an adequate account of how the church must negotiate a world "after Christendom." To explore that question I must explore what might be called Bonhoeffer's political ethics, which are expressed primarily by his critique and attempt to find an alternative to the traditional Lutheran doctrine of the two kingdoms.

3. BONHOEFFER'S SEARCH FOR A POLITICAL ETHIC

Bethge reports that at a conference sponsored by the Church Federation Office in 1932, Bonhoeffer (even though he was the youngest speaker at the conference) vigorously attacked the idea of the "orders of creation" introduced by traditional Lutherans. That Bonhoeffer would reject the two-kingdom tradition was inevitable given the direction he had begun in *Sanctorum Communio* and *Act and Being*. Creation simply cannot be self-validating because Christians have no knowledge of creation separate from redemption. "The creation is a picture of the power and faithfulness of God, demonstrated to us in God's revelation in Jesus Christ. We worship the creator, revealed to us as redeemer."[60] Whatever Christians have to say about worldly order, it will have to be said on the presumption that Christ is the reality of all that is.

58. This passage comes from Bonhoeffer's wonderful essay "The Question of Baptism," written in 1942 in response to a controversy in the Confessing Church (*No Rusty Swords*, p. 160). Bonhoeffer observes that it is very understandable that in a secularized church there is a desire for a pure, authentic, truthful set of believers to exist. Such a desire is understandable, but full of dangers because it is far too easy for a community ideal to take the place of the real community of God or for such a community to be understood as a contribution made by man.

59. Bonhoeffer, *Ethics*, p. 68.

60. Bonhoeffer, *The Prayerbook of the Bible*, p. 163.

Bonhoeffer soon returned to the issue of the orders of creation in a address to the Youth Peace Conference in Czechoslovakia in July 1932. Again he attacks those who believe that we must accept certain orders as given in creation. Such a view entails the presumption that because the nations have been created differently each one is obliged to preserve and develop its own characteristics. He notes this understanding of the nation is particularly dangerous because "just about everything can be defended by it." Not only is the fallenness of such order ignored, but those who use the orders of creation to justify their commitment to Germany fail to see that "the so-called orders of creation are no longer *per se* revelations of the divine commandment, they are concealed and invisible. Thus the concept of orders of creation must be rejected as a basis for the knowledge of the commandment of God."[61]

However, if the orders of creation are rejected, then Bonhoeffer must provide some account of how Christians understand the commandment of God for their lives. In *Creation and Fall* Bonhoeffer notes that the Creator does not turn from the fallen world but rather God deals with humankind in a distinctive way: "He made them cloaks." Accordingly the created world becomes the preserved world by which God restrains our distorted passions. Rather than speaking of the orders of creation, Bonhoeffer begins to describe God's care of our lives as the orders of preservation.[62] The orders of preservation are not self-validating: "they all stand under the preservation of God as long as they are still open for Christ, they are *orders of preservation*, not orders of creation. They obtain their value wholly from outside themselves, from Christ, from the new creation."[63] Any order of the world can, therefore, be dissolved if it prevents our hearing the commandment of Christ.

The question, of course, is what difference for concrete ethical reflection changing the name from creation to preservation may have. Bonhoeffer is obviously struggling to challenge the way the Lutheran "two order" account fails to be christological as well as serving as a legitimation of the status quo. In *Christ the Center*, the lectures in Christology Bonhoeffer delivered at Berlin in 1933, he spelled out in more detail some of the implications of his christological display of the orders of preservation. For example, he observed that since Christ is present in the church after the cross and resurrection, the church must be understood as the center of history. In fact, the state has only existed in its proper form only so long as there has been a church, because the state has its proper origin with the cross. Yet the history of which the church is the center is a history made by the state. Accordingly the visibility of the

61. Bonhoeffer, *A Testament to Freedom*, p. 106.
62. Bonhoeffer, *Creation and Fall*, p. 139.
63. Bonhoeffer, *No Rusty Swords*, pp. 166–67.

church does not require that the church must be acknowledged by the state by being made a state church, but rather the church is the "hidden meaning and promise of the state."[64]

But if the church is the "hidden meaning" of the state, how can the state know that the church is so if the church is not visible to the state? How is this "hiddenness" of the church for the state consistent with Bonhoeffer's insistence in *Sanctorum Communio* on the church's visibility? Bonhoeffer clearly wants the boundaries of the church to challenge or at least limit the boundaries of the state, but he finds it hard to break Lutheran habits that determine what the proper role of the state is in principle. Thus he will say that the kingdom of God takes form in the state insofar as the state holds itself responsible for stopping the world from flying to pieces through the exercise of its authority; or, that the power of loneliness in the church is destroyed in the confession-occurrence, but "in the state it is restrained through the preservation of community order."[65] Understandably it does not occur to Bonhoeffer that he does not need to provide an account in principle of what the state is or should be.

In his *Ethics* he seems to have abandoned the language of "orders of preservation" and instead uses the language of the "mandates."[66] According-ing to Bonhoeffer the Scriptures name four mandates—labor, marriage, government, and the church.[67] The mandates receive their intelligibility only as they are created in and directed toward Christ. Accordingly the authorization to speak on behalf of the church, the family, labor, and government is conferred from above and then "only so long as they do not encroach upon each other's domains and only so long as they give effect to God's commandment in conjunction and collaboration with one another and each in its own way."[68] Yet Bonhoeffer does not develop

---

64. Bonhoeffer, *Christ the Center*, p. 65.

65. Bonhoeffer, *A Testament of Freedom*, pp. 96–97.

66. Bonhoeffer, *Ethics*, pp. 73–78.

67. Bonhoeffer rightly worries how to justify the identification of the mandates. He rejects the Lutheran attempt to derive the orders from the world and attempts to justify them from the Bible. He observes, "it is perhaps not by chance that precisely these mandates seem to have their type in the celestial world. Marriage corresponds with Christ and the congregation; the family with God the Father and the Son, and with the brotherhood of men with Christ; labor corresponds with the creative service of God and Christ to the world, and of men to God; government corresponds with the communion of Christ in eternity; the state corresponds with *telos* of God." *Ethics*, p. 295. Bonhoeffer's effort is clearly speculative and I think not much should be made of his naming different mandates in different contexts.

68. Bonhoeffer, *Ethics*, p. 246. Benjamin Reist provides an enlightening discussion concerning the tension between Bonhoeffer's stress on the space the church must occupy and his use of the two-sphere language bequeathed to him by the Lutheran tradition. See Reist, *The Promise of Bonhoeffer* (Philadelphia: Westminster, 1969), pp. 85–90.

how we would know when one domain has encroached on the other or what conjunction or collaboration might look like.[69]

It is clear what Bonhoeffer is against, but it is not yet clear what he is for. For example he is clearly against the distinction between person and office he attributes to the Reformation. He notes this distinction is crucial for justifying the Reformation position on war and on the public use of legal means to repel evil. "But this distinction between private person and bearer of an office as normative for my behavior is foreign to Jesus. He does not say a word about it. He addresses his disciples as people who have left everything behind to follow him. 'Private' and 'official' spheres are all completely subject to Jesus' command. The word of Jesus claimed them undividedly."[70] Yet Bonhoeffer's account of the mandates can invite the distinction between the private and public, which results in Christian obedience becoming invisible.

Bonhoeffer's attempt to rethink the Lutheran two-kingdom theology in the light of his christological recovery of the significance of the visible church, I think, failed to escape from the limits of the habits that have long shaped Lutheran thinking on these matters. However there is another side to Bonhoeffer's political ethics that is seldom noticed or commented on. Bethge notes that though Bonhoeffer was shaped by the liberal theological and political tradition, by 1933 he was growing antiliberal not only in his theology but in his politics. Increasingly he thought liberalism—because of either a superciliousness or a weak laissez-faire attitude—was leaving decisions to the tyrant.[71]

Nowhere are Bonhoeffer's judgments about political liberalism more clearly stated than in a response he wrote in 1941 to William Paton's book, *The Church and the New World Order,* a book that explored the church's responsibility for social reconstruction after the war. Bonhoeffer begins by observing that the upheavals of the war have made Continental Christians acutely conscious that the future is in God's hands and no human planning can make men the masters of their fate. Consequently the churches on the Continent have an apocalyptic stance that can lead to otherworldliness, but may also have the more salutary effect of making the church recognize that the life of the church has its own God-given laws, which are different than those that govern the life of the world.

69. While generally praising Bonhoeffer's *Ethics* and in particular his account of the mandates because they "do not emerge from reality" but descend into it, Karl Barth suggests there still may remain just a hint of North German patriarchalism in Bonhoeffer's understanding of some having authority over others. Karl Barth, *Church Dogmatics* III/4 (Edinburgh, U.K.: T & T Clark, 1961), p. 22. Barth's comment is interesting just to the extent that his own account of the political implications of the gospel has been criticized for exhibiting the same "arbitrariness" he finds in Bonhoeffer.

70. Bonhoeffer, *Ethics*, pp. 134–35.

71. Bethge, *Dietrich Bonhoeffer*, p. 289.

Accordingly the church cannot and should not develop detailed plans for reconstruction after the war, but rather remind the nations of the abiding commandments and realities that must be taken seriously if the new order is to be a true order.[72]

In particular Bonhoeffer stresses that in a number of European countries an attempt to return to full-fledged democracy and parliamentarianism would create even more disorder than that which obtained prior to the era of authoritarianism. Democracy requires a soil that has been prepared by a long spiritual tradition and most of the nations of Europe, except for some of the smaller ones, do not have the resources for sustaining democracy. This does not mean the only alternative is state absolutism, but rather what should be sought is that each state be limited by the law. This will require a different politics than the politics of liberalism.

In his *Ethics* Bonhoeffer starkly states (and he clearly has in mind the French Revolution) that "the demand for absolute liberty brings men to the depths of slavery."[73] In his response to Paton, he observes that the Anglo-Saxon word that names the struggle against the omnipotence of the state is freedom and the demand for freedom is expressed in the language of "rights and liberties."[74] But "freedom is a too negative word to be used in a situation where *all* order has been destroyed. And liberties are not enough when men seek first of all for some minimum security. These words remind us much of the old liberalism which because of its failures is itself largely responsible for the development of State absolutism."[75]

Bonhoeffer takes up this history again in his *Ethics* suggesting that these developments cannot help but lead to godlessness and the subsequent deification of man, which is the proclamation of nihilism. This godlessness is seldom identified by hostility to the church, but rather

---

72. Bonhoeffer, *No Rusty Swords*, pp. 109–10.

73. Bonhoeffer, *Ethics*, p. 38. This aspect of Bonhoeffer's work has been attacked in Germany by Klaus-Michael Kodalle in his *Dietrich Bonhoeffer: Zur Kritik seiner Theologie* (Gutersloh, Germany: Guterslohes Verlagshaus, 1991). Wolfgang Huber defends Bonhoeffer against Kodalle in his "Bonhoeffer and Modernity," in *Theology and the Practice of Responsibility: Essays on Dietrich Bonhoeffer*, Wayne Whitson, ed. (Valley Forge, Pa.: Trinity Press, 1994), pp. 5–19. I fear I am equally unsympathetic with Kodalle's critique and Huber's defense just to the extent they each remain determined by the categories of liberal political theory. Huber challenges Kodalle's dualism of individual and community, but fails to see that the heart of Bonhoeffer's challenge is ecclesial.

74. In his wonderful "Thoughts on the Day of the Baptism of Dietrich Wilhelm Rudiger Bethge" Bonhoeffer observes, "We thought we could make our way in life with reason and justice, and when both failed, we felt that we were at the end of our tether. We have constantly exaggerated the importance of reason and justice in the course of history." *Letters and Papers from Prison*, p. 298.

75. Bonhoeffer, *True Patriotism*, p. 113.

this "hopeless godlessness" too often comes in Christian clothing. Such "godlessness" he finds particularly present in the American church, which begins by seeking to faithfully build the world with Christian principles and ends with the total capitulation of the church to the world. Such societies and the churches have no confidence in truth with the result that the place of truth is usurped by sophistic propaganda.[76]

The only hope, if Europe is to avoid the plunge into the void after the war, is in the miracle of a new awakening of faith and the institution of God's governance of the world that sets limits to evil. The latter alternative, what Bonhoeffer calls "the restrainer," is the power of the state to establish and maintain order.[77] In his reply to Paton he suggests that such an order limited by law and responsibility, which recognizes commandments that transcend the state, has more "spiritual substance and solidity than the emphasis on the rights of man."[78] Such an order is entirely different from the order of the church, but they are in close alliance. The church, therefore, cannot fail its responsibility to sustain the restraining work of the state.

Yet the church must never forget that her primary task is to preach the risen Jesus Christ because in so doing the church "strikes a mortal blow at the spirit of destruction. The 'restrainer,' the force of order, sees in the church an ally, and, whatever other elements of order may remain, will seek a place at her side. Justice, truth, science, art, culture, humanity, liberty, patriotism, all at last, after long straying from the path, are once more finding their way back to their fountain-head. The more central the message of the church, the greater now will be her effectiveness."[79]

Above I suggested that Bonhoeffer's attempt to reclaim the visibility of the church at least put him in the vicinity of trying to imagine a non-Constantinian church. Yet in his *Ethics* he displays habits of mind that clearly seem committed to what we can only call a "Christian civilization." But Larry Rasmussen suggests that Bonhoeffer in the last stages of his *Letters and Papers from Prison* began to move away from any Christendom notions.[80] In particular Rasmussen directs attention to the "Outline for a Book" Bonhoeffer wrote toward the end of his life. Rather than finishing the *Ethics*, which he expressed regret for not doing, if he had lived I believe, as Rasmussen believes, that Bonhoeffer would

76. Bonhoeffer, *Ethics*, pp. 41–42.
77. Ibid., p. 44.
78. Bonhoeffer, *True Patriotism*, p. 113.
79. Bonhoeffer, *Ethics*, p. 45.
80. Larry Rasmussen, *Dietrich Bonhoeffer: Reality and Resistance*, pp. 85–86. I am sure Rasmussen is right but I obviously have a different account of what Bonhoeffer means when he says Christians must acknowledge the "world come of age."

have first written the book envisaged in his "Outline." I do so because the book hinted at in the "Outline" would have allowed him to extend his reflections about the limits of liberal politics and in what manner the church might provide an appropriate alternative.

In his "Outline" Bonhoeffer begins with "a stocktaking of Christianity." In particular he suggests that what it means for mankind to have "come of age" is the dream that humans can be independent of nature. As a result human creations have turned against their creators, making those that sought freedom enslaved to their self-created chains. The church provides no alternative, trapped by its invisibility and unwilling to risk itself on behalf of the world. Such a church is no more than a stopgap for the embarrassment of our suffering and death.[81] In the second chapter of his book Bonhoeffer, in terms reminiscent of *Sanctorum Communio*, suggests he will begin with the question "Who is God?" in order to recover the God who is found only through our "participation in the being of Jesus." Bonhoeffer proposes to end his book with an account of the church that will "have to take the field against the vices of *hubris*, power-worship, envy, and humbug, as the roots of all evil. It will have to speak of moderation, purity, trust, loyalty, constancy, patience, discipline, humility, contentment, and modesty."[82]

Finally Bonhoeffer says he intends to explore the importance and power of example, "which has its origin in the humanity of Jesus and is so important in the teachings of Paul," and whose importance has been underestimated.[83] I cannot say that if Bonhoeffer would have had the opportunity to write the book suggested in his "Outline," he would have forever left Constantinianism behind. But I remain convinced that Bonhoeffer's attempt to think through what the recovery of the visible church entails—the implications of which he was beginning to see in his last proposed book—is an invaluable resource for the challenges that those of us who must live after Bonhoeffer cannot ignore. He is now part of God's exemplification given for our redemption.

---

81. Bonhoeffer, *Letters and Papers from Prison*, pp. 380–83. Bonhoeffer's description of the human project to safeguard life against accidents (p. 380) has only recently become a theme in the work of postmodern theorists. In his "Thoughts on the Day of the Baptism," he observes "for the greater part of our lives pain was a stranger to us. To be as free as possible from pain was unconsciously one of our guiding principles" (p. 298). Bonhoeffer clearly saw that the attempt to escape suffering was the breeding ground for self-willed tyranny.

82. Bonhoeffer, *Letters and Papers from Prison*, p. 383.

83. Ibid., p. 383.

2

BONHOEFFER ON TRUTH
AND POLITICS

1. BONHOEFFER'S PASSION FOR TRUTH

It is not accidental that my account of Bonhoeffer as a political theologian makes him an ally of John Howard Yoder. Bonhoeffer, like Yoder, sought to recover the visibility of the church amid the ruins of Christendom from the beginning to the end of his life. To so interpret Bonhoeffer risks making him subject to the same criticism so often directed at Yoder—i.e., Bonhoeffer's account of the church makes the church politically irrelevant. Those tempted to so criticize Bonhoeffer, of course, have to give some account for the political character of his life. For example, they might suggest that Bonhoeffer's life was more political than his theology or even (as I suggested in the first chapter) that Bonhoeffer's theology is particularly well suited for totalitarian contexts but fails to provide an adequate account of how Christians should live in democratic societies.

In this chapter I hope to counter those tempted to make these kinds of criticisms by developing Bonhoeffer's understanding of the relation between truth and politics. In short I will try to show that Bonhoeffer rightly understood that the gift the church gives to any politics is the truthful proclamation of the gospel. As far as I know, Bonhoeffer's understanding of truth and politics has seldom been commented on or analyzed. One of the reasons may well be the general assumption that truth and politics, particularly in democratic regimes in which compromise is the primary end of the political process, do not mix.[1] Yet I hope to show that Bonhoeffer saw clearly that such a view of politics abandons the political realm to violence.

I should be candid that (as we say in the South) I also have a dog in this fight. Because I am so influenced by Yoder I am often accused of abandoning the politics necessary to achieve relative justice.[2] My oft-made claim that the first task of the church is not to make the world more just but to make the world the world is interpreted as a call for Christians to withdraw from the world. By focusing on Bonhoeffer's understanding of how the church serves the world by being God's truthful witness, I hope to direct attention to the same theme in my own work. For it has always been my conviction, a conviction I believe I learned from Barth, that the character of a society and state is to be judged by the willingness to have the gospel preached truthfully and freely.[3] By drawing on

---

1. For example, John Rawls observes: "The zeal to embody the whole truth in politics is incompatible with an idea of public reason that belongs with democratic citizenship." "The Idea of Public Reason Revisited," in John Rawls, *The Law of Peoples* (Cambridge, Mass.: Harvard University Press, 2002), p. 133. A few pages later Rawls makes the same claim, noting not only that the insistence on whole truth is incompatible with democratic citizenship but also with "the idea of legitimate law" (p. 138). I suspect Rawls assumes that the phrase "the whole truth" is a correlate of his understanding of comprehensive or perfectionistic moral positions. However, one should at least ask Rawls whether, if politics cannot deal with the "whole truth," is it not the case that "smaller truths" might be important for any politics that would be an alternative to naked power?

Hannah Arendt's account of the relation between truth and politics remains one of the most interesting we have. According to Arendt, to look on politics from the perspective of truth—and by truth she meant "factual truth"—is to stand outside the political realm. She notes, "truthfulness has never been counted among the political virtues, because it has little to contribute to that change of the world and of circumstances which is among the most legitimate political activities." *The Portable Hannah Arendt*, ed. with an introduction by Peter Baehr (New York: Penguin, 2000), p. 570. Arendt is not recommending lying in politics, but rather trying to explain why the political realm so often seems immune to truthfulness. She notes that a politics that acknowledges the need for the existence of impartial institutions, such as universities, improves the possibility of truth prevailing in public (p. 571). Yet she observes that such institutions remain exposed to all the dangers arising from social and political power.

2. See, for example, Jeff Stout's appendix in the new edition of his *Ethics after Babel* (Princeton, N.J.: Princeton University Press, 2001), pp. 334–58. Stout has developed his criticisms not only of my work but of Milbank's and MacIntyre's in his *Democracy and Tradition: Religion, Ethics, and Public Philosophy* (Princeton, N.J.: Princeton University Press, 2003). Stout's position requires a more substantial response than I can give here; however, his challenge is extremely important and sets a fruitful agenda for future discussion.

3. Barth challenged Hitler's regime on the grounds that Hitler was trying to determine what the church could preach. He did so from the conviction "that it is the preaching of

Bonhoeffer's understanding of the significance of truthfulness, I hope to show the political significance of the Christian refusal to lie.

Bonhoeffer was a relentless critic of any way of life that substituted agreeableness for truthfulness. For example in a speech he gave in 1932 at the Youth Peace Conference in Czechoslovakia, he attacked attempts to secure unity by focusing on "practical" issues rather than fundamental issues of theology. According to Bonhoeffer, when theological questions are ignored, truth plays into the hands of the forces that the ecumenical movement was meant to counter. For example, Bonhoeffer observes that because there is no theology of the ecumenical movement, "ecumenical thought has become powerless and meaningless, especially among German youth, because of the political upsurge of nationalism."[4] Bonhoeffer observes:

> No good at all can come from acting before the world and one's self as though we knew the truth, when in reality we do not. This truth is too important for that, and it would be a betrayal of this truth if the church were to hide itself behind resolutions and pious so-called Christian principles, when it is called to look the truth in the face and once and for all confess its guilt and ignorance. Indeed, such resolutions can have nothing complete, nothing clear about them unless the whole Christian truth, as the church knows it or confesses that it does not know it, stands behind them. Qualified silence might perhaps be more appropriate for the church today than talk which is very unqualified. That means protest against any form of the church which does not honour the question of truth above all things.[5]

Bonhoeffer saw little point to theological engagement if truth does not matter. He was, for example, quite critical of his fellow students at Union Theological Seminary. In his report of his study at Union in 1930–1931, he noted that the upbringing and education of American students was essentially different from the education German students receive. According to Bonhoeffer, to understand the American student, you need to experience life in a hostel, which produces a spirit of comradeship as well as a readiness to help one another. The unreservedness of life together, "the thousandfold 'hullo,'" manifests the American desire before all else to maintain community. In America, in the tension between the attempt to say the truth and the will for the community, the latter

---

justification of the Kingdom of God, which founds, here and now, the true system of law, the true State." Karl Barth, *Community, State, and Church*, with an introduction by Will Herberg, trans. G. Ronald Howe (Garden City, N.Y.: Anchor, 1960), p. 126.

4. Dietrich Bonhoeffer, *No Rusty Swords*, trans. Edwin Robertson and John Bowden (New York: Harper & Row, 1965), p. 159.

5. Ibid., p. 160.

always prevails. Fairness, not truth, becomes the primary commitment necessary to sustain community for Americans. As a result "a certain levelling in intellectual demands and accomplishments" shapes the life of the American educational institutions. Intellectual competition and ambition are lacking, making innocuous the work done in seminar, discussion, and lecture.[6]

Bonhoeffer's views of his fellow students reflected his general account of American religious and political life. His observation that America represents a form of "Protestantism without Reformation" is often quoted, but why he thought such a characterization appropriate is seldom explored. Bonhoeffer thought the "Protestant fugitives" who came to America did not come to enact another struggle. Rather Protestants claimed the right "to forgo the final suffering in order to be able to serve God in quietness and peace. . . . In the sanctuary there is no longer a place for strife. Confessional stringency and intolerance must cease for the person who has himself shunned intolerance. With his right to flee the Christian fugitive has forfeited the right to fight. So, at any rate, the [American] Christian understands the matter."[7]

Because the American student of theology sees the question of truth primarily in the light of this understanding of community, preaching cannot aspire to the truthful proclamation of the gospel. Rather "preaching becomes an edifying narration of examples, a ready recital of his own religious experiences, which are not of course assigned any positively binding character."[8] As a result, the relation of denominations to each other in America is not one that represents a struggle for the truth in preaching or doctrine. One might think, Bonhoeffer reflects, that such a situation would be favorable for the possibility of the unity of the churches of Jesus Christ. If the struggle for truth no longer divides the church, then surely the unity of the church must already exist. Yet just

6. Ibid., p. 87.

7. Ibid., pp. 102–3. Though these judgements about American Christianity come early in Bonhoeffer's career, if the work in the *Ethics* is any indication he never changed his mind. For example, he contrasts the French and American revolutions, observing the latter was not based on the emancipation of man, but on the limitation of all earthly powers by the sovereignty of God. Yet the process of secularization in America is as advanced as that in Europe. Bonhoeffer suggests that "the claim of the congregation to build the world on Christian principles ends only with the total capitulation of the Church to the world, as can be seen clearly enough by a glance at the New York church registers. If this does not involve a radical hostility to the Church that is only because no real distinction has ever been drawn here [America] between the offices of Church and state. Godlessness remains more covert. And indeed in this way it deprives the Church even of the blessing of suffering and of the possible rebirth which suffering may engender." *Ethics*, ed. Eberhard Bethge and trans. Neville Horton Smith (New York: Macmillan, 1962), pp. 40–41.

8. Bonhoeffer, *No Rusty Swords*, p. 88.

the opposite is the case. "Precisely here, where the question of truth is not the criterion of church communion and church division, disintegration is greater than anywhere else. That is to say, precisely where the struggle for the right creed is not the factor which governs everything, the unity of the church is more distant than where the creed alone unites and divides the church."[9]

Christians came to America having fought hard to renounce confessional struggles. Subsequent generations born free of the battles for which their forebears fought no longer think it necessary to fight about anything. The struggle over the creed which occasioned the flight of their fathers and mothers becomes—for their sons and daughters—something that is itself unchristian. "Thus for American Christianity the concept of *tolerance* becomes the basic principle of everything Christian. Any intolerance is in itself unchristian."[10] Because Christians in America have no place for the conflict truthfulness requires, they contribute to the secularization of society;[11] a society, moreover, which finds itself unable to subject politics to truth and the conflict truthfulness requires.[12] Tolerance becomes indifference and indifference leads to cynicism.

Bonhoeffer's criticism of American theology, education, and politics reflects his lifelong passion to speak the truth. For example, in a letter to Bishop Ammundsen on August 8, 1934, Bonhoeffer discusses the upcoming conference at Fano and the address he was to give. Bonhoeffer confesses he is more worried about those who identify with opposition to Hitler than with the German Christians. The former will be worried that they should not appear unpatriotic, but they must recognize that

9. Ibid., p. 96.
10. Ibid., p. 103.
11. Bonhoeffer had little use for the kind of education available at Union Theological Seminary. He thought the "theological atmosphere" at Union was accelerating the process of secularization of American society. According to Bonhoeffer the criticism from Union directed at fundamentalists and "Chicago humanists" is necessary, but no basis is given for rebuilding after demolition. He was particularly critical of the students at Union who had turned their backs on all genuine theology in order to study economic and political organizations. Theology in America had been transformed into ethics. Even if Barth is studied, the basic suppositions of those who read him are "so inadequate that it is almost impossible for them to understand what he is talking about." Ibid., p. 90.
12. In a diary entry dated June 24, 1939, Bonhoeffer observes, "there hardly ever seem to be 'encounters' in this great country, in which the one can always avoid the other. But where there is no encounter, where liberty is the only unifying factor, one naturally knows nothing of the community which is created through encounter. The whole life together is completely different as a result. Community in our [German] sense, whether cultural or ecclesiastical, cannot develop here." Dietrich Bonhoeffer, *A Testament to Freedom: The Essential Writings of Dietrich Bonhoeffer*, ed. Geoffrey B. Kelly and F. Burton Nelson (San Francisco: HarperSanFrancisco, 1990), p. 498.

those who come together at Fano do so not as Germans, Danes, or Swiss but as Christians. Bonhoeffer continues:

> Precisely because of our attitude to the state, the conversation here must be completely honest, for the sake of Jesus Christ and the ecumenical cause. We must make it clear—fearful as it is—that the time is very near when we shall have to decide between National Socialism and Christianity. It may be fearfully hard and difficult for us all, but we must get right to the root of things, with open Christian speaking and no diplomacy. And in prayer together we will find the way. I feel that a resolution ought to be framed—all evasion is useless. And if the World Alliance in Germany is then dissolved—well and good, at least we will have borne witness that we were at fault. Better that than to go on vegetating in this untruthful way. Only complete truth and truthfulness will help us now. I know that many of my German friends think otherwise. But I ask you urgently to appreciate my views.[13]

"Only complete truth and truthfulness will help us now" was not just a reflection of Bonhoeffer's understanding of the challenge presented by the rise of Hitler. For Bonhoeffer, Hitler or no Hitler, the peace and justice any social order might try to achieve was impossible without truth. "There can only be a community of peace when it does not rest on *lies* and *injustice*."[14] The mistake of Anglo-Saxon thought is the subordination of truth and justice to the ideal of peace. Indeed, such a view assumes that the very existence of peace is proof that truth and justice have prevailed. Yet such a view is illusory just to the extent that the peace that is the reality of the gospel is identified with the peace based on violence. No peace is peace but that which comes through the forgiveness of sins. Only the peace of God preserves truth and justice. So "neither a static concept of peace (Anglo-Saxon thought) nor even a static concept of truth (the interpretation put forward by Hirsch and Althaus) comprehends the Gospel concept of peace in its troubled relationship to the concepts of truth and righteousness."[15]

For Bonhoeffer nothing less than the truth of the gospel was at stake in the confrontation with Hitler. Bethge observes that Bonhoeffer's famous radio address in 1933, which criticized the *Führer* concept, was

13. Bonhoeffer, *No Rusty Swords*, pp. 286–87.

14. Ibid., pp. 168–69. John Paul II often sounds very much like Bonhoeffer just to the extent that the pope maintains no freedom is worth having that is not disciplined by the truth. Jean Bethke Elshtain draws on Bonhoeffer and John Paul II in her book *Who Are We? Critical Reflections and Hopeful Possibilities* (Grand Rapids: Eerdmans, 2000). Elshtain rightly thinks Bonhoeffer and John Paul II to be allies, particularly given our current cultural challenges.

15. Bonhoeffer, *No Rusty Swords*, p. 169.

not based on liberal democratic ideas, but rather reflected Bonhoeffer's concern with authority.[16] According to Bonhoeffer, in the past, leadership was expressed through the office of the teacher, the statesman, and the father, but now the "Leader" has become an end in himself. When leadership was based on office, leadership required commitment to standards that were public and therefore capable of some rational justification. But the new leadership is based on choice, answering to nothing other than its own self-justification.[17]

Sociologically Bonhoeffer attributes this change to the breakdown of German society after the First World War. After the war the German people felt lost, dominated by techniques intended to subjugate nature now turned against their makers, distrusting all political, philosophical, and religious ideologies, and overwhelmed by the insignificance of the individual confronted by the dull power of the mass. The significance of the individual and the possibility of real community seemed to be forever destroyed. "The individually formed, autonomous personality and the idea divorced from reality seemed to have gone bankrupt. And from this need there now arose the passionate call for a new authority, for association, for community."[18] Hitler, the leader who exploited this hunger for significance, mocks God and in so doing becomes himself an idol no longer subject to truthful correction.

Bonhoeffer's criticism of American religious and political life as well as his analysis of the rise of Hitler can make uncomfortable reading for some who admire his opposition to Hitler but do not consider Bonhoeffer's own understanding of why Hitler must be opposed. Bonhoeffer's assumption that truth matters makes him an unlikely ally of the widespread assumption that—since no one knows the truth—the best we can do ecclesially and politically is to be tolerant. Moreover, it may be objected that it is by no means clear what Bonhoeffer took truth to be. I hope to show that the best way to respond to those who fear the "conservative" implications of Bonhoeffer's passion for truth as well as his understanding of truth is to be found in his essay that appears in *Ethics*, "What Is Meant by 'Telling the Truth'?" Not only does this essay make clear that, from the beginning to the end of his life, truth mattered to Bonhoeffer, but even more importantly we see that he understood that far more significant than giving us a "theory of truth" is giving us an account of what it means to be truthful.

16. Eberhard Bethge, *Dietrich Bonhoeffer: A Biography* (Minneapolis: Fortress, 1999), pp. 259–60. The address can be found in *No Rusty Swords*, pp. 190–204.
17. Bonhoeffer, *No Rusty Swords*, pp. 194–96.
18. Ibid., p. 194.

2. BONHOEFFER ON "TELLING THE TRUTH"

Joseph Fletcher claims Bonhoeffer's essay "What Is Meant by 'Tell-ing the Truth'?" "is as radical a version of the situational method as any Christian relativist could call for."[19] Fletcher's description of Bonhoeffer's position is so far off the mark I am tempted to call Fletcher a liar. He surely must have known better or, at least, been a better reader than his description of Bonhoeffer's position seems to suggest. However, given the mischaracterizations of positions so prominent in Fletcher's work it may be a mistake to attribute to Fletcher the intentional deception that Bonhoeffer thinks is often characteristic of the liar; which is but a reminder that it is at least as difficult to describe lying as it is to learn to speak truthfully.

Fletcher may well have been misled by Bonhoeffer's claim that " 'tell-ing the truth' may mean something different according to the particular situation in which one stands. Account must be taken of one's relation-ship at each particular time. The question must be asked whether and in what way a man is entitled to demand truthful speech of others."[20] It is also true that Bonhoeffer argues that in formal terms the description of the lie as a discrepancy between thought and speech is inadequate. There is a way of speaking that can be correct but still a lie, i.e., when a notorious liar for once tells "the truth" in order to mislead or when a correct statement contains a deliberate ambiguity or omits something essential necessary to know the truth.[21]

Bonhoeffer's account of the lie is determined by his understanding of reality. We are obligated to speak truthfully about reality but we must

19. Joseph Fletcher, *Situation Ethics: The New Morality* (Philadelphia: Westminster, 1966), p. 149.

20. Bonhoeffer, *Ethics*, p. 326.

21. Ibid., p. 331. A fascinating exercise would be to compare Bonhoeffer's account of lying with that of Augustine's. On the surface Bonhoeffer seems to be denying Augustine's account of the lie as the use of speech to say what I know is not the case in order to deceive. However I think Augustine's careful analysis of lying, which may well involve silence, is much closer to Bonhoeffer's account than would first appear. Though Bonhoeffer does not claim, as does Augustine, that one may never lie, the general direction of Bonhoeffer's understanding of lying is quite similar to Augustine's. For a subtle and compelling account of Augustine's position see Paul Griffiths, "The Gift and the Lie: Augustine on Lying," *Communio* 26 (spring 1999): 3–29. Griffiths has now written a book, *Lying: An Augustinian Theology of Duplicity* (Grand Rapids: Brazos, 2004) that develops this essay by putting Augustine in conversation with other accounts of lying.

Bonhoeffer's observations about the problem of the notorious liar is quite fascinating when compared to Norman Mailer's reflections on Colin Powell's presentation before the United Nations on February 5, 2003. Mailer observes that Powell was able to show Hussein had violated every rule he could get away with. According to Mailer he was able to do so because Hussein "has a keen nose for the vagaries of history. He understood the longer one

remember that reality names not only what is "out there" but our relation to what is "out there." According to Bonhoeffer every word we speak should be true. To be sure, the veracity of what we say matters; but the relation between ourselves and others that is expressed in what we say is also a matter of truth or untruth. "The truthful word is not in itself constant; it is as much alive as life itself. If it is detached from life and from its reference to the concrete other man, if 'the truth is told' without taking into account to whom it is addressed, then this truth has only the appearance of truth, but it lacks its essential character."[22] Bonhoeffer observes that some may object to this understanding of truthfulness on the grounds that truthful speech is not owed to this or that individual person, but to God. Bonhoeffer responds that this is of course correct as long as one remembers that God is not a "general principle, but the living God who has set me in a living life and who demands service of me within this living life."[23]

Bonhoeffer acknowledges that the concept of the living truth is dangerous just to the extent that it may give the impression that the truth can be tailored to fit this or that situation, making it difficult to tell the difference between truth and falsehood. The complexity of Bonhoeffer's account, however, does not lead him to equivocate about lying. For example, he says that one might think that the man who stands behind his word makes his word a lie or a truth, but that is not enough because "the lie is something objective and must be defined accordingly."[24]

Bonhoeffer gives the example of a child who is asked in front of the class by a teacher if his father often comes home drunk. In fact, the student's father often does come home drunk, but in answer to the teacher the child denies that the teacher's description is true. According to Bonhoeffer, the child rightly lies in answer to a question that should have never been asked in a classroom. Bonhoeffer explains that "the family has its own secret and must preserve it," which the teacher has failed to respect. Ideally

---

could delay powerful statesmen, the more they might weary of the soul-deadening boredom of dealing with a consumate [*sic*] liar who was artfully free of all the bonds of obligation and cooperation. It is no small gift to be an absolute liar. If you never tell the truth, you are virtually as safe as an honest man who never utters an untruth. When informed that you just swore to the opposite today of what you avowed yesterday, you remark, 'I never said that,' or should the words be on record, you declare that you are grossly misinterpreted. Confusion is sown rich in permutations." Norman Mailer, "Only in America," *New York Review of Books* 50/5 (March 27, 2003): 49. Mailer's account of the "consumate liar" is different than my argument that Bill Clinton could not be a liar—he could not be a liar because he could no longer distinguish truth from falsehood. It was all spin. See my "Why Bill Clinton Is Incapable of Lying: A Christian Analysis," in *Judgment Day at the White House*, ed. Gabriel Fackre (Grand Rapids: Eerdmans, 1999), pp. 28–31.

22. Bonhoeffer, *Ethics*, p. 328.
23. Ibid., pp. 326–27.
24. Ibid., p. 332.

the child would have the ability to answer the teacher in a manner that would have protected the family as well as the rule of the school. But that is to expect more from a child than should be expected. Bonhoeffer does not deny that "the child's answer can indeed be called a lie; yet this lie contains more truth, that is to say, it is more in accordance with reality than would have been the case if the child had betrayed his father's weakness in front of the class. According to the measure of his knowledge the child acted correctly. The blame for the lie falls back entirely upon the teacher."[25]

It is against this background that we can appreciate Bonhoeffer's claim that "telling the truth is something which must be learnt."[26] He acknowledges that this will sound shocking to anyone who thinks telling the truth depends on moral character and if we have a good character then not lying is child's play. But if the ethical cannot be divorced from reality, then continual practice in learning to discern and appreciate reality is a necessary ingredient in ethical action. That we must learn to tell the truth, that we must develop the skills of description to tell the truth, is the background presumption necessary to understand Bonhoeffer's remark that only the cynic claims "to speak the truth" at all times and places.[27]

Bonhoeffer's insistence that politics can never be divorced from truth is prismatically illuminated by his understanding of cynicism. In a letter to Bethge in December 1943, Bonhoeffer reports that he is working on his essay "What is 'speaking the truth'?" in which he is trying to draw a sharp contrast between trust, loyalty, and secrecy and the "cynical" conception of truth. According to Bonhoeffer "anyone who tells the truth cynically is lying."[28] Yet cynicism is the vice that fuels the habits necessary to sustain a politics that disdains the truth.

25. Ibid., p. 330.

26. Ibid., p. 327. In *Culture and Value*, ed. G. H. von Wright, trans. Peter Winch (Chicago: University of Chicago Press, 1977), p. 35e, Wittgenstein observes: "No one *can* speak the truth; if he has still not mastered himself. He *cannot* speak it;—but not because he is not clever enough yet. . . . The truth can be spoken only by someone who is already at home in it; not by someone who still lives in falsehood and reaches out from falsehood towards truth on just one occasion."

Wittgenstein, perhaps more than anyone, knew that speaking truthfully was a skill that not only required attention to what we say but how we say it. Moreover, we can only learn to speak truthfully when our pride has been defeated.

27. Dietrich Bonhoeffer, *Letters and Papers from Prison*, ed. Eberhard Bethge, trans. Reginald Fuller, Frank Clark, and John Bowden (enlarged ed.; New York: Touchstone, 1997), p. 163.

28. Ibid. This remark, like much else Bonhoeffer has to say, often sounds quite similar to some of Wittgenstein's remarks about lying and how hard it is to avoid lying. For example in *Culture and Value* (p. 39e), Wittgenstein observes: "How hard I find it to

For example, in *Letters and Papers from Prison* Bonhoeffer writes to Bethge (December 1943) describing a fellow prisoner who has simply come undone in prison. Bonhoeffer relates that this man now consults Bonhoeffer about every little thing as well as reporting to Bonhoeffer every detail of his life, such as when he has cried. Bonhoeffer's fellow prisoner simply has no life that he does not expose. This occasions in Bonhoeffer a remarkable reflection in which he tells Bethge that he has been thinking again about what he wrote recently about fear:

> I think that here, under the guise of honesty, something is being passed off as "natural" that is at bottom a symptom of sin; it is really quite analogous to talking openly about sexual matters. After all, "truthfulness" does not mean uncovering everything that exists. God himself made clothes for men; and that means that *in statu corruptionis* many things in human life ought to remain covered, and that evil, even though it cannot be eradicated, ought at least to be concealed. Exposure is cynical, and although the cynic prides himself on his exceptional honesty, or claims to want truth at all costs, he misses the crucial fact that since the fall there must be reticence and secrecy.[29]

Bonhoeffer is quite aware that secrecy can also be the breeding ground of the lie. The reticence and the secrecy Bonhoeffer is intent on protecting is the reticence that sustains relationships such as marriage and the family that should not be subjected to the gaze sponsored by ideological formations. What concerns him is how language itself is debased, made incapable of truth, by its misuse in the interest of "community." Each word, for example the word of command, which rightly is used in public service, must be rightly used if we are to be truthful. Commands—if used in the family—can sever the bonds of mutual confidence that sustain the trust crucial to family life.[30] But

---

see what is *right in front of my eyes!* . . . You can't be reluctant to give up your lie, and still tell the truth."

Later Wittgenstein comments, "Someone who knows too much finds it hard not to lie." A remark I suspect Bonhoeffer might appreciate.

29. Bonhoeffer, *Letters and Papers from Prison*, p. 158.

30. Bonhoeffer, *Ethics*, p. 328. I suspect this kind of reflection is what informs Bonhoeffer's observation in *Letters and Papers from Prison* (p. 148) that husbands and wives should have the same mind about matters even in the literary sphere. He confesses that he and his fiancée Maria are not yet on the same wavelength about writers. He worries that she reads poets such as Rilke whom he regards as "decidedly unhealthy." Bonhoeffer's attitudes about these matters can be interpreted as an exemplification of an unrepentant male point of view. Certainly it would have been interesting how Bonhoeffer's views on these matters might have developed if he and Maria would have had the time to marry and live together. That said, I think he is right to think that it is extremely important that marriage provide the time for husbands and wives to discover common judgments about matters that matter. Such judgments do not always or even in most cases entail agreement.

from Bonhoeffer's perspective modern developments have rendered words incapable of truthful expression:

> It is a consequence of the wide diffusion of the public word through the newspapers and the wireless that the essential character and the limits of the various different words are no longer clearly felt and that, for example, the special quality of the personal word is almost entirely destroyed. Genuine words are replaced by idle chatter. Words no longer possess any weight. There is too much talk. And when the limits of the various words are obliterated, when words become rootless and homeless, then the word loses truth, and then indeed there must almost inevitably be lying. When the various orders of life no longer respect one another, words become untrue.[31]

It is against this background, moreover, that we can appreciate what Bonhoeffer thought was at stake for the church in the confrontation with Hitler. As early as *Act and Being,* Bonhoeffer maintained that humans cannot place themselves into the truth without the help of revelation because the untruth of human self-understanding is only made apparent within the truth that revelation creates. Humans can only "recognize themselves as having been created anew from untruth for truth. But they recognize themselves as that only from within truth, within revelation—that is, in Christ, whether judged or pardoned."[32] Accordingly "the lie is primarily the denial of God as He has evidenced Himself to the world. 'Who is a liar but he that denieth that Jesus is the Christ?' (I John 2:22)."[33]

Lies are nothing less than contradictions of the word of God and the reality that is created by God. The purpose of our words, in unity with the word of God, is to "express the real, as it exists in God; and the assigned purpose of our silence is to signify the limit which is imposed upon our words by the real as it exists in God."[34] For Bonhoeffer, the source of the

31. Bonhoeffer, *Ethics*, pp. 329–30. Wendell Berry provides a contemporary complaint similar to Bonhoeffer's observation about the degradation of our language. He observes that a movement may lose its ability to speak truthfully when its enemies preempt its language. His example is organic farming, which became an end in itself making possible huge "organic" monocultures. This has made possible the attempt of the United States Department of Agriculture to label food that has been genetically engineered as well as irradiated to be called organic. Berry comments, "Once we allow our language to mean anything that anybody wants it to mean, it becomes impossible to mean what we say. When 'homemade' ceases to mean neither more nor less than 'made at home,' then it means anything, which is to say that it means nothing." *In the Presence of Fear* (Great Barrington, Mass.: Orion Society Publication, 2001), pp. 34–35.

32. Dietrich Bonhoeffer, *Act and Being*, trans. H. Martin Rumscheidt (Minneapolis: Fortress, 1996), pp. 81–82.

33. Bonhoeffer, *Ethics*, p. 332.

34. Ibid., p. 332.

lie is always our penchant for abstraction. Therefore the true meaning of correspondence with reality is neither civility nor opposition to the factual, but rather the attempt to understand reality without the real man—Jesus Christ. To attempt to live without Jesus Christ, the One before whom all factual reality derives its ultimate foundation and its ultimate annulment, is to live in "an abstraction to which the responsible man must never fall victim; it is to fail to make contact with reality in life; it is to vacillate endlessly between the extremes of servility and revolt in relation to the factual."[35]

I do not think Bonhoeffer believes that every word we use must gain its immediate intelligibility from Christ. As Rowan Williams suggests, the truth to which christological dogmas gesture is not so much a concern with rationality or comprehensive elucidation of all that is, but more with the "need to preserve the possibility of the kind of encounter with the truth-telling Christ that stands at the source of the Church's identity."[36] The threat to truth for Christians comes not from the difficulty of developing an unproblematic correspondence theory of truth, but rather from the lies that speak us disguised as truth.[37] Those are the lies Bonhoeffer rightly feared made possible the rise of Hitler, and the ongoing lies necessary to sustain Hitler in power. The failure of the church to oppose Hitler was but the outcome of the failure of Christians to speak the truth to one another and to the world.

3. LIVING IN TRUTH

Some may find the account I have given of Bonhoeffer's understanding of truth and politics troubling. The implications of Bonhoeffer's understanding of truthfulness for politics could even suggest he favored

35. Ibid., p. 198. In the section of the *Ethics* in which he discusses the "Concept of Reality," Bonhoeffer says, "Henceforth one can speak neither of God nor of the world without speaking of Jesus. All concepts of reality which do not take account of Him are abstractions" (p. 61).

36. Rowan Williams, *On Christian Theology* (Oxford, U.K.: Basil Blackwell, 2000), p. 82.

37. Bernard Williams has explored the relation between truth and truthfulness in an extremely helpful way in his *Truth and Truthfulness* (Princeton, N.J.: Princeton University Press, 2002). He notes that his concern throughout his book is with the "value of truth" even though "to speak of the value of truth is no doubt a category mistake: truth as a property of propositions or sentences is not the sort of thing that can have a value." However he defends his use of the phrase as a means to direct attention to what he calls the "virtues of truth," that is, "the qualities of people that are displayed in wanting to know the truth, in finding it out, and in telling it to other people" (pp. 6–7). According to Williams those virtues are sincerity and accuracy. I am particularly attracted to Williams's account of accuracy as the virtue at odds with "wishing." "Realism," therefore, is understood as the desire not to let my belief be undercut by what I wish to be the case.

a theocracy. Even though I do not share the general presumption that theocracy is a "bad idea,"[38] Bonhoeffer remained far too Lutheran to entertain a theocratic alternative. For example, in his essay "The Church and the New Order in Europe," written in 1941 in response to William Paton's *The Church and the New Order*, Bonhoeffer observes that there is a new recognition that the political order also is under the lordship of Christ. The political order, therefore, cannot be considered a domain that lives on its own terms apart from God's plan. "The commandments of God indicate the limits which dare not be transgressed, if Christ is Lord. And the Church is to remind the world of these limits."[39] Accordingly the church cannot and should not try to develop a detailed plan for postwar reconstruction. Rather the church should remind the nations of the reality that the commandments entail if the new order is to be a "true order."

In particular, Bonhoeffer suggested that the "chaos" behind the war could not be overlooked if the new order was to be true and just. National Socialism was made possible because there was just enough justice in some of Germany's claims against the "peace" established in the railway wagon at Compiègne to make credible Hitler's presentation of himself as a prophet of justice.[40] For Bonhoeffer there is no way to the future that does not truthfully acknowledge the sins of the past.

Bonhoeffer saw clearly the challenge modern politics presents for those committed to truthfulness. His views on the politics of the lie we confront are quite similar to Hannah Arendt's understanding of the lies associated with modern politics. Arendt observes that the politics of the lie we experience in our day are quite different from the traditional political lie. In traditional politics, by which I assume she means the kind of politics Machiavelli represented, the lie was assumed a necessity in diplomacy and statecraft to protect secrets or intentions that had never been made public or could not be made public.[41] In contrast, the

38. To his credit and for our instruction Allen Verhey has recently written an extremely intelligent analysis and defense of theocracy. See his *Remembering Jesus: Christian Community, Scripture, and the Moral Life* (Grand Rapids: Eerdmans, 2002), pp. 333–507.

39. Dietrich Bonhoeffer, *True Patriotism*, trans. Edwin H. Robertson and John Bowden (New York: Harper & Row, 1973), p. 109.

40. Bonhoeffer, *True Patriotism*, pp. 111–12.

41. For example, see Ruth Grant's extremely subtle analysis of Machiavelli and Rousseau on the necessity of hypocrisy in her *Hypocrisy and Integrity* (Chicago: University of Chicago Press, 1997). Grant observes, "While most in need of honesty as a political virtue, liberal democratic regimes are most likely to produce the conditions that undermine that virtue. Oddly enough, in light of these reflections on the thoughts of Machiavelli and Rousseau, liberalism can be criticized not for being hypocritical, but for refusing to acknowledge the necessity of hypocrisy. At the outset, we noted the peculiar susceptibility of liberal democracies to charges of hypocrisy. This is a function of both aspects of what I have called the 'paradox of democracy'; liberal democratic regimes make particularly

modern political lie deals not at all with secrets but with what is generally known. For example Arendt calls attention to

> highly respected statesmen who, like de Gaulle and Adenauer, have been able
> to build their basic policies on such evident non-facts as that France belongs
> among the victors of the last war and hence is one of the great powers, and
> "that the barbarism of National Socialism had affected only a relatively small
> percentage of the country." All these lies, whether their authors know it or
> not, harbor an element of violence; organized lying always tends to destroy
> whatever it has decided to negate, although only totalitarian governments
> have consciously adopted lying as a first step to murder.[42]

I believe Bonhoeffer's passion for the truth meant he would have
stood against the lies that speak through us in modernity—lies all the
more powerful because we believe we speak them by our own volition.
We are, after all, "a free people." Moreover, we live in a manner that
seems to make our lies true because we are so determined to make them
true.[43] The clarity of Bonhoeffer's truthful witness to the truth was made
possible by the clear evil he opposed. Yet such clarity is apparent only
retrospectively. Most of Bonhoeffer's fellow Christians did not see the
truth with Bonhoeffer's unflinching clarity.

In his book *Living in Truth*, Vaclav Havel calls attention to the innocent
act of a manager of a fruit and vegetable shop who puts in his window,

---

strong claims to be able to provide open and honest political processes at the same time
that those processes are structured so as to increase dependencies conducive to hypocritical political behavior" (p. 176). Bonhoeffer might well agree with Grant's contention that
some forms of hypocrisy may not only be necessary but justified in democratic regimes,
but I do not think he would regard that as a "good thing."

For a good critical analysis of the oft-made assumption that liberal democracies can
be the more truthful form of democracy because such polities provide a place for the
"marketplace of ideas," see Williams, *Truth and Truthfulness*, pp. 206–32.

42. Arendt, *The Portable Hannah Arendt*, p. 565. In *Truth and Truthfulness* Williams provides
an extremely important chapter on the significance of narratives, particularly historical narratives, for our being truthful. However, he rightly denies that there can be such a thing as
"the truth" about the past, but rather truth about the past names "the hope that hopeful but
truthful stories can go on making sense, and that while they do, they will be told" (p. 266).

43. Arendt tells the medieval anecdote about the sentry that was given to practical jokes
who one night sounded the alarm just to give his townsfolk a scare. Everyone rushed to
the walls. As a result he was the last one to rush to the walls. Arendt comments that the
story illustrates how hard it is to lie to others without lying to oneself. She comments, "The
tale suggests to what extent our apprehension of reality is dependent upon our sharing the
world with our fellow-men, and what strength of character is required to stick to anything,
truth or lie, that is unshared. In other words, the more successful a liar is, the more likely
he will fall prey to his own fabrications." *The Portable Hannah Arendt*, p. 566.

Wittgenstein remarks that "nothing is so difficult as not deceiving oneself." *Culture
and Value*, p. 34e.

among the onions and carrots, the slogan "Workers of the world, unite." Why, Havel asks, does the shop owner put the sign in his window? Is he genuinely enthusiastic about the possibility of the workers of the world uniting? Does he want to communicate his enthusiasm for this ideal to his fellow citizens? Does he have any idea what it might mean for workers to be so united?

Havel suspects that the majority of shopkeepers who put such a sign in their window never think about what they are doing nor does the sign express their true opinions. The poster was delivered from the headquarters along with the onions. The shop owner put the sign in his window because he had always done so and if he did not he could get in trouble. Moreover the greengrocer thinks nothing is at stake because he understands that no one really believes what the slogan says. What is important is the subliminal message the sign communicates. Havel suggests that the sign's real message is: "I, the greengrocer XY, live here and I know what I must do. I behave in the manner expected of me. I can be depended upon and am beyond reproach. I am obedient and therefore I have the right to be left in peace."[44]

To help us understand what is happening with the display of this sign, Havel suggests a thought experiment. Suppose the greengrocer had been asked to display the sign "I am afraid and therefore unquestioningly obedient." Even though the new sign expresses the truth, Havel observes that the greengrocer would be ashamed to display such a sign. He is, after all, a human being with some sense of his own dignity. The display of the sign "Workers of the world, unite" allows the greengrocer "to conceal from himself the low foundations of his obedience, at the same time concealing the low foundations of power. It hides them behind the facade of something high. And that something is *ideology*."[45]

I suspect most of us think there to be a great distance between the sign in the greengrocer's window and the rise of National Socialism in Germany. Yet I think Bonhoeffer rightly saw that the Christian acceptance that truth does not matter in such small matters prepared the ground for the terrible lie that was Hitler. In order to expose the small as well as the big lies a community must exist that has learned to speak truthfully to one another. That community, moreover, must know that to speak truthfully to one another requires the time granted through the work of forgiveness. Such patient timefulness is a gift from the God the community believes has given us all the time we need to care for the words

44. Vaclav Havel, *Living in Truth*, ed. Jan Vladislav, trans. Erazim Kohák (London: Faber & Faber, 1986), p. 42.
45. Ibid.

we speak to one another.[46] Any politics absent such a people is quite literally doomed to live lies that are the breeding ground of violence.[47] Bonhoeffer believed that the church is the sign that God has placed in the windows of the world to make possible a truthful politics.

This means that Bonhoeffer's observations about the character of theological education in America are not what might be considered his personal prejudices. Rather they are a challenge to teacher and student alike that few things are more important than our holding ourselves, as well as being held by the church, to speak the truth. As odd as it may sound given the accommodated character of the church in liberal societies, if the church does not itself preach the gospel truthfully then politically we condemn ourselves and those to whom we are pledged to witness to what Bonhoeffer called "the void."[48] A sobering observation, but one that at least directs those of us who count ourselves Christian

46. For a powerful account on the importance of word care for Christians, see Stephen Fowl, *Engaging Scripture* (Oxford, U.K.: Blackwell, 1998), pp. 161–71. One of the offices John Howard Yoder thought crucial for the church was what he called "agents of linguistic self-consciousness." He noted, however, that this is a dangerous office in the church because the tongue is hard to govern. The demagogue, the poet, the journalist, the novelist, the grammarian are all in the business of steering society with the rudder of language. The problem is that too often concepts become reified by such people because it is through such concepts that they make themselves indispensable. Therefore Yoder urges the teacher to watch for the "sophomoric temptation" to make verbal distinctions without substantial necessity. *The Priestly Kingdom: Social Ethics as Gospel* (Notre Dame, Ind.: University of Notre Dame Press, 2001), pp. 32–33.

47. For a fascinating and powerful account of the relationship between lies and violence, see Robert Dodaro, OSA, "Eloquent Lies, Just Wars, and the Politics of Persuasion: Reading Augustine's *City of God* in a 'Postmodern' World," *Augustinian Studies* 25 (1994): 77–138. Dodaro argues that Augustine saw the lies that shaped Roman politics and political leaders drew their intelligibility from the attempt to beat death by achieving political glory that would ensure immortality. Dodaro thinks the same process is at work in our own politics as exemplified in attempts to justify the first Gulf War.

An analysis of relationship between the acknowledgment of death, our ability to live truthful lives, and violence would be extremely informative. For example, Bonhoeffer observes, "the miracle of Christ's resurrection makes nonsense of that idolization of death which is prevalent among us today. Where death is the last thing, fear of death is combined with defiance. Where death is the last thing, earthly life is all or nothing. Boastful reliance on earthly eternities goes side by side with a frivolous playing with life. . . . The drastic acceptance or rejection of earthly life reveals that only death has any value here. To clutch at everything or to cast away everything is the reaction of one who believes fanatically in death." *Ethics*, pp. 16–17. And, of course, where death is everything, violence cannot be kept at bay.

48. Bonhoeffer saw clearly that "the void" becomes possible as the alternative to Christianity. In the extraordinary story he tells in the section of the *Ethics*, "Inheritance and Decay," he rightly suggests that "it was only from the soil of the German Reformation that there could spring a Nietzsche" (p. 28). In a manner that anticipates recent "postmodern" doubts about reason, Bonhoeffer notes that "contempt for the age of rationalism is a suspicious sign of failure to feel the need for truthfulness. If intellectual honesty is not

to the task God that has given us, that is, to be a people capable of speaking truthfully to ourselves, to our brothers and sisters in Christ, and to the world.[49]

---

the last word that is to be said about things, and if intellectual clarity is often achieved at the expense of insight into reality, this can still never again exempt us from the inner obligation to make clean and honest use of reason" (p. 34). Finally he notes, "Luther's great discovery of the freedom of the Christian man and the Catholic heresy of the essential good in man combined to produce the deification of man. But, rightly understood, the deification of man is the proclamation of nihilism" (p. 39). For Bonhoeffer's explicit use of the language of "the void," see p. 44 of the *Ethics*.

49. Wittgenstein observes, "You cannot write anything about yourself that is more truthful than you yourself are. That is the difference between writing about yourself and writing about external objects. You write about yourself from your own height. You don't stand on stilts or on a ladder but on your bare feet." *Culture and Value*, p. 33e. This remark is extremely important if what Christians believe is true—namely, we can only know the truth about ourselves by receiving it as a gift from God. So we can never trust our "truth," but rather must continually look to that truth that is God if we are to truthfully see ourselves.

II

TRUTHFUL PERFORMANCES

3

PERFORMING FAITH

The Peaceable Rhetoric of God's Church

James Fodor
Stanley Hauerwas

INTRODUCTION[1]

Christian faith evokes diverse and sometimes competing images and associations. For some, it conjures up a fairly coherent, albeit complexly interrelated array of experiences, dispositions, attitudes, and beliefs.

1. The argument developed in this essay is a joint effort, the happy result of genuine collaboration. As our readers follow its movements, recapitulations, and provisional resolutions, we hope they will discern themes at once common to Christian faith but also peculiar to the distinctive styles of its respective authors. Those familiar with Hauerwas's work will readily identify motifs and emphases that have become characteristic of his oeuvre over the years. Nonetheless, because the essay brings together two rather different but, we trust, compatible ways of inflecting Christian faith, an argument that has been formulated, advanced, revised, negotiated, and tested through numerous conversations and long discussion between us, our hope is that the reader will discern in the final product an original performance. By "original" we do not mean unique or altogether new but fully collaborative, melodious, amicable, and above all edifying. When it comes to performance, it is hard to know exactly where the substance of an argument leaves off and its execution

For others, faith names not so much the defining subjective features of religious consciousness as the objective content of Christian religion. Faith is thus construed as a set of doctrines, a peculiar body of teaching and instruction. In short, faith is a divine "deposit"—with the church or the Bible acting as its repository.

Although these two broadly defined ways of speaking strive to do justice to the divine source as well as to the richness, density, and historical scope of Christian life, both prove deeply dissatisfying. One of the difficulties of speaking of faith principally in subjective terms, especially in modernity, is that it cuts off Christianity and effectively quarantines it within the narrow, inner realm of the private. Although Christian faith no doubt encompasses the full range of human experience and alters, adjusts, and transforms human dispositions and attitudes, it is nonetheless grounded in a reality prior to and far greater than the human. Likewise, speaking of faith in terms of a deposit induces images and impressions that are at once static and lifeless. Like a meteor fallen to earth, Christian faith objectively understood as "revealed data" connotes something that is simply "there"—inert and self-contained because delivered once and for all, intact, whole. "Keeping the faith" thus comes to mean "neither adding to nor taking away," that is to say, the reception of a deposit and its faithful transmission without alteration, corruption, or diminution from one generation to the next. What is overlooked by both subjective and objective accounts of faith is the sense in which Christian existence is first and foremost an activity—a performance, if you will.[2]

---

begins or, for that matter, who contributed what—who took the lead and who followed, who intervened to change the direction or pace of the argument, who corrected and modified it. Some scientific disciplines have a convention of listing contributors to an article in order of significance for the research. If we followed such a convention, Fodor would clearly be listed first. But since ours is less a scientific undertaking and more an exercise in the mutual exploration and rhetorical negotiation of Christian faith, this convention proves unsuitable and inappropriate. Given the fact that the quality and power of Christian religious reflection is unavoidably communal, drawing upon a rich and ancient tradition with a vast chorus of voices, we are content to leave our readers with the task of judging this work not according to which of its two authors contributed what, but according to how well they move together in a performance that persuasively exhibits the rhetorical power and coherence of Christian faith.

2. Since the mid-1980s, a number of important studies have been devoted to the performative aspects of Christian faith. See, for example, Nicholas Lash, "Performing the Scriptures," in *Theology on the Way to Emmaus* (London: SCM, 1986), pp. 37–46; Frances Young, *The Art of Performance: Towards a Theology of Holy Scripture* (London: Darton, Longman & Todd, 1990); Michael G. Cartwright, "The Practice and Performance of Scripture: Grounding Christian Ethics in a Communal Hermeneutics," in *The Annual of the Society of Christian Ethics, 1988*, ed. D. M. Yeager, pp. 31–54; and "Practices, Politics, and Performance: Toward a Communal Hermeneutic for Christian Ethics" (Ph.D. diss.,

If Christian faith is from start to finish a performance, it is so only because Christians worship a God who is pure act, an eternally performing God. Trinity and creation are the language Christians use to speak of this God. Indeed, God performs peaceably and most excellently precisely because God is God's own *causi sui*. That is to say, only God as Trinity can perform in such a way as not to be alienated from who God is. It may be that the Christian faith is "primarily an account of divine action" and "only secondarily an account of the believing subject";[3] nonetheless, the very character of Christian speech is distorted when its rhetorical property is ignored. The Christian God is found in Israel and in Jesus. God refuses to be known apart from our life in God, which means that to be made part of God's speech lies at the heart of the Christian understanding of God. In short, our God is a performing God who has invited us to join in the performance that is God's life. Before developing explicitly these theological claims, we need to say a few words regarding first the character of performance and the fruitfulness of its contribution to a better appreciation of theology and ethics, and then the way theology is from start to finish a rhetorical enterprise.

Theology, Improvisation, and the Performing Arts

In the last twenty years or so, a new field of investigation and inquiry, called performance studies, has come into existence.[4] Although the term is associated mostly with music, it also applies to the performing arts in general.[5] "The past few decades have witnessed a virtual explosion in scholarly writing about musical performance. A vast literature on historical performance practice, the psychology of performance, the relation

---

Duke University, 1988); Allen Verhey, "Scripture and Ethics: Practices, Performances, and Prescriptions," in *Christian Ethics: Problems and Prospects,* ed. Lisa Sowle Cahill and James F. Childress (Cleveland: Pilgrim, 1996), pp. 18–44; Walter Brueggemann, *Texts under Negotiation: The Bible and Postmodern Imagination* (Minneapolis: Fortress, 1993); Hans Urs von Balthasar, *The Action,* trans. Graham Harrison (vol. 4 of *Theo-Drama: Theological Dramatic Theory;* San Francisco: Ignatius, 1994); and Samuel Wells, *Transforming Fate into Destiny: The Theological Ethics of Stanley Hauerwas* (Carlisle, Scotland, U.K.: Paternoster, 1998), hereinafter cited as *Transforming Fate*. Each of these studies points up the centrality of the dramatic and the performative in Christian faith, albeit with accents and emphases on different features.

3. This accords with John Webster's point. See his article on "Faith" in *The Blackwell Encyclopedia of Modern Christian Thought,* ed. Alister E. McGrath (Oxford, U.K.: Blackwell, 1993), pp. 208–10.

4. Indeed, separate journals, like *Text and Performance Quarterly* and *Literature in Performance,* are devoted exclusively to these issues.

5. A closely related, though distinct, term is "performance art," which refers to "a hybrid form of performance, originating in futurist and dadaist performances, that often draws on visuals, media art, dance, and music and appropriates its materials from pop culture,

between analysis and performance, and 'interpretation' broadly defined has emerged during that time."[6] This rapidly expanding field of inquiry encompasses a broad spectrum of topics: structure and meaning in performance; performance as process; the role of intuition in performance; the relation between creator or composer, performer, and listener; the meaning of "authentic" performance; the "text(s)" of performance; and the inevitable partiality of interpretation and the need for judgment and choice among more or less convincing performances. To be sure, performance studies concerns not only instrumental and vocal music but also drama, ballet, opera, dance, and certain narrative forms of poetry.

Performance suggests itself as a potentially illuminating and instructive category for Christian reflection and self-understanding, both ethically and politically but also aesthetically and rhetorically, because it is a category richly suggestive of analogical relations between various facets of religious life.[7] For one thing, understanding Christian existence as a kind of performance helpfully encapsulates the sense in which both the intelligibility and the assessment of faith are of one piece. That is to say, the intelligibility (and hence the persuasiveness) of Christian faith springs not from independently formulated criteria, but from compelling renditions, faithful performances. In George Lindbeck's words, "Reasonableness, in religion and theology, as in other domains, has something of that aesthetic character, that quality of unformalizable skill, which we usually associate with the artist or the linguistically competent. . . . In short, intelligibility

---

often blurring the boundary between art and life. Performance art can be loosely improvisatory, relying on environment, chance, and even found objects, or tightly scripted; it can function as antiaesthetic statement, political or cultural intervention, social practice, or theatrical or narrative art." Carol Simpson Stern and Bruce Henderson, *Performance: Texts and Contexts* (New York: Longman, 1993), p. 546; see also pp. 382–83. It is particularly important to our case that improvisation not be thought equivalent to "spontaneity," if the latter means "undisciplined" action. Improvising, after all, is only possible within a disciplinary set of skills. A "disciplinary set of skills" is another way of describing what we mean by tradition.

6. John Rink, ed., *The Practice of Performance: Studies in Musical Interpretation* (Cambridge: Cambridge University Press, 1995), p. ix. See also H. M. Brown and S. Sadie, eds., *Performance Practice: Music before 1600* and *Performance Practice: Music after 1600* (London: Macmillan, 1989); and R. Jackson, *Performance Practice, Medieval to Contemporary: A Bibliographic Guide* (New York: Garland, 1987).

7. Performance is, of course, a much more encompassing and multifaceted phenomenon than that captured either by "performance studies" or "performance art." Stern and Henderson use the term very broadly to refer to three continuums of human activity that are customarily studied across disciplines in the humanities, the arts, and the social sciences (anthropology, ethnography, history, the fine arts, to name but a few). In short, the term "embraces cultural and literary performance as well as performance art, which includes a variety of activity from aesthetic to political, individual to collective." Stern and Henderson, *Performance*, p. 546.

comes from skill, not theory, and credibility comes from good performance, not adherence to independently formulated criteria."[8]

Moreover, concentrating on performance helps retain the importance of historical and temporal contingencies for understanding Christian existence. Timing is indispensable to all good performances. Musical improvisation or extemporization is a kind of performance especially attuned to matters of time, and in that sense it lends itself well to fertile descriptions not only of the ethicist's work in particular but of the general art of living well under God.[9] Albert Jonsen, for instance, is surely right to draw attention to the ways in which rhetorical and casuistic invention are features of the ethicist's craft in much the same way that improvisation and invention are part of the artistry and virtuosity of an accomplished musician.[10]

In its most simple definition, improvisation refers to the process of creating music in the course of performance.[11] Just as ethicists invent and improvise arguments from topics, concepts, and arguments already laid down in the tradition, so too classical musicians extemporize the

8. George A. Lindbeck, *The Nature of Doctrine: Religion and Theology in a Postliberal Age* (Philadelphia: Westminster, 1984), pp. 130–131.

9. Improvisation, like performance, is itself a multifaceted phenomenon and varies according to the historical period, genre, and musical culture. Whereas improvisation is not a major factor in Chinese and Japanese art music, it is of enormous importance in the music of sub-Saharan Africa—although with respect to the latter the formal distinction between improvised and composed genres may not be as clearly defined as in other music cultures. In any event, every musical performance involves to some extent elements of improvisation, though its degree varies according to period and place; and to some extent every improvisation rests upon a series of conventions or implicit rules. "Some improvisational systems are governed by theoretical rules strictly applied by performers. The degree to which a musician departs from a written or memorized work and the extent to which performances differ from each other may also be considered a function of improvisation. Thus, the presence or nature of improvisation is affected by, but does not depend upon, the concept of composition, the use of notation and oral tradition, and the nature of performance practice." See "Improvisation, extemporization," in *The New Harvard Dictionary of Music*, ed. Don Michael Randel (Cambridge, Mass.: Harvard University Press, 1986), pp. 392–94.

10. Albert R. Jonsen, "The Ethicist as Improvisationist," in Cahill and Childress, eds., *Christian Ethics*, pp. 218–34. Jonsen's thesis is that ethicists "invent and improvise arguments" in much the same way that classical musicians extemporize on particular musical scores. Both move—make judgments, execute actions—from themes already laid down. While improvisation allows and indeed encourages the virtuoso to stray, wander, explore, it nonetheless demands that she remain close to home. Improvisation "departs from the composition and must return to it; and, indeed, even as it flows from the artist's virtuosity, it must remain at least remotely true to the composer's inspiration" (pp. 225, 224). All of which is to say that improvisation is a difficult art because under constant negotiation.

11. "Musical performance which is created as it is played, without a notated score or detailed preparation": Paul Griffiths, "Improvisation," in *The New Oxford Companion to Music* (vol. 1; ed. Denis Arnold; Oxford, U.K.: Oxford University Press, 1984), p. 903. "The

melodies, keys, rhythms, and other musical elements set forth in their respective tradition. The invention of the concerto form for orchestra and solo instrument in the seventeenth and eighteenth centuries, for example, "allowed the soloist an opportunity to show technical skill by departing from the composer's notation and playing freely for some time. These 'cadenzas' came just before the end of the first movement, following the statement of themes and their recapitulation, so that the player might pick up the melodies already established in the notated score and modify them in harmony, rhythm, modulation of key, and phrasing."[12]

The central point of comparison between musical improvisation and casuistical moral judgment is that neither set of practices can be produced without reference to prior exemplifications. Significant models and exemplars (memorable performances) are necessary to determine the scope but also to set a standard against which a musician plays or an ethicist reflects and judges. Performance in both instances is evaluated primarily by its ability to improvise, to balance individual inventiveness with adherence to a tradition of prescribed conventions—which means that elements of risk and unpredictable achievement are inescapable features of any good performance. As Jonsen puts it,

> improvisation is like invention in that both take definite material as the base and frame for creative interpretation. Rhetorical invention finds the common and special topics suited to the case and allows the orator to work creatively with the actual circumstances of persons, times, and places. The orator invents with the standard materials and with the unique elements that a particular case presents. Musical improvisation provides musicians with melodies and key and lets them display notes, harmonies, and rhythms that expand, emphasize, and reorder the original set composition. The simile is not, of course, perfect but it begins, I think, to reveal how ethicists work with their materials, which are the general concepts of morality and the particulars of issues, questions, and cases.[13]

---

creation of music while it is being performed." Philip D. Morehead, *The New American Dictionary of Music* (New York: Penguin, 1991), p. 245. "The invention of music . . . at the same time that it is being performed." Christine Ammer, ed., *The HarperCollins Dictionary of Music* (3d ed.; New York: HarperCollins, 1995), p. 194. "The creation of a musical work, or the final form of one, as it is being performed." Stanley Sadie, ed., *The Norton/Grove Concise Encyclopedia of Music* (rev. and enlarged ed.; New York: Norton, 1994), p. 383.

12. Jonsen, "The Ethicist as Improvisationist," p. 224.

13. Ibid., p. 224. While Jonsen's general point about the limitation of the simile of improvisation is well taken, we have difficulty with his description of how the orator/ ethicist purportedly improvises his or her ethical judgment. To speak of "general concepts of morality" makes it appear that these are raw materials that are simply there; it is then the ethicist's job to coordinate or apply them vis-à-vis "the particulars of issues, questions, and cases."

Performance (and in particular improvisation) proves indispensable both in providing access to but also in offering a means of assessment of Christian faith. A more sustained and careful exploration of the notion of improvisation is therefore required and will be supplied in due course. For the present, however, it is important to recognize several clear dangers of overemphasizing performance, even though it remains a crucial notion. One of the liabilities in beginning with "performance studies" as a means of exhibiting the character of Christian theology and life is that the former becomes too easily associated with, if not subsumed under, the rubric "performing arts" or "fine arts." That the so-called arts should define and determine faith is a view we in no way wish to endorse. Neither do we want to reinforce the tendency, so strong in modernity, to use these descriptions to designate separate realms of human existence. Because we refuse strong compartmentalization of human life into discrete spheres or separate districts, we avail ourselves of these studies modestly and with some degree of qualification. Part of our strategy throughout this essay, therefore, is to avoid calling attention to rhetoric as if it were a discrete activity.

A further danger of focusing on improvisation as a key to explicating the character of Christian life is that it concentrates too exclusively, too one-sidedly, on "active" aspects of human performance and thus fails to characterize adequately the dialectical movement between acting and suffering, self-dispossession and self-constitution, that is part of any good performance. For if improvisation is a kind of activity or movement, it is equally a kind of suffering, a pause in or cessation of movement, an undergoing, a receptivity. In other words, performance that is truly improvisatory requires the kind of attentiveness, attunement, and alertness traditionally associated with contemplative prayer. All of which is to say that the virtuoso is played even as he or she plays. For music plays the performer as much as if not more than the performer plays the work; likewise, language speaks the speaker as much as if not more than the speaker speaks the language. As music precedes and thus makes possible the performer, so language precedes and makes possible the speaker.

Theology as Rhetorical Performance

Examining the character of performance skills invites the comparison, hinted at earlier, between musical improvisation and rhetorical invention. This analogy in turn raises the question of whether and to what extent theology itself is a rhetorical performance. Regardless of medium—be it musical sounds or human speech—competent performers in both will display the necessary dexterity, finesse, and inventiveness to warrant their recognition as excellent performers within their respective traditions and communities of practice.[14] With regard to the Christian tradition, one might say that the very grammar of faith points up a vital sense in which the doing of theology is intrinsically performative. Word and deed are inseparable in Christian life and practice; nevertheless, because word and action do not always or completely coincide, Christians have always been concerned about "getting it right."[15] What

14. The skills of improvisation are more common than they are often given credit. A number of studies note important similarities between jazz improvisation and linguistic competence, for example. See Alan M. Perlman and Daniel Greenblatt, "Miles Davis Meets Noam Chomsky: Some Observations on Jazz Improvisation and Language Structure," in *The Sign in Music and Literature*, ed. Wendy Steiner (Austin: University of Texas Press, 1981), pp. 169–83. The virtue of these studies is that they alert us to how ordinary and pervasive in human life are improvisatory skills. Amélie Rorty, for one, helpfully draws attention to the ways in which even everyday practices like conversation (real conversations rather than an exchange of monologues, which often passes for the genuine article) presuppose the type of close attention, flexibility, and finesse exhibited in practices more commonly associated with the performing arts. True conversational skills, then, are closer to musical improvisation, for example, than we might at first suspect. As Rorty describes it, "in a real conversation, the participants do not know, ahead of time, what they will say, or even sometimes what they think. But at any moment in the conversation, there are an indefinite number of relevant, consecutive true things they could say and think. Closure is given by the minutiae of interactions: the look of puzzlement on an interlocutor's face, the excitement of common pursuit, an ironic remark. The more subtly partners in a conversation understand each other—the more they are familiar with one another's gestures, facial expressions, and reactions—the more condensed and improvisatory their conversation is likely to be. Like jazz musicians, they sometimes lapse into a familiar riff for a little rest, finding something in that riff that leads them in a new direction. Not only conversations and music-making, but many of our central actions—designing a playground or a curriculum, cooking a meal, selecting a Supreme Court Justice, hanging paintings for an exhibition—take this form." Amélie O. Rorty, "Virtues and Their Vicissitudes," in *Ethical Theory: Character and Virtue* (vol. 8 of *Midwest Studies in Philosophy;* ed. Peter A. French, Theodore E. Uehling, Jr., and Howard K. Wettstein [Notre Dame, Ind.: University of Notre Dame Press, 1988]), pp. 136–48; p. 144. Sharon Welch draws on jazz to display the importance of listening for the development of community in her "Communitarian Ethics after Hauerwas," *Studies in Christian Ethics* 10/1 (1997): 82–95. Welch nicely reminds us that to improvise first means to respond.

15. Concern about "getting things right" is evidence of the diligence and attention essential to Christian faith. Because theology concerns those things which matter, and matter finally, theologians, of all people, care intensely about *how* things are said; which means that the genre in which faith is conveyed and exhibited is by no means an incidental matter. In one obvious sense, therefore, linguistic vigilance and intellectual sensitivity and alertness are indispensable to the theologian's work. Such skills and sensibilities prove virtuous insofar as they serve to check ideologically distorting propensities that continually threaten to undermine Christian life, or indeed any significantly rich and complex form of life, religious or otherwise. If obsessively pursued as ends in themselves, however, such that standards of linguistic accuracy and precision become divorced from the particular, concrete, historical realities to which they apply, then the goal of getting things right quickly transforms itself into a preoccupation with getting things *just* right. The

"getting it right" means in terms of faith is somewhat elusive, given that circumstances and situations in which the church finds itself are always changing, sometimes in small and imperceptible ways, sometimes in ways that are marked and drastic. Whether these changes are minuscule or expose major shifts, transitions, and developments, improvisation is a constant feature of Christian witness by virtue of the contingencies of created existence.

Because theology is first and foremost a way of talking, a way of thinking, a way of using language to make sense of God, the world, and ourselves, it is indelibly marked by both poetic and rhetorical qualities.[16] As Rowan Williams puts it, "Theology is a language used by a specific group of people to make sense of their world—not so much to *explain* it as to find words that will hold or reflect what . . . is sensed to be solid, authoritative, and creative of where we stand. Thus theology is always involved with doing new or odd things with speech."[17] Theology is rhetoric—what else could it be?—inasmuch as rhetoric is "a way of talking, and a way of transforming and negotiating with or in language."[18] Its proper exercise never occurs in abstraction from specific historical contexts.

---

latter differs markedly from the former; getting things *just* right assumes that everything can be put in order, accorded its proper place. Getting things right, on the other hand, is a less ambitious but for all that a more vigilant and exacting enterprise, since it sets for itself the goal of locating a suitable word in its season. Sadly, whenever theologians commit themselves to system-building, they find that they have little time to engage in the continual struggle and hard, intellectual labor of finding a "timely" word. Fascinated by order and seduced by standards of precision and comprehensive rigor that effectively remove theology from the vagaries of time (part of the beauty to which such systems aspire is, after all, the promise of "timeless" perfection), system-builders have little patience with rhetoric. ("Having little patience with rhetoric" is in effect another way detractors fail to notice, precisely and especially when they make such claims, that they themselves are using rhetoric.) Indeed, the idea of negotiating in and with language in order to find the appropriate way to say things seems, at best, an indulgence reserved for poets and other wordsmiths blessed with sufficient leisure. At worst, a concern with the rhetorical workings of theological discourse appears to system-builders as a diversion from, if not a betrayal of, theology's true calling. What is lost whenever system replaces rhetoric is, ironically, the willingness to start again. Understanding theology as rhetorical performance at least holds out the possibility of retaining time and risk as integral features of theology's ongoing task. As any good performer knows, excellence, proficiency, virtuosity cannot be had without commitment to practice and constant rehearsal. And practice holds no fear, even for master performers, for although it implies a willingness to start again, practice does not entail starting all over again. Such commitments are indeed far removed from the world of system-builders.

16. Although the mode of doing theology may be intrinsically performative and improvisatory, and will therefore exhibit these features, theology's object is not performance per se but an eternally performing God, a God who is pure act.

17. Williams, quoted in Todd Breyfogle, "Time and Transformation: A Conversation with Rowan Williams," *Cross Currents* 45/3 (fall 1995): 293–311; p. 296.

18. Ibid., p. 296.

Its form cannot be separated from its content. That is to say, because theology cannot be rightly understood apart from a consideration of who is doing it, with whom, and to what ends, its task is perpetually self-renewing, and in that sense unfinished. In addition to social and political factors, the complex set of practices that constitute theology involves a host of other dimensions: linguistic, rhetorical, ethical, and aesthetic, to name a few. Furthermore, if theologians are to remain true to their task, they must write in such a way that their readers have to work with them, "perform" along with them when reading.[19] The rhetorical formation of an audience proves intrinsic to theology's craft inasmuch as readers must to be schooled and apprenticed in order to sense with the theologian the pressures that shift her language this way and that. Theology, from beginning to end, is the performing of a rhetoric.[20]

How a distinctively Christian understanding of rhetoric might accord with, diverge from, or even contest nonreligious or philosophical understandings of rhetoric, Aristotle's, for instance, is not our present concern.[21] The extent to which Christian theology is or ought to be beholden to classical, Renaissance-humanist, or modern understandings of rhetoric is likewise too extensive and involved a topic to broach, given the more limited concerns of this essay.[22] To be sure, Christian rhetoric is also performative and inventional, just like its nonreligious or philosophical cousins; it too engages with the socially situated, practical concerns of everyday life; it too displays a deep affinity with time.[23] But even these similarities, when understood within the Chris-

19. The performative logic of the Christian narrative is, as Samuel Wells rightly points out, inescapably self-involving. "The text makes such a demand on us that we cannot properly read it unless we are performing it." *Transforming Fate*, p. 91.

20. In making such a claim we are borrowing—and slightly adapting—Williams's expression, made in reference to Gillian Rose; namely, that her "philosophy [is] the performing of a rhetoric." "Time and Transformation," p. 296.

21. Two important secondary sources on Aristotle's *Rhetoric* are Eugene Garver, *Aristotle's Rhetoric: An Art of Character* (Chicago: University of Chicago Press, 1994); and Amélie O. Rorty, ed., *Essays on Aristotle's Rhetoric* (Berkeley: University of California Press, 1996).

22. The intimate relations between Greco-Roman rhetorical practices and Christian faith have long been recognized. See, for example, George Kennedy, *The Art of Rhetoric in the Roman World* (Princeton, N.J.: Princeton University Press, 1972). Although we do not have the space in this essay to examine the ways in which the distinctive Christian practices of theological persuasion transcend and transform Aristotelian categories, we recommend James L. Kinneavy's intriguing study, *Greek Rhetorical Origins of Christian Faith: An Inquiry* (Oxford, U.K.: Oxford University Press, 1987). Kinneavy argues that "many of the major features of the concept of persuasion, as embodied in Greek rhetoric of the Hellenistic period, are semantically quite close to the Christian notion of faith" (p. 4).

23. The significance of time (and timing) to rhetoric cannot be overstated. Of particular importance for rhetoric—in its classical, Christian, and modern manifestations alike—is the notion of *kairos*. As Walter Jost and Michael Hyde indicate, the links between rhetoric and *kairos* are apparent not only in the work of such modern philosophers and rhetori-

tian story, are finally more apparent than real. For what sets Christian rhetoric apart from all other rhetorical performances is its peaceable character. That Christian rhetoric is not only inventional but peaceable is perhaps its most defining trait. Our account will therefore consist of an extended conceptual-rhetorical unfolding of the eternally peaceable drama of the mystery of God whom Christians worship as Father, Son, and Spirit.

Theologically locating our discussion thus is crucial if we are to appreciate the way in which Christian rhetoric and Christian ethics are mutually implicative. Our primary objective, then, is to display the intimate connections between the rhetorically and ethically performative dimensions of Christian theology by accentuating some of the latter's distinguishing features: time, gift, self-divestment (*ekstasis*), "overacceptance," and reincorporation. We begin, then, by constructively and critically engaging the work of John Milbank (on difference in relation to Trinity and creation) and Sam Wells (on the church's practice of "overacceptance" and reincorporation) in order to set the groundwork for our own proposals toward a pedagogy of performance.

GOD AS PURE, PEACEABLE PERFORMANCE

Christians believe that no human action (or any other action for that matter) can be described as autonomous activity, a self-generating move-

---

cians as Martin Heidegger, for whom *kairos* serves as a central organizing concept in his transcendental analysis of *Dasein*, they are also pivotal in pre-Socratic Greek drama and literature (Pythagoras, Empedocles, Hesiod), in Aristotle, in classical Roman rhetoric, and in the rhetoric of Renaissance humanism. See Walter Jost and Michael J. Hyde, eds., *Rhetoric and Hermeneutics in Our Time: A Reader* (New Haven and London: Yale University Press, 1997), pp. xiv ff. To be sure, the exact role of and emphasis on time is different in each of these types of rhetoric, and it is again different for Christian forms of rhetoric. While there may be some superficial similarities between Heideggerian *kairos*, or even the uses of *kairos* in classical rhetorical theory and the Christian notion of *kairos* as the "fullness of time," these are finally quite dissimilar since deployed in radically different traditions. For example, although *kairos* may refer in classical rhetorical theory to "the principle or power *(dunamis)* by which the opportune moment calls forth an intuitive, appropriate response from the rhetor," and in that sense "such *kairos* remains beyond the control of the rhetor, coming rather as gift or even magic *(goetia)*," the giftedness of time to the Christian does not pose the same tension between receptivity and activity inasmuch as it is set within an eschatological horizon of God's action. This is not to say that Christian rhetoric is unconcerned with invention or discovery, but that the problematic is radically different because set within a distinctly different story. Even Heidegger's appropriation of *kairos*, despite its links with the early Christian concern with the "fullness of time," is more a distortion of rather than a borrowing from Christianity.

ment. To act is to share in the divine life, for human reality exists solely within God's reality.[24] Because the source or ground of human activity resides not in ourselves but in God, any movement we make, any action we perform, entails an actualization of the divine act in our own temporal and finite context. Far from erasing the distinction between God's act and our actions, this claim affirms that any human action truly and properly performed will be nothing short of, and nothing other than, "a movement into our createdness."[25] Which is but another way of saying that to act according to what we are created to be is to act truly and to act morally. In sum, because all this life *is* God's act, it follows that performing actions that are fully human is by definition to be "caught up in the eternal movement of God's commitment to his creation."[26]

When Christians speak of the eternally performing God, a God who not only creates but redeems, they are not referring to some univocal Being but to Father, Son, and Spirit. Indeed, because the Christian God is Trinity and not Being, this makes all the difference to how the character of human actions is understood as participatory in, and thus derivative of, God's action. This is especially important if Jesus Christ is viewed as God's true and most defining act. Because Christ is regarded by his followers as God's most memorable and excellent performance (complete, holy, and finally efficacious because inclusive of all difference), the implication is that Christian lives, too, can become "holy performances."[27] However, if human acts neither persist alongside nor stand over against God's pure act nor are swallowed up or absorbed into God's complete performance, how can we register the difference they make? More specifically, how is the manifold diversity of human actions "accommodated" or preserved in God's pure, undivided act? No satisfactory response to these questions can be provided without reflecting further on Christian understandings of Trinity and creation; for unless

24. See Rowan Williams, "*Sapientia* and the Trinity. Reflections on the *De Trinitate*," in *Collectanea Augustiniana* (vol. 1; ed. T. J. van Bard; Leuven, Netherlands: Leuven University Press, 1990), p. 321.

25. Ibid., p. 326. Such claims entail that all attributions of God are analogical—a point which, when forgotten, invites disaster.

26. Rowan Williams, *Open to Judgement: Sermons and Addresses* (London: Darton, Longman & Todd, 1994), p. 85. Redescribing Christian existence as "enacting the faith" serves as a reminder that human agency and action are creaturely acts: they can be rightly understood only within the context of creation. Human actions acquire their true shape and dynamic only in reference to the more determinative, because prior and all-encompassing, act of God.

27. The language of "holy performances" unavoidably carries considerable ethical overtones, which is but another way of restating the claim that the goodness or worth or reality of human actions is always measured in relation to God's actions. Or, to put it in an interrogative mood, what else is the Christian moral life if not remaining alert to the movement of God's grace in every movement, becoming alive to God in every action?

these matters are addressed, the ramifications for human performance under God will be distorted if not missed altogether.

Milbank on Peaceable Difference: Trinity, Creation, and the Church

In his various writings, John Milbank sets forth in great detail, as well as much erudition and sophistication, a harmonious ontology of pure relationality as rooted in an understanding of God as Trinity. According to Milbank, the Christian faith owes no allegiance to the idea of the univocity of Being, which can only uphold difference coercively and violently, but is instead moved by a trinitarian understanding of God, an absolute that is itself difference, inclusive of all difference, and thus able to affirm difference in a peaceful manner.[28] Christianity, in other words, exhibits *a peculiar mode* of difference, one which ascribes ontological priority to peace rather than conflict, one which transmits differences nonviolently by sustaining those differences in a continuous, internal harmony. Indeed, precisely because Christianity is "totally different," it exposes all other cultural-linguistic systems as threatened by an incipient nihilism insofar as they are governed by monistic conceptions of Being rather than by a differential ontology peaceably sustained in the Trinity of Father, Son, and Spirit. The fact that Christianity has always understood God as the God "who is also difference, who includes relation, and manifold expression" means that any conception of God as monistic is proscribed.[29] The Christian God, in other words, is one who makes possible "a true melodic progression" by his openness, in love, to all differences.[30]

Creation reveals a God who is open to all differences. "As the reality which includes and encompasses every difference, God is also the God who differentiates"—that is, the God who creates.[31] For creation is nothing other than God's free, gratuitous self-positing of difference. But this creative act, ceaselessly called out of its own eternal power of differentiation, is never an imposition on, an arbitrary limitation of, a preexisting reality. It is, rather, creation *ex nihilo* and thus by its very "nature" peaceable.[32] Because God is the one who creates freely in his

28. John Milbank, *Theology and Social Theory: Beyond Secular Reason* (Oxford, U.K.: Basil Blackwell, 1990), p. 429.

29. John Milbank, "The Second Difference: For a Trinitarianism without Reserve," *Modern Theology* 2/3 (April 1986): 213–34; p. 213.

30. John Milbank, " 'Postmodern Critical Augustinianism': A Short *Summa* in Forty-Two Responses to Unasked Questions," *Modern Theology* 7/3 (April 1991): 225–237; p. 229.

31. Milbank, *Theology and Social Theory*, p. 423.

32. As Milbank remarks elsewhere, "creation out of nothing eschew[s] the idea of a 'chaotic' realm over against the divine, in eternal conflict with it." Thus, wherever "there

self-differentiation and self-donation, the entire created order is "in-corporable" into God's life. The divine life is, moreover, eternal peace: it is both unending (in the sense that it continually accommodates all difference) and also aesthetically pleasing and perfectly beautiful (in that it refuses to countenance the loss of even a single difference).

The full brilliance and splendor of God's all-inclusive peace has been revealed most clearly in Jesus Christ. The full specification of God's perfect peace, in other words, is most excellently displayed in the life, death, and resurrection of Jesus. For only in the perfect saving of this one man from the destruction of death do we witness God's refusal to accept the loss of any difference.[33] "Creation *ex nihilo* and the resur-rection of the dead" are therefore positive expressions of God's limit-less inclusion of all difference, but also "protocols against the myth of scarcity, of limited being."[34]

The practical, ethical problem with which the church is left, and to which it must respond, is: How does Christian faith reconcile the doctrine of God as Trinity (and thus as the pure generation of difference) with the doctrine that all creation, including human existence, participates through Christ in the life of the Trinity (and thus peaceably includes and incorporates all difference)?

On secular accounts—that is to say, from nontrinitarian points of view—all differences are by definition negatively related.[35] Difference "enters the existing common cultural space only to compete, displace or expel"; "in the public theatre, differences arise only to fall; each new difference has a limitless ambition to obliterate all others, and therefore to cancel out difference itself."[36] The best that secular peace can hope for, then, is a "tolerable" regulation or management of conflict by one coercive means or another.[37] However, because Christians believe in a God who is pure act in trinitarian relation, difference does not and cannot interpose itself violently: the peaceableness exhibited by the church must also be infinitely patient of difference. How does this manifest itself?

After all, it is quite clear that Christians, too, "do not live in a world where differences just lie benignly alongside each other, without mu-

---

is a positing of a sacred over against a chaotic other, then the supremacy of the sacred can always be deconstructed, for it appears that there is something more ultimate that includes both the sacred and chaos, that governs the passage between them. Is not this passage itself chaotic?" "Postmodern Critical Augustinianism," p. 230.

33. John Milbank, "Enclaves, or Where Is the Church?" *New Blackfriars* 73/861 (June 1992): 341–52; p. 348.

34. Ibid., p. 350.

35. According to a secular outlook, difference is always subterfuge, severance, a mani-festation of a violent rupture. See Milbank, *Theology and Social Theory*, p. 376.

36. Ibid., p. 290.

37. Ibid., p. 334.

tual interference, but, rather, every difference is in itself an 'overlap', a disturbance within some area of common space."[38] But this does not mean that the church is obliged to interpret every disturbance violently, as a virtual war. On the contrary, because Christians understand difference affirmatively in God, inasmuch as creation is viewed as God's free, gratuitous self-positing of difference and not an imposition on, or an arbitrary limitation of, a preexisting reality, the church is free to blend or reconcile all differences. Because the Christian multiple is not a multiple set dialectically over against the one but is instead an infinite flow of excessive charitable difference emanating from, and finally returning to, a single divine spring,[39] differences are preserved rather than eradicated. Charity is the resource that makes the blending in God of all differences possible. To the extent that the church's life is animated by charity, and inasmuch as charity's source and mode of expression is essentially trinitarian (that is, a constant outgoing and excess, which is never finally threatened by difference), the life of the church is enlivened by a power that accords every difference its place.

How exactly does this preservation of differences manifest itself in practical, concrete terms within the life of the church, part of whose present reality includes the spatio-temporal world of God's good creation? The only answer that is forthcoming, it appears, is an agnostic one. Although the church cannot claim to know in advance the full details of the story, it nonetheless has some inkling of its general shape and eventual outcome. Perhaps a knowing that has the form of an "unknowing" is all that Christians can rightly expect if their lives are truly lived in hope. And though Christians live in expectation of the *eschaton*, the "fullness of time" when all things will be made one in God, that hope does not pretend to lift the church out of time. Explicating the character of Christian hope, therefore, means that considerably more can and must be said regarding the "timing"—and indeed the time it takes—to abide in, to keep the faith. Performance analogies are especially apt in this respect.

Following Saint Augustine's lead,[40] Milbank discovers in music an appropriate analogy for the life of faith, arguing that while the church

38. Ibid., p. 289.
39. Ibid., p. 410.
40. Augustine's early treatise *De musica* is clearly a pivotal work, which has profoundly influenced subsequent Christian theology. See St. Augustine, *On Music*, Books I–VI, trans. R. Catesby Taliaferro (Annapolis, Md.: St. John's Bookstore, 1939). See also a fascinating series of studies on the theological import of Augustine's treatise on music, *Augustine on Music: An Interdisciplinary Collection of Essays*, ed. Richard R. La Croix (Lewiston, N.Y.: Edwin Mellen Press, 1988). The fact that the order displayed in Augustine's *De musica* is one which has its ultimate basis of harmony and meaning not in the visual, nor even the acoustic, but in the numerical raises interesting questions regarding the relation between the practice and performance of mathematics and the performance and practice of music.

"is open to difference—to a series of infinitely new additions, insights, progressions towards God, it also strives to make of all these differential additions a harmony, 'in the body of Christ'."[41] Indeed, insofar as music is "a consistently beautiful, continuously differential and open series," it serves as an appropriate model of the peaceable accommodations of interpretive differences within the church.[42] Just as every musical note exists in a position fully defined by the unfoldings of the entire sequence, so too every interpretive difference emerges in relation to the overall historical development of the church's life and self-understanding. Music's endlessly peaceable progression mirrors the church's infinitely expansive interpretive practices.[43] As the undivided musical sequence undergoes continuous alteration and revision in its accommodation of each additional note, so too the church displays an unending capacity to expand in a noncoercive, nonviolent way. In one sense, of course, the whole musical sequence is nothing other than the *differentia* of its parts.[44]

41. Milbank, "Postmodern Critical Augustinianism," pp. 227–28.

42. Ibid., p. 228. See also *Theology and Social Theory*, pp. 404ff. Milbank is well aware of the objection that even in music there is dissonance, interruption, and discord as well as consonance and harmony. As Frances Young notes, "Within a particular work the role of repetition, recurring themes, development and recapitulation, and conversely internal oppositions, contrasting themes, tempos, moods, keys, and so on, is even more important. The dynamics of music, or any other art form, depend on disjunctive as well as unitive features, on dissonance as well as its resolution in harmony." *Art of Performance*, p. 66. Milbank is aware of the various ways in which the tragic impinges upon Christian life, but he believes that tragedy is not finally determinative inasmuch as it presupposes "the dominance of a spatial perspective." The vision of the church, however, is not that of a particular bounded space but an unending "process of peaceful transmission." "Enclaves, or Where Is the Church?" pp. 351, 348. It is a temporal (and in particular the eschatological) rather than a spatial vision that informs the life of the church, and which allows Milbank to acknowledge the reality of those losses of difference without at the same time conceding that they are finally irredeemable. As he puts it, "if anything is to be saved, it can only be saved in the passing moment of its loss, and if anything is to remain it can only remain through recollection, which repeats what has vanished and so intimates its eternity. As everything passes and only 'is' through the trace of its vanishing, nothing even of what has been violently or tragically surrendered (under force of circumstances) is irrecoverable" (ibid., p. 351). Ironically, however, as much as Milbank wishes to emphasize the importance of time, and movement through time, his description of how the church is to remain in time, "keep" time with all its dissonances and interruptions, is curiously absent. In short, what Milbank fails to provide is a pedagogy of the church's peaceable performance.

43. At this point the analogy is a bit misleading, both with regard to the practice of musical composition and with regard to the church's infinitely expansive capacities to generate ever new interpretations. In both cases, differences are never introduced atomistically, one difference at a time, but in clusters, patterns, or configurations, each with varying degrees of complexity. This does not undermine the analogy as such but complicates it, underscoring the difficulty of its particular implementation in the day-to-day life of the church.

44. See Milbank, *Theology and Social Theory*, p. 405.

Although the church may confidently claim this work as its own, it must nonetheless not lose sight of the fact that "it is God himself who is differentiation, ensuring that this process is 'music', not the ceaseless rupture and self-destruction of a differentiation poised 'univocally' between an 'indifferent' transcendence and an anarchic finitude."[45]

To be sure, in music there are also "continuous endings and displacements, yet these are not necessary violence, because *only in the recall* of what has been displaced does the created product consist. Violence would rather mean an unnecessarily jarring note, a note wrong because 'out of place', or else the premature ending of a development."[46] The church is therefore called not to exclude or reject but to affirm, welcome, and accept difference in the hope that everything will in the end be reconciled to God in Christ. In the meantime, its interpretive practices will never be fully transparent either to the world or to itself, for Christians live by faith and hope, not sight. Since Christians can never claim "to know" the finality of what they treat as final, the church's posture remains one of hope.[47]

Theatrical Improvisation: A Contribution to Christian Ethics

Musical performance is not the only analogy from the performing arts that elucidates the character of Christian life. In a fascinating study, Samuel Wells employs the analogy of improvisation in the theater as a way of explicating the ethical nature of Christian existence.[48] Theatrical improvisation proves useful, Wells explains, because it involves "immersion in the Christian narrative," through which we learn the skills of patience, courage, hope, peaceableness, constancy: this takes moral effort. In a crisis, the community trusts the habits formed from those skills, and concentrates on doing the obvious. In this way it "overaccepts" issues that come to it from its own experience and from the wider society, and transforms "fate into divine destiny."[49] This immersion in and acquired facility and practiced dexterity with respect to the improvisational skills of Christian faith helps account for the way the church trusts, in times of crisis, its own habituation and formation of character, what makes the Christian community's faithful performance distinctive in its commitment to peace.[50] The peaceableness of Christian witness is rooted in the manner

45. Milbank, "Augustinianism," p. 237.
46. Ibid., p. 228 (emphasis added).
47. Ibid., p. 231. Because patience is inextricably wedded to hope, peaceableness will necessarily be part of hope's modality as well.
48. Wells, *Transforming Fate*, pp. 2, 191. In a manuscript soon to be published by Brazos Press, Wells develops the suggestion begun in *Transforming Fate*.
49. Ibid., p. 2.
50. See ibid., p. 9.

in which Jesus accepts his cross "as the way of disarming the powers that oppress us, and in the vindication of his nonviolent witness in the resurrection."[51] Christological considerations, but also Trinity and creation, are therefore clearly central to the performative ethic of the church.

Wells's leading insight is that the practice of "overaccepting" or improvising in theatrical drama provides a model for the formation of Christian imagination.[52] Within the world of theater, the art of "overaccepting" means fitting the remarks of the previous actor into a context enormously larger than his or her counterpart could have supposed.[53] What this amounts to, Christianly speaking, is being exercised in the habit of regarding all offers as potential gifts. In short, what it means to be ethically well-formed is having one's imagination trained to regard the world not as a given but as truly a gift from God. A better way to describe Christian ethics, then, is not as a choosing or deciding what is the right thing to do but being educated in the art of rightly accepting gifts.[54] Performing the Christian faith chiefly entails "working out how to accept (or 'overaccept') things that present themselves as 'givens' but which are not."[55] Although the language of acceptance, and in particular overacceptance, may sound inappropriately passive, all too accommodating, this is far from the case, given that the task of the Christian imagination is "to *change* or *challenge* the presumed 'necessities' of the world" rather than to comply with or conform to the world's offer.[56]

Faithfully enacting the Christian story, then, is effectively to "out-narrate" the world by situating the world's "givens" within a more determinative, peaceable, and hence more encompassing, narrative.[57] "This is

51. Ibid., p. 9.

52. See ibid., p. 209. It would be interesting to explore how the difference between drama, which is Wells's prime example, and music, which is Milbank's, changes one's understanding of improvisation and its relation to theology.

53. See ibid., p. 209. Wells draws predominantly on the work of Keith Johnstone, *Impro: Improvisation and the Theatre* (New York: Theatre Arts Books, 1979).

54. The highly distinctive Christian art of receiving and giving gifts must, of course, be set within a theological framework that includes such related notions as end of sacrifice, resurrection, plenitude, and confidence. See John Milbank, *The Word Made Strange: Theology, Language, Culture* (Oxford, U.K.: Blackwell, 1997), pp. 228ff.

55. Wells, *Transforming Fate*, p. 212.

56. Ibid., p. 212 (emphasis added).

57. The language of "out-narrating" is John Milbank's but it is clearly consonant with Wells's use of "overaccepting." See Milbank, *Theology and Social Theory*, p. 330. Milbank's notion of "out-narrating" contrasts with that of "argument." Because the various stoic-liberal-nihilist tendencies of secular reason are themselves finally a *mythos*, which means that they cannot be refuted by argument but only out-narrated, if we can persuade people that Christianity offers a much better story, adopting an argumentative rather than a rhetorical mode is not only futile but deeply compromising. Perhaps better that all arguments we have to make depend on the rhetorical force of the narrative that forms us.

exactly what the Christian community does with offers that come to it from wider society. It overaccepts in the light of the Church's tradition and story seen in eschatological perspective—a perspective much wider than urgent protagonists may have imagined."[58] "Overacceptance" thus signifies the practice of rendering the apparent given as gift by placing the latter within a wider story. Reconceiving Christian ethics in this way has the added virtue of placing the emphasis squarely on the giver rather than the recipient. Not only does this have the auspicious and positive consequence of promoting an eschatological rather than a teleological vision, it also signals the fact that what is central to the Christian life is not the will but the imagination, not so much our power as God's. The more Christians stretch their imaginations through the improvisatory habits of overacceptance, cooperation, and adaptation, the more they become open to the giftedness of the world and to its giver, God.[59]

The site where this analogy with theatrical improvisation occurs most vividly for Wells is in the relation between providence and the written text of Scripture.[60] Although Scripture is for the Christian the definitive story of God's way with the world, it is by no means the entire story. "Whenever the Christian community faces a trying situation, it does

58. Wells, *Transforming Fate*, p. 209. Wells's point is effectively illustrated by Tom Wright, who, in his book *The New Testament and the People of God* (London: SPCK, 1992), characterizes world history as a five-act drama. "The story," according to Wright, "moves through creation, the Jews, and Jesus, and finishes with the eschaton. The Church finds itself in Act Four. While secular society supposes itself to be in a one-act play . . . , the Church knows itself to be bounded in past and future by God's decisive acts. Hence the Church can overaccept the pressing secular demands by outnarrating them—fitting them into a much larger story, one which begins at creation and ends with the eschaton, where the main character is God, and where the definitive event is Jesus Christ."

59. Wells anticipates and successfully meets the objection that making the imagination central to Christian ethics places an undue burden on the Christian's creative effort to improvise, overaccept every offer as given, and transform it instead into a gift. That sounds too much like something *we* do. However, Wells rightly reminds the objector that the most vital resource of the Christian imagination is memory, not creativity. "What is required is an imagination that enables us to keep the story going. This is where it is important to remember that the story is not just our story. The originality lies in the story already: this is the sense in which we are continuing to perform the Christian story whose decisive elements have already been set in place." *Transforming Fate*, p. 204. Because it is God's story, already set in motion and superintended by God, its truthful telling is not finally dependent on our efforts—either to get it going, keep it going, or ensure its outcome. As Wells puts it, "improvising within a narrative is less a constant striving after being original, and more a matter of remembering" (p. 217). This last remark ameliorates the strict opposition between memory and creativity indicated earlier. One could say, in this regard, that creativity exhibits the peculiar way Christians are trained and encouraged to remember their story.

60. Wells, *Transforming Fate*, p. 216.

not have an 'answer' in a script, but it is able to respond in a manner analogous to 'overaccepting', by placing the event within the larger, providential story which is under God's superintendence and direction. The response cannot be violent, since that would contradict God's way of dealing with the world as revealed in Jesus Christ. Neither can the response be to block—that is, to end the story—since that would imply that the larger story were incapable of incorporating the situation."[61] What is required, rather, is receiving each apparent given as gift (that is, in such a way that it peaceably and harmoniously becomes part of the continuing story). Reincorporation, then, is the reverse side of improvisation; both form part of a single, peaceable dynamic.

If overacceptance names the posture of creative openness to all givens as potential gifts, then "reincorporation" designates a profound awareness of the end of the story that, precisely because it is an eschatological awareness, commits Christians to a kind of patience and hope that will not foreclose on the end of the story but will search instead for ways to keep it going. As Wells puts it, "When elements found earlier in the story begin to be reincorporated, then some pattern emerges and a sense of completion is possible. Christian ethics seen from an eschatological perspective is always profoundly aware that the story has an end and that this end reincorporates earlier (perhaps all earlier) parts of the narrative."[62]

These, then, are the salient features of Wells's fascinating and insightful study of how theatrical improvisation (construed in terms of overacceptance and reincorporation) is analogous to the performative, yet peaceable, character of Christian existence. Wells's approach displays a distinct affinity with and dependence upon the work of John Milbank. Although Milbank does not treat the phenomenon of performance directly and as such, his reflections on "difference" in relation to the Christian doctrines of Trinity, creation, Christ, and the life of the

---

61. Ibid., p. 216. Preaching is, of course, the paradigmatic practice for this task.

62. Ibid., p. 218. Although we agree with this claim broadly conceived, there is nonetheless something suspiciously Hegelian about it, which gives us pause. The language of the reincorporation of all differences smacks too much of *Aufhebung*. Part of what is needed here is a Kierkegaardian kind of intervention, where emphasis is on a repetition that defies and resists synthesis. Another way of articulating this worry is to say that one ought to be highly wary of too tight and neat formulations of doctrines of God's providence that begin to sound like theodicies. Indeed, Wells's language of transforming fate into divine destiny through improvisation and overacceptance, because in God there is always a larger story (p. 219), comes uncomfortably close to theodicy. Another way to put this is to say that although Christians are profoundly aware that the story has an end and that this end will reincorporate all earlier parts of the narrative, they do not claim to know when and how this will be accomplished.

church betray striking similarities to Wells's understanding and use of "overacceptance" and "reincorporation." In one sense, Milbank sets up a problematic to which Wells's theological appropriation of improvisation constitutes a response.

"Timely" Interventions on Performance

Like Wells's analysis of the theatrical model of improvisation, Milbank speaks of the process of reincorporating and assimilating difference as something that can be appreciated only retrospectively.[63] At one time (i.e., from the then present but clearly limited point of view), many differences struck us as nothing short of violent interruptions, jars, dislocations, ruptures, and were thus refused, excluded. Likewise, what currently appear within the Christian tradition as premature endings at another time were understood differently; what we now with hindsight want to name violent and tragic exclusions in the tradition were formerly included and welcomed as something obvious, perhaps even necessary. If that is so, then how do the improvisatory practices of the church—analogous with practices in musical or theatrical performance that Milbank and Wells respectively espouse—help Christians resolve the temporal tensions between, for example, habit and moral effort? How do they actually aid us, instruct us, train us, in "keeping time" as we perform the exacting, disciplined art that is the church's peaceful witness?

Milbank's project—and in a less sustained but more focused way, Wells's investigation—is more properly concerned with providing "supra-ethical religious affirmation[s] which recast the ethical field in terms of religious hope"[64] than in setting forth ethical prescriptions about what we must do in specific situations.[65] To be sure, setting forth

63. As Wells puts it, "reincorporation is a backward-looking art." *Transforming Fate*, p. 235.

64. Milbank, "Enclaves, or Where Is the Church?" p. 343.

65. It is precisely for this reason that Milbank refuses to endorse any particular brand of "pacifism." Pacifism is not recommended as a moral position for the same reason that Milbank cannot condone any form of "ethics": neither one can guide our decision about the appropriate moment to act. As Milbank puts it, "The formal specification of truth as peaceful relation cannot be applied as a criterion authorizing non-resistance." "Church," p. 349. Applying something called "pacifism" as a criterion, in other words, does not tell us *when* it is appropriate to resist nonviolently or for that matter how and with regard to whom. Those are matters of judgment, which are acquired through the practice (performance) of nonviolence. What is ironic about Milbank's insight regarding the vital importance of time and timing in the Christian witness of peace is that his very recognition of its centrality should so blind him to the way that his own supraethical account of peace as harmonic differentiation and melodic progression is in danger of becoming a timeless model.

moral criteria or ethical principles will be of no help here. They will not tell us *when* and *how* and *with regard to whom* we Christians should act. Ethics, after all, is entirely a matter of proper description, rightly naming in God the realities of our world. However, more needs to be said about the ways in which these theological descriptions arise. If it is the case, and surely it is, that supraethical religious affirmations recast the ethical field in terms of religious hope, how is it, for example, that Christians come to describe certain situations as trying or as crises? Why is something "obvious" in one context and not in another? Surely, improvisation cannot simply mean "being so trained in one's tradition that one trusts the obvious is the appropriate."[66] That is to put the matter in too stark and insufficiently nuanced a manner. While the Christian practices of overacceptance and reincorporation may helpfully indicate ways in which the peaceable witness of the church retains its integrity, they do not go far enough in showing why the appropriate response may at one time be "trusting what is obvious in the tradition," while at another trusting "the obvious" should not be trusted.[67] In short, the danger into which both Wells and Milbank fall is that of advocating an overly undifferentiated, an all too timeless model of faithful performance. Such models neglect to treat adequately what "keeping time" in Christian performance entails.[68]

Christian faith, then, is not only intrinsically performative, it is also inescapably "timeful." Perhaps the most crucial feature of the church's performance is its eschatological orientation. That eschatology and teleology are not one and the same hardly goes without saying. For an eschatological vision alone is capable of delivering the church from having to structure its ethics around an incomplete *telos*, the realization of which it feels obliged somehow to bring about.[69] Keeping this eschatological perspective in view helps avert a temptation to which Chris-

---

66. Wells, *Transforming Fate*, p. 230.

67. In several places in Wells's work he uses the language of "doing the obvious"—in moments of "crisis" or in "trying" situations. See *Transforming Fate*, pp. 2, 216, 230, 233. In one sense, of course, it is true that if the Christian community is well-trained in performing the faith it will do "the obvious" in such circumstances. But neither "the obvious" nor what constitutes a "crisis" or a "trying situation" is simply there. If Wells's analysis is to be fully persuasive, more attention needs to be given to the temporal conditions under which these descriptions hold and for whom, how they arise in the first place, and how they may change over time. These matters are clearly resistant to the kind of generalization implied in Wells's analysis.

68. To his credit, Wells does recognize (like Milbank) the indispensable importance of time to performance. He rightly remarks that "salvation saves humans within time, not from time." *Transforming Fate*, p. 168. However, like Milbank he goes on to make claims that curiously neglect these important "timeful" aspects of Christian performance.

69. See Wells, *Transforming Fate*, p. 48.

tians all too easily and frequently succumb: assuming the responsibility (which is clearly not theirs but God's) of ensuring that the story comes out right. In other words, recognizing and explicitly acknowledging an eschatological rather than a teleological orientation serves as a helpful reminder that the story centers on a sovereign God and not on the acting human subject.[70] Because the Christian story has, so to speak, already ended victoriously and definitively in Jesus, the church is free to bear witness, peaceably and patiently, to that ending. Only by concentrating on Christ as its true and final end will the church give up its struggle to bring about the end prematurely and instead gladly give itself over to the long, patient labor of becoming a sacrament of Christ's peaceable presence. For it is only in "keeping" time that we learn how to save it—or, perhaps better, we are saved in and through time. [71]

TOWARD A PEDAGOGY OF FAITHFUL PERFORMANCE

Neither performance nor improvisation is an instance of simple, undifferentiated doing. Rather, they are timeful, disciplined, ruled unfoldings of action. As such, they require attention, alertness, and concentration, all of which bespeaks the hard labor of patience intrinsic to Christian faith. This kind of attention, of course, is not something that can be mastered or attained once and for all, but requires continual practice, repeated rehearsals, ongoing performance, fresh improvisations. Time and repetition are thus uneliminable features of performance theologically construed.

In performance Christians are called upon to recognize time aright, to attune themselves to a time that is God's time. The context in which this attunement occurs is properly called worship. Liturgical time, in other words, takes Christians out of what the world teaches them to think of

70 See ibid., p. 147. Having an eschatological rather than a teleological outlook also encourages the church to learn about its hope by seeking it, by performing the faith so as to live in hope.

71. The temptation is to cut corners and avoid the long, arduous discipline of becoming an accomplished actor. Shortcuts are appealing to a novice, although for a virtuoso musician and a seasoned performer such an attitude will be looked on with pity and disdain. For all experienced performers have acquired a sense of what it means to live as creatures of God's good creation precisely in their valuation of time. For them, time is not something to evade; time, rather, is their most cherished resource. It is not to be squandered or foreshortened but to be "saved," put to work, redeemed. For it is only in "keeping" time that we learn how to save it—or, perhaps better, how that we are saved in and through time. Gerard Loughlin gives systematic power to these admittedly assorted and somewhat disconnected observations on time. See his *Telling God's Story: Bible, Church, and Narrative Theology* (Cambridge, U.K.: Cambridge University Press, 1996).

as the standard or normative measurements of time and orients them to, sets them firmly within, God's eschatological horizon. Worship marks the time of Christ that breaks into "our" time, the time that Christians are lulled into thinking is always here. In this regard, the regular, continual pattern of gathering for worship may be viewed as the church's rehearsal. Worship thus becomes a kind of performance before the performance, a preparation beforehand for whatever witness the church might be called upon to give. Being schooled in the basic rhythms and movements that constitute Christian faith means that the church's witness is more than something spoken, debated, written about, discussed; it is a faith that is enacted, performed, fleshed out. In order for such a witness to be faithful and true, in order for it to be convincing, the church must be attuned to the times.[72] Only by continually practicing, rehearsing, performing the faith will Christians have any chance of learning what it means to keep God's time.

Because rhetoric is always about time and timing, it follows that for Christians as well as non-Christians rhetoric is preeminently a practical skill, an "ability to adapt to circumstances and audiences without relying on theoretical rules."[73] Although Christian judgments are, like their non-religious and secular counterparts, irreducible to calculation and logic, they nonetheless strive to be timely—by which we mean that Christians cultivate forms of discernment in accordance with God's time such that whatever we do or say might be appropriate or adequate to whom we speak. This does not mean that Christians invariably "get it right," but it does suggest that Christian discourse is finally definable against and accountable to that which is not of its own making—yet another way to speak of gift. The gift of godly speech is bequeathed freely and gratuitously, to be sure, but this does not preclude effort and regular practice and constant rehearsal on the part of the recipients of that gift. Indeed, worship is where Christians most learn about the movements of God's time.

Although ordinary time is altered and transformed in the performing arts (theater, dance, music) just as it is profoundly reoriented, converted, during worship, there is nonetheless a deep disanalogy between the two.[74] It is often remarked how a truly good musical or dramatic performance moves, transports, transfixes its audience, so caught up in the performance

72. Being attuned to the times also requires that a Christian be cognizant of the difference between the times—i.e., between earthly temporal frameworks and those of God's kingdom.

73. Jost and Hyde, *Rhetoric and Hermeneutics*, p. xv.

74. See, for example, T. P. Dolan, "The Mass as Performance Text," in *Essays in Early English Drama*, ed. John A. Alford (East Lansing, Mich.: Michigan State University Press, 1995), pp. 13–23. The irreplaceable importance of both music and liturgy resides in the fact that both oblige us to rethink time. See Rowan Williams, *Open to Judgement*, p. 248.

that all sense of time is lost. But to speak of losing time in worship is not quite correct, for time is not so much forgotten, erased, or transcended as it is radically altered, realigned. As Frances Young puts it, "Music moves through time, change and development, rhythm as well as melody, being of its essence; yet paradoxically we may speak of time standing still or of experiencing 'timelessness' when caught up in its 'higher' or 'deeper' reality."[75] Putting oneself into, and thus truly participating in, a performance—either as performer or observer or auditor—is therefore not an attempt to escape time by transcending it. That would amount to bad faith. Rather, being truly present to a performance is to enter fully into time—perhaps for the first time—precisely to the extent that one allows what heretofore has been regarded as the standard measurement of time to be converted and reconfigured by what God's time shows itself truly to be. True performance engages and transfigures, rather than evades, time.[76]

The Patient Obedience of Christian Performance

That Christians are saved in and for time, not from time, means that they are committed to cultivating the virtues that characterize good

75. Young, *The Art of Performance*, p. 22.

76. This applies equally to musical as well as theatrical performance. Indeed, with respect to the latter, one of the most important reasons theatrical drama has such profound effect on us is because it reorients us to time. To be sure, as Alasdair MacIntyre notes, the reason "the dramatic narrative of the play is able to represent off-stage life [is] just because and insofar as that life is itself structured as dramatic narrative." Address delivered at the inauguration of Paul Joseph Philibert, O.P., S.T.D., as president of the Dominican School of Philosophy and Theology, Berkeley, California, February 8, 1987.

In a fascinating study, Anne Righter argues that only with the advent of Shakespearean theater, with its general recognition of the theatrical nature of life, was a new relationship of actors and audience possible. Before this development the audience related quite differently to the drama. Fourteenth-century playgoers, for example, were urged to associate illusion with their own lives and reality itself with the dramas enacted before them in the mystery play. Likewise, the same was true with regard to the dramatic space of the cathedral and the performance of the Mass. "From the West Portal of Chartres, the images of the Twelve Months and their labours look out across the cornlands of the Beauce, reminding the worshipper that as he enters the cathedral he turns away from the world of springtime and harvest, where birth implies destruction and the future flows irrevocably into the past. Within the walls of a medieval church, as within the mind of God Himself, 'all time is eternally present'. St Francis stands beside John the Baptist; the prophets of the Old Testament mingle with those of the New, and within the confines of a single, painted scene, Noah simultaneously constructs his ark, releases the dove, and sees the waters vanish from the earth. The liturgy itself affirms the perpetual contemporaneity of The Passion. Annually, the Church rejoices because Christ has been born again in Bethlehem; as the winter draws near an end He enters Jerusalem, is betrayed, crucified, and the long Lenten sadness ended at last, rises from death on Easter morning." See *Shakespeare and the Idea of the Play* (New York: Barnes & Noble, 1962), p. 15.

performers, accomplished improvisers, persuasively peaceable rheto-
ricians. Being disciplined in obedience is perhaps the key virtue of a
good and faithful performer. This is a skill that can be acquired only in
communities that foster an "ecology of hope," what Nicholas Lash calls
"schools of stillness, of attentiveness; of courtesy, respect and reverence;
academies of contemplativity."[77] Patient listening and attentiveness are
skills that are exercised, honed, and refined in Christian community.
Moreover, within the life of the church this type of respectful, attentive
listening is acquired primarily in liturgy; this is where Christians learn
what Rowan Williams calls "repentant attention"—reverence toward
one another and receptivity to God.[78] Attentive listening cannot be had
without its two inseparable companions, obedience and patience. Indeed, Christians must be instructed in patience as well as in action, for
patience forms a part of all true action.

Patience is learning what it means to serve, to attend time. For knowing
how to wait means having a sense of time, appreciating what it means to
live with something *over* time. Patience is crucial to a life of faith, given
that part of the condition of our contingency, one of the features of our
creaturely existence, is that we constantly meet up with resistances of
various sorts: the sheer otherness of another person; the surprise and
unexpectedness of events; the mute hardness and incorrigibility of the
world. In the face of all these resistances, the practice of patience alone
makes belief in God's providence endurable. To be sure, Christians trust
in a God who has promised that all things will be reconciled without
loss in Christ. Nonetheless, providence is also "God's working slowly
through and with the free interrelations of persons."[79] Without patience
Christians would abandon trust in God for self-invention. Fostering a
silent, attentive openness to God, to one another, and to the world means
that we are less likely to impose our own story. We are less prone to
rewrite the script. To be sure, we have an inkling of the whole, but we
know little about the details and less about the order of its unfolding.
Christians are ignorant of precisely how the world will come out. But
one thing Christians do know is that their identity is hid with Christ.
Whatever wholeness or unity they have, therefore, is kept and formed by
God; which means that patience is irreplaceable if their trust is truly in
a God who acts in, through, with—and in many cases, in spite of—their
own actions and inactions. In short, the patience of a good performer
requires a doing but also and equally important a suffering, an undergoing, a giving up, a receptivity, a capitulation. This giving up, however, is

77. Nicholas Lash, "The Church in the State We're In," *Modern Theology* 13/1 (January
1997): 121–37; p. 131.
78. Williams, *Open to Judgement*, p. 200.
79. Ibid., p. 194.

more a giving over or dispossession of oneself in the performance rather than a concession to fatalism.

The **Ekstasis** *of Faithful Performance*

One of the traits of faithful performance is the way in which the performer is drawn out of him- or herself and is "possessed" or "taken over" by the work.[80] This ability to let go of oneself, to dispossess oneself in the very execution of the act, is a skill that is not learned quickly or easily and certainly not on one's own. Indeed, if acquired at all, it is learned in communion and fellowship with others over the course of an entire Christian life. The power of performance, then, originates not so much in the performer but in his or her attunement to the work that is being performed, worked out, through and by the performer. Without the requisite alertness and respectful, disciplined attention to the creative rhythm of things, the performance falls flat; it fails to move or convince or enthrall performer and audience alike. In this sense, true performance takes us out of ourselves *(ekstasis)* only to return us to ourselves fuller, richer, more deeply changed.

Although these "ecstatic" moments are also features of self-absorbing play, where the participant becomes so wrapped up in the activity that it may be more correct to say that the game plays him than he plays the game, there is something more involved in performing the faith than a temporary suspension or loss of self-control. To be sure, self-absorbing play induces a certain self-forgetfulness or obliviousness. But the loss of control that attends genuine performances of faith is, paradoxically, at the same time an expression remarkable for its discipline and self-control because all are profound engagements with memory. It is a loss of control because the performer gives her- or himself over to the drama of God's action, a movement larger than his or her own biography. In the first instance, it is the game; in the other, it is the power of God. But true performance is more a work of remembrance than it is of creativity, since the narrative drama we enact is always larger than our own particular, individual stories. Self-divestment therefore invites a certain privation, a peculiar giving up that is also a giving over—which means that, with regard to Christian faith, the "loss" of self-control is not so much a forfeiture of responsible agency as it is the cultivation

---

80. Fidelity in performance, as we shall see, encompasses both the work and its performer. Although the two are certainly distinguishable for analytical purposes, they are clearly inseparable when it comes to description. In the account that follows, then, "performer" and "performance" will be used more or less interchangeably, since any hard-and-fast distinction between them eventually breaks down. Here the language of reciprocity or mutual inclusion is perhaps more nearly appropriate.

of a certain sense of wonder and awe. It is what might be called contemplative receptivity.

Good performers of the Christian faith, like good musicians, are those who have refined the art of allowing themselves to be played by the work even as they perform it. The work plays them as much as, if not more than, they play the work. Christian performance is faithful, powerful, and compelling precisely inasmuch as its execution becomes a form of prayer; that is, "an opening of ourselves as best we can to the life of God, letting God live in us."[81]

R. S. Thomas's poem "The Musician" wonderfully captures this sense of oneness between performer and what is performed.[82]

> A memory of Kreisler once:
> At some recital in this same city,
> The seats all taken, I found myself pushed
> On to the stage with a few others,
> So near that I could see the toil
> Of his face muscles, a pulse like a moth
> Fluttering under the fine skin,
> And the indelible veins of his smooth brow.
>
> I could see, too, the twitching of the fingers,
> Caught temporarily in art's neurosis,
> As we sat there or warmly applauded
> This player who so beautifully suffered
> For each of us upon his instrument.
>
> So it must have been on Calvary
> In the fiercer light of the thorns' halo:
> The men standing by and that one figure,
> The hands bleeding, the mind bruised but calm,
> Making such music as lives still.
> And no one daring to interrupt
> Because it was himself he played
> And closer than all of them the God listened.

The intimate fusing of music and musician, the work and its performer, speaks to the mystery of God as Trinity, part of which John's Gospel powerfully portrays: "My Father is working and I work, My Father speaks and I am what he speaks; he acts and I am what he does" (see John 10:37–38). Not only is the Father in Jesus and Jesus in the

81. Williams, *Open to Judgement*, p. 141.
82. The poem appears in R. S. Thomas, *Collected Poems 1945–1990* (New York: Sterling, 2002) and is also cited in Young, *Art of Performance*, p. 185.

Father (John 10:38; 14:11), but with the outpouring of the Spirit that relation of mutual inclusion extends to Christ's entire body, the church (John 17:20–21)—those for whom Jesus' prayer is one of unity: "that they may all be one; even as you, Father, are in me, and I in you, that they also may be in us" (John 17:21). The church's grammar, therefore, echoes that played out, performed, by the life and death of Jesus; which means that the music Jesus makes will be, in Thomas's words, "such music as lives still." The ongoing performance of the church *is* God's life in the world, exactly to the extent that the church's own performance is of one piece with a trinitarian grammar that bespeaks a life of "mutual inclusion."

The church is therefore called to perform the good news of God's redeeming love in Christ. That is its vocation. What it means to be a good performer of the gospel, then, is not simply a matter of finding the right words—although it is clearly that—but it is also a matter of finding the right key in which to sing our song, the right meter and cadence in which to say our poem, the right register in which to play our piece. All performances of God's called people, in other words, are repeat performances, at once emulating the one true performance of God in Christ but also an extension and variation—an improvisation, if you will—of that singularly defining performance.[83] The elements of continuity and discontinuity, sameness and difference, old and new, make assessing the faithfulness of Christian performance an ongoing task.

Spending Time on the Hard Road to Peace

God has not only given Christians a story but has included, incorporated, them in it as well; we as a church have been given ample time to tell the story. That we have the time to perform it—not once but repeatedly, inventively, faithfully—is an assurance that arises not from our own abilities as actors and performers but from God, who is the story's author, the playwright, the choreographer, the producer, the composer as well as the conductor of the work. Fidelity in performance therefore demands a certain attention and receptivity, an alertness on our part to

83. A common error is to link improvisation too strongly with a certain Romantic notion of creativity. This is especially the case when the subject is broached in relation to the performing arts. In modern aesthetics, especially, creativity, improvisation (extemporization), and innovation are defined relative to individual genius. However, as Wells rightly reminds us, within Christian tradition it is memory more than creativity that is the true resource for improvising the faith. Perhaps a better way to express this point is to say that creativity is another way Christians describe what happens when they remember, and thus reenact, their story.

the movement of God's grace in every move. In that sense, performance is more a discipline of discovery than accomplishment.[84]

Fine performances are always a matter of timing, and thus the church must cultivate patience and practiced obedience to get this timing right. In light of its high call to incorporate all differences peaceably, the church often finds itself fretting, either because it feels that there is not enough time (time is running short) or because there is too much time (things are taking too long). But because the church believes in the providence of God's grace, a grace that is working according to its own pace and rhythm, the church must neither rush ahead nor lag behind. It must learn to keep God's time.

Learning to keep God's time is in a number of important respects analogous to the difficult art of listening to (or performing) music well. Rowan Williams wonderfully captures this sense in his thought experiment regarding future technological prospects of musical recordings.[85] "Imagine, if you will, an advertisement for a new recording of the St. Matthew Passion, or The Magic Flute or Shostakovich's Fourth Symphony, that ran something like this: 'We all love the great classics; but think how much of your busy life you can waste listening to *slow* recordings! At last, thanks to the latest technology, we can offer you a recording that takes 10% less time than any other on the market, with *no* reduction in musical quality.'" The rather obvious point of Williams's thought experiment is that "there's something odd . . . in the suggestion that sheer brisk speed is a virtue in itself where music's concerned."[86] Indeed, one of the inescapable facts about music is that "it takes time, and it arrogantly imposes *its* time on us. It says, 'There are things you will learn only by passing through this process, by being caught up in this series of relations and transformations.'"[87] Any attempt to hurry,

---

84. In what may seem paradoxical, gaining experience in performance by continual practice and rehearsal does not necessarily make one a better Christian. In some respect, "better" remains an empty category, given the continually changing situations of the church in the world. However, becoming a practiced performer does at least hold out the promise of inculcating a certain kind of readiness for the unexpected, which, for worshipers of a surprising God, is a skill ever in demand.

85. Oddly enough, the advent of musical recording technology has been closely linked to a peculiarly modern interest in questions of "authenticity" in performance. Richard Taruskin perceptively observes how the intelligibility of "a notion of the reified *Werk*—the objectified musical work-thing to which fidelity is owed"—arises in direct correlation with technological advances in musical recording. Questions of authenticity are thereby exacerbated as greater and greater fidelity is achieved in musical recording. See *Text and Act: Essays on Music and Performance* (Oxford, U.K.: Oxford University Press, 1995), p. 10.

86. Williams, *Open to Judgement*, p. 247.

87. Ibid., p. 247. Although music—or for that matter any of the other "performing arts"—is said to impose itself, such an imposition is nonviolent. As Williams goes on to explain, engaging in the performing arts (either as spectators or auditors or as actors and

retard, or otherwise alter deeply that process and think that one is truly listening to or performing the music is delusional. One of music's most profound but largely unappreciated lessons for the church is that it "keeps and is kept by time, and requires my time, which is my flesh and blood, my life, for its performance and reception."[88] Good music, like the performance of faith, takes time; it will not be rushed. And in that respect, learning to appreciate and understand and play music is to engage in a supremely moral activity. Why? Because these skills amount to exercises in "a recovery of the morality of time."[89] Acquiring the obedience of listening and following is a preeminently ethical practice. What is learned in performing the faith, then, is something of what it means "to work with the grain of things."[90]

God calls to us in time, in the world; which means that time is not to be evaded or transcended but redeemed. As the church that proleptically embodies God's kingdom we are called to peace, to the reconciliation and harmonious incorporation of all differences in the body of Christ. Because peace is, like unity, an achievement and not a given, the church is called to keep time. For without time the continuing, hard, patient labor of forgiveness and reconciliation proves impossible. "Salvation saves humans within time, not from time."[91] The great virtue of understanding the life of faith in terms of musical performance and the performing arts in general is that they teach us to live as creatures of time, to view time not as an enemy to be vanquished but as a friend to be embraced. Time is God's gift and thus time proves a reliable confidante and friend insofar as it marks and measures the peaceable rhythms of our faithfulness.

For Jews, no less than for Christians, peace remains a hope, a duty, and a promise. As Rabbi Jonathan Sacks puts it, "Peace is always our last prayer, never our first, because we know how hard peace is to achieve."[92] Until we enter into that rest, that final peace of God's kingdom, we are called to a patient, obedient working with time. Continually performing and improvising the faith is, of course, fraught with risk. We fear that in giving our time, we may lose it, be robbed of it. But this is to forget that time is God's gift to us, which means that in giving time we receive

---

performers) means that "we choose to yield something of ourselves, a portion of our time, a period of our life; no one forces this, no one and nothing can compel our contemplation except the object in its own right." Ibid., pp. 249–50.

88. Ibid., p. 248.

89. Ibid., p. 249. Williams puts it well when he says: "To listen seriously to music and to perform it are among our most potent ways of learning what it is to live with and before God." Ibid., p. 249.

90. Ibid., p. 250.

91. Wells, *Transforming Fate*, p. 168.

92. Sacks, quoted in Lash, "Church in the State We're In," p. 131.

it back surcharged.[93] Appreciating time as gift allows us confidently to submit our performances to a judgment that will come in its own time. Indeed, we know that the excellence, beauty, and faithfulness of our timeful actions remain open to judgment but also that their ultimate success is measured not according to human standards of excellence, success, or achievement but according to their "epiphanic depth," their openness and transparency to God.[94] Should we be so surprised to discover, then, that the God who shows himself in our halting and awkwardly amateurish attempts to keep time, to perform the faith, is a playful, performing—indeed a dancing—God? Not only is the Christian God a dancing God, but he is one who, with outrageous generosity and uncontainable joy, has invited us to join in the dance.

TOWARD A CONCLUSION

To be sure, the Christian faith is far too rich and complex to be captured by a single analogy—whether of musical performance or theatrical improvisation. Nevertheless, analogies derived from the performing arts prove wonderfully insightful and instructive. In this respect, Samuel Wells's fine analysis and theological commentary on how theatrical improvisation illuminates a central ethical dynamic in Christian life is truly welcome. Indeed, both Wells and Milbank go a long way toward offering an account of how the church embodies a peaceable trinitarian harmony that reincorporates all differences into itself nonviolently. It is to such peaceable, timeful practices that Christians are called; these are skills that set the church apart from those who wish to manage conflict with conflict, who think that violence can be contained only with further violence. Informed by an eschatological vision, the church finds itself called not only to a different performance but also an entirely different way of performing. That way is the way of peace.

Peace both surrounds and constrains the forms of life that constitute God's faithful company; yet the church nonetheless toils hard to embody that peace. It never ceases to practice and refine forms of reverent, patient, and expectant attention, without which its life would be unintelligible because indistinguishable from all other earthly forms of life. Although attention is a gift, it is also and at the same time hard work.

93. Williams speaks of this as the "double giftedness" time. "In that double gift—time given away, time given back—we are taken more deeply into the wisdom of God." *Open to Judgement*, p. 250.

94. "Epiphanic depth" forms the subject of Rowan Williams's essay, "Interiority and Epiphany: A Reading in New Testament Ethics," *Modern Theology* 13/1 (January 1997): 29-51.

"It draws out of us our most strenuous energy."[95] What tends to be over-looked (or at least downplayed) in Milbank's but also to a lesser extent in Wells's account is the sense in which the peaceable performance of the church in the world is nothing short of an "endless uphill labour of transfigurative harmony."[96] "Setting the common life of the Church too dramatically apart from the temporal ways in which the good is realised in a genuinely contingent world" is a warning both Milbank and Wells would do well to heed.[97] While they are right to emphasize the irreplace-able importance of peaceful performance, harmonic reincorporation, and overacceptance, they are in danger of failing to keep time.[98]

It is not easy—perhaps it is not even wise—to attempt to describe in too general a fashion what faithful performance looks like for those called to keep time with the slow, reconciling, peaceful movement of God's grace. The church is too often fickle and unsteady in its commit-ments, unfaithful in its performance, impatient in its actions. We are too often tempted to trust more in our own timing than God's. Conse-quently, in many of our well-intentioned strategies, our cleverly devised schemes and plans to save time—even and especially in our theological designs—we end up losing time, falling out of step, precisely because we fail to pay sufficient heed to the hard bodily practices that teach us how to dwell in time.[99]

What, then, might a pedagogy of peaceful Christian performance amount to? There is, of course, no single answer to that question. How-ever, several possibilities suggest themselves, not all of which appear obvious at first glance. Indeed, one of the most unexpected ways we, as performers of the faith, might be open to the concrete, artful ways of God is captured in the story Williams relates of the young Chilean

95. Williams, *Open to Judgement*, p. 250.

96. Nicholas Lash, *Believing Three Ways in One God: A Reading of the Apostles' Creed* (Notre Dame, Ind.: University of Notre Dame Press, 1993), p. 111.

97. Rowan Williams, "Saving Time: Thoughts on Practice, Patience, and Vision," *New Blackfriars* 73/861 (June 1992): 319–26; p. 323.

98. Rowan Williams's observation is telling in this respect. Milbank provides a much too formal picture of a harmonic ontological relation because it he concentrates more on the end than the processes of its historical unfolding. In spite of the fact that peace is conceived as something already given though not fully realized, Milbank nevertheless pays little attention to the specific, historically contingent ways in which this peace is "learned, negotiated, betrayed, inched forward, discerned and risked." Williams, "Saving Time," p. 321. In other words, the relation between the musical and the numerical harmony is not specified sufficiently.

99. In other words, learning to execute in coordinated peaceful harmony those actions which constitute the life of Christ's body on earth means being trained in the difficult, bodily virtues of self-control, gentleness, patience, compassion, and forbearance. Only by settling into our bodily and earthly existence can we find some hope of negotiating well the timeful character of our life as participants and actors in God's drama.

teacher in Australia who developed dance and drama with the mentally handicapped.[100]

The story concerns a British television documentary, *Stepping Out*, which depicts the fascinating account of the Laura Hodgkinson Sunshine Home in Sydney, Australia. It begins with "scenes showing the very first stages, as these young people in their twenties and thirties gradually learned controlled breathing, co-ordinated movement, learned to relax into their bodies and *live* in them. Then we saw the build-up, as costumes and masks were tried on, the music become more adventurous, the dancing more subtle; and the emergence of thirty-one-year-old Chris as the natural soloist of the group, dancing to Villa-Lobos and Puccini, portraying the death of Madame Butterfly with total conviction, a kind of level ritual pathos which few professionals could manage. You watched the awkward, superficially lumpy and vacant face of a 'retarded' man turn into a tragic mask: every inch, every corner of the body answering the music with discipline, accuracy, complete engagement. And the climax, a breathtaking performance in the Sydney Opera House, no less, was greeted with a standing ovation."[101]

Witnessing such a performance, watching grace in action, makes a person delighted and glad to be a human being. Here we catch a glimpse of what it means to embody, together in many members, God's grace. Moreover, here in the dance we begin to appreciate the kind of apprenticeship that is necessary if grace is to be truly present, concretely enacted.

> But *put* grace and you will *find* grace. Invite the unlovely partner to sit opposite you, breathing slowly and deeply, and to mirror your gestures: the slow circling of an arm, the opening of a hand. That's how our Chilean teacher began. That's how dancing begins. Sit and watch. I'll give you grace and you can give it back. You can answer me because you are like me. You are alive too. Here are the signs of my life, the patterns I make, the beauty I create: and so can you. . . .
>
> Listen to this invitation. Sit down, all of you handicapped, lumpish, empty, afraid, and start to feel that you too are rooted in a firm, rich earth. Opposite you is someone who, it seems, doesn't need to learn. His

100. Rowan Williams, "My Dancing Day," in *Open to Judgement*, pp. 72–75.

101. Ibid., p. 72. Not wishing to moralize the experience of watching *Stepping Out*, Williams deflects the predictable, cynical response of many modern viewers by drawing attention to something deeper and far more revealing. "You might have started out (I did) prepared to feel a little moved, rather patronising—how touching, how pathetic, how cute—but the only final response worth making was humble, awed delight. We'd been watching grace, in every sense. We'd been watching love, the patient, humorous, grave care of the teacher, getting these people to value and admire their bodies, giving words and hugs of encouragement to each one as they prepared to perform" (pp. 72–73).

roots are very deep, very deep indeed; he knows he is lovely and loved. Dancing is natural to him, he has no paralysing, self-conscious dread, no self-protection to overcome. So he begins: he stretches out his arms, wide as he can. And so do you. Then he rises up, arms to the sky. And so do you. Then he takes your hand and swings you loose and leaves you to improvise the music—on your own, then combining with the others, then alone again, then with one or two, then all together, and alone again.[102]

This is what our Beloved has done for us. He has called us to his dance. He has invited us to join with him in the grace of his movements, performing them just as he has taught us, so that we might awaken bodily and fleshly to a graceful performance that God is enacting in us and through us. God in Christ therefore gives us "the fusion of his mind and imagination and flesh—his glorious body. The signs of his life, the patterns he makes, the presence of his beauty—all this is his body, signing to us, inviting us, making us alive. He repeats over and over his central gesture—arms flung wide, then palms carried upwards as he stands on the earth, carrying us, embracing us. As we watch, we know; our roots grow deeper downwards. We can afford to dance, dance the useless dance of love for its own sake. . . . Dancing is natural to him; bit by bit it becomes natural to us. He can't help himself; and, in due course, neither shall we be able to help ourselves."[103]

102. Ibid., pp. 73–74.
103. Ibid., p. 74.

4

CONNECTIONS CREATED AND CONTINGENT

Aquinas, Preller, Wittgenstein, and Hopkins

*A main source of our failure to understand is that we do not com-
mand a clear view of the use of our words.—Our grammar is lacking in this sort of perspicuity. A perspicuous representation produces just that understanding which consists in seeing connexions.
Hence the importance of finding and inventing intermediate cases.
The concept of a perspicuous representation is of fundamental significance for us. It earmarks the form of account we give, the way
we look at things. Is this a Weltanschauung?*

Ludwig Wittgenstein[1]

1. THE CURIOUS CASE OF THE MISSING FOOTNOTES: A NOT VERY MYSTERIOUS MYSTERY

In *With the Grain of the Universe*, the Gifford Lectures delivered at
the University of Saint Andrews (2001), I argue that natural theology is

1. Ludwig Wittgenstein, *Philosophical Investigations*, trans. G. E. M. Anscombe (New
York: MacMillan, 1953), p. 222.

unintelligible divorced from a full doctrine of God.[2] Even more strongly I contend that if you could "prove" the existence of God, if you had evidence that something like a god must exist, then you would have evidence that the God that Jews and Christians worship does not exist.[3] In support of these claims I suggest that Thomas Aquinas would agree with this understanding of the status of our knowledge of God. I therefore conclude that those who have appealed to Aquinas to justify the assumption that "natural theology" is a necessary first step to sustain theology based on revelation have distorted Aquinas's understanding of Christian theology.

I did not claim that this understanding of natural theology or of Thomas Aquinas was original. I had learned from George Hendry that the "little coda"—"and this everyone understands to be God"—that ends each of the proofs is an indication that Aquinas understood the "proofs" were not proofs.[4] David Burrell was, however, my main teacher for this understanding of Aquinas. His analysis of Aquinas's philosophical moves made it clear, at least clear to me, that Aquinas was first and foremost a theologian.[5] But I had forgotten that it was neither Hendry nor Burrell who first shaped my reading of Aquinas. It was Victor Preller. It is therefore with some embarrassment that I note that nowhere in *With the Grain of the Universe* do I acknowledge my indebtness to Preller's *Divine Science and the Science of God: A Reformulation of Thomas Aquinas.*[6]

I am not sure when I first read *Divine Science and the Science of God,* but I am almost certain it was before I left graduate school in 1968. In graduate school I was allegedly being trained to be an "ethicist," but "ethics" only named for me a way to explore the challenge made at that time by some well-known philosophers who argued that it is not so much religious language which might be false; but rather that theological convictions are meaningless because they do not and cannot do any real work for informing us about the ways

---

2. Stanley Hauerwas, *With the Grain of the Universe: The Church's Witness and Natural Theology* (Grand Rapids: Brazos, 2001), p. 15.

3. Ibid., p. 29.

4. Ibid., p. 26; George Hendry, *Theology of Nature* (Philadelphia: Westminster, 1980), p. 14.

5. The first book by Burrell that forever changed how I read Aquinas was his *Analogy and Philosophical Language* (New Haven: Yale University Press, 1973). His *Aquinas: God and Action* (London: Routledge & Kegan Paul, 1979) is his most sustained defense of his understanding of Aquinas. I think the "natural theology" reading of Aquinas was persuasive to many only because they forgot his account of why charity is the form of the virtues. What Aquinas says about the virtues cannot be abstracted from his understanding of our knowledge of God.

6. Victor Preller, *Divine Science and the Science of God: A Reformulation of Thomas Aquinas* (Princeton, N.J.: Princeton University Press, 1967).

things are.[7] I am sure I read Preller because I had been told that the criticisms he develops in chapter 4 of *Divine Science and the Science of God* against the various strategies to "save" the meaningfulness of religious language were very important, as indeed they were and are. I am also sure that at David Burrell's urging I reread Preller in my early years at Notre Dame.[8]

This makes it all the more embarrassing that I failed to acknowledge my debt to Preller in *With the Grain of the Universe*. I have always maintained that a "creative idea" is just forgetting where you read it. So it is not surprising that I forgot Preller's influence on me. Such a "forgetting," moreover, may be partly due to the success of Preller's argument (albeit its delayed success). You can now learn the main outlines of his account of Aquinas from many different sources, which makes it possible to forget that it was Preller who led the way.[9] But we should not forget that *Divine Science and the Science of God* was so against the grain of neoscholastic interpreters of Aquinas that Preller had difficulty gaining a hearing.

The other reason that explains my failure to acknowledge Preller's influence is much more commonplace—I had lost or loaned my copy of *Divine Science and the Science of God* without it being returned. However, rereading *Divine Science and the Science of God* for this essay made clear, at least to me, that I could have made the case I tried to make in *With the Grain of the Universe* more strongly if I had remembered Preller's more detailed arguments in his book. Preller thought and said better in 1967 what I was trying to say in 2001.

That I had forgotten how much I owed to Preller, however, provides an opportunity I want to exploit in this essay. However, my primary interest lies not in defending the position I took in my Gifford Lectures, but rather in exploring a problem I think he and I share in common. Put simply, I take the problem to be: given our arguments against natural theology, how does or can the worship of the God Preller and I worship display the truthfulness of those convictions for those who do not share our faith? Though this is often seen as an apologetical task, I think it is a mistake to so limit the inquiry such a question produces. It is not just

7. The issues raised in Anthony Flew and Alasdair MacIntyre, eds., *New Essays in Philosophical Theology* (London: SCM, 1961), were never far from my attempt to reintroduce the language of the virtues in ethics.

8. For Burrell's review of Preller's book see his "Religious Life and Understanding," *Review of Metaphysics* 22/4 (June 1969): 681–90. I also had the honor of meeting Victor several times when I was at Princeton.

9. I am thinking in particular of Gene Rogers, *Thomas Aquinas and Karl Barth: Sacred Doctrine and the Natural Knowledge of God* (Notre Dame, Ind.: University of Notre Dame Press, 1995); and William Placher, *The Domestication of Transcendence: How Modern Thinking about God Went Wrong* (Louisville: Westminster/John Knox, 1996).

a matter of what we have to say to those who do not share our common worship, but equally it is a question that must be asked and answered by those who are internal to the practice of Christian worship, if we believe that what we believe is true. That is, we are ready to risk our lives for what we believe is true. I hope to show that Preller and Wittgenstein represent in different but complementary ways the recovery of the contingent character of all that is. Moreover, Wittgenstein and Preller school us how to recognize the contingent character of our lives without attempting to subvert the frightening character of the contingent through explanations.

In the "Foreword" to *Divine Science and the Science of God,* Preller makes clear that his book is not an attempt to provide a philosophical defense or proof of theological language or propositions. Rather, "at most I have stated some of the things that must be true of human thought and language if theological claims are not to be rejected out of hand" (p. vii).[10] Or as he puts it later in the book:

> It is the program of natural theology to lead the intellect through a series of judgments which hopefully will result in a negative insight productive of the further judgment that the intellect has encountered a non-intelligible level of experience incapable of formulation in a conceptually meaningful question. The conclusion of natural theology is then the paradox that the human intellect is ordered to a reality that it cannot know and is seeking an intelligibility that it cannot understand. In judging the world to be radically unintelligible, we are implicitly seeking God, and in talking about "God" we are judging the world. All the language of natural theology is language about that which is sought after but unknown. It is incapable, therefore, of conforming the mind to that which is sought. It conveys no *knowledge*

---

10. Toward the end of an article written in 1989 entitled "Sexual Ethics and the Single Life," Preller makes a quite similar claim about the status of the arguments he develops in the essay, which defends a more "traditional sexual ethic" on the basis that all human actions gain their moral intelligibility by being ordered to God. He observes that he does not expect his arguments to be convincing to those who accept the description of actions based on the individualistic and naturalistic presumptions of our culture. He observes, "there are no hard rules of rationality to which I can appeal. All that I, or any other supporter of traditional morality can do is ask the new reformers and modern libertarians to look again at their model and ask themselves seriously if it can be used to justify the pursuit of a just and peaceful society which is anything other than a context for the unbridled pursuit of human gratification and pleasure. And I can also ask them if they honestly believe that such a pursuit of gratification is conducive to the sort of character they themselves would like their friends and neighbors to possess. The model of human nature they use to justify their demands for radical change in traditional sexual ethics may be in some sense compatible with virtuous character, loving relations, and a just social order, but it is in no way conducive to such goods." The essay appears in Philip Turner, ed., *Men and Women: Sexual Ethics in Turbulent Times* (Cambridge, Mass.: Cowley, 1989), pp. 143–44.

of God—even of an imperfect sort—and it terminates in the judgment that there is that of which we have no knowledge. (Pp. 179–80)

These remarks beg for further elucidation, e.g., does Preller want to deny, contrary to Aquinas, that the mind can be conformed to know that which cannot otherwise be known?[11] What could it possibly mean to say we have "encountered a non-intelligible level of experience?"—non-intelligible, maybe, but how could that be an "experience"? Rather than engage these questions directly, I first want to call attention to a challenge I believe Preller and I both face. That Preller claims to do no more in *Divine Science and the Science of God* than to say "some things that must be true of human thought and language if theological claims are not to be rejected out of hand" is a background presumption necessary to sustain my contention in *With the Grain of the Universe* that God is known only through witness. Put differently, Preller and I argue that there can be no coercive argument to compel acknowledgement that God is God. Yet I worry that my argument, as well as Preller's, may fail to say all that needs to be said. It is one thing to argue that God cannot be proved. It is quite another matter to suggest that nothing more can be said about why belief in the God that cannot be proved may nonetheless "make sense" in the world as we know it. Indeed, "make sense" may be a weak way of putting the matter. Surely Christians have claimed and continue to claim that their faith is about the way things are. Preller's (and my) refusal to assume some knockdown arguments must exist to justify the Christian faith seems to suggest to those committed to more rationalistic accounts that we can say no more than "Try it; you will like it."

I think Preller (and I) have a response to this challenge. The response, however, requires me to renarrate the case Preller makes in *Divine Science and the Science of God* in the light of some of the developments in Wittgenstein's work. When Preller wrote *Divine Science and the Science of God* he was obviously more influenced by Wilfrid Sellars than Wittgenstein. Of course anyone familiar with Wittgenstein's work cannot help seeing how many of the arguments Preller uses in his book can readily be described as Wittgensteinian. Preller could have easily been influenced by Wittgenstein through Sellars; or it may even be the case, as David Burrell has long argued, that Aquinas really anticipated some of the lessons we

11. It is very important that anyone trying to answer this question notice that Preller says that "natural theology" is incapable of so adequating the mind. Yet Preller shows quite well how natural theology may prepare us for acknowledging the limits of our knowledge of God. It is important that "nature" and "grace" be distinguished, but not bifurcated. For my attempt to think through these matters, see *Sanctify Them in the Truth* (Nashville: Abingdon, 1998), pp. 37–59.

now attribute to Wittgenstein. So Preller appears Wittgensteinian because
he is such an able reader of Aquinas. However, I am not so much interested
in the question of influence. But I do hope to show that reading Preller
through Wittgensteinian eyes provides some of the intellectual and moral
tools we need to suggest why Christians rightly believe that their faith in
God is also a claim about the way things are, making possible continued
conversation with those who do not share our faith.

I need to be clear about the character of what I am trying to do in this
essay. I cannot pretend that what I am about can bear the grand description of "an argument." To be sure, I will report on arguments—quite good
arguments I believe—that Preller and Wittgenstein develop. However, I
cannot pretend that displaying the similarity between Preller's arguments
against arguments for God's existence and the change in Wittgenstein's
thought from the *Tractatus* to the *Investigations* is anything more than
an attempt at illuminating a family resemblance. At best I try to make
some connections that I hope some may find illuminating. In the final
section of the essay, however, I will make a few suggestions about how
one might go on if the resemblance between Preller's theology and
Wittgenstein's philosophy works in the way I try to develop below. Finally, as I suggested above, I hope in the process of comparing Preller
and Wittgenstein to illumine the position I developed in *With the Grain
of the Universe* as well as to suggest why Christian witness necessarily
involves the assertion of claims about the way things are. The necessity
of witnesses suggests that Christians must work to find ways to listen
as well as talk with those who do not share our faith.

2. PRELLER'S ARGUMENT IN BRIEF

The heart of Preller's argument in defense of his understanding of
what he takes to be Aquinas's views is quite simple.[12] "God, for Aquinas,
is 'outside of the general category of intelligible things' because his
'intelligibility' cannot be defined in terms of our conceptual system—it
does not appear in the 'light of reason'."[13] In short if God is not part of

---

12. Some may object I am conflating Preller's views with those of Aquinas, but I see no
alternative. *Divine Science and the Science of God* is appropriately subtitled "A Reformulation
of Thomas Aquinas." In his review of Preller's book David Burrell observes that whatever
Preller's linguistic reformulation of Aquinas is, "Aquinas may be endlessly discussed" (p.
682). As far as I can see, however, given the argument Preller makes in the book there is
no way to distinguish his views from his reformulation of Aquinas.

13. Preller, *Divine Science and the Science of God*, p. 155. Pages in parentheses in text
are from *Divine Science and the Science of God*. I have wondered if Preller's understanding
of Aquinas, which was so much against the grain of the Thomism of his day, may have at
least been made possible by his reading of works of Aquinas other than the *Summa*. For

the metaphysical furniture of the universe, then God cannot be made to function "as an *intelligible* link—even the *first* link—in a conceptual progress or causal chain, [because if God so functioned] then of necessity any defect or problem associated with 'contingent reality' will be built into the concept of God" (p. 135).

Aquinas's use of the name "God" is therefore determinatively theological, drawing its rationality from revelation (p. 144). But even revelation does not justify the presumption that we can speak of God unproblematically. Thus the five ways, which seek to tie God into the world by extrapolating a notion of causality or perfection from our conceptual system, cannot be successful. Preller's detailed analysis of the five ways is crucial for his overall argument. He must show (and I think he does) not only that the five ways fail but that Aquinas knew they must fail. Preller observes that, of all the categories introduced in the five ways, "contingency and necessity" in the third proof are least removed from the "creational notion" that informs Aquinas's use of the proofs. For it is Preller's notion—a contention that David Burrell has continued to develop—that Aquinas reads all the arguments for God from the viewpoint of creation: "The human mind is ordered to God the *Creator* as to One Unknown. The intellect implicitly demands that the 'existence' of the world be measured and made necessary by a free *intentional or conceptual act*. It does not know, however, in what way that is possible" (p. 164). That is why Preller rightly notes that the "contingency" implied in the third proof is not the "contingency" implicit in the relationship between creator and creature. Preller acknowledges that the fifth way based on the governance of creation may not be "finally incompatible" with Aquinas's doctrine of God, but Aquinas elsewhere acknowledges that God's "providence over all cannot be proved" (p. 134). Moreover Preller argues that the Aristotelian presuppositions of the first three ways are incompatible with the fifth.

In short, the "proofs" cannot be successful because, according to Preller, the five ways are quite incompatible with Aquinas's doctrine of God. God chooses to place himself at man's disposal by grace, that is, by gift. "Even that gift, however, becomes man's possession—at his disposal—only in the 'light of Glory' when reality is seen in terms of God's intentions. In this life 'God' remains a word in *another* language—a word *mentioned but not used in our language*" (p. 156).[14]

---

example, the internal quotation comes from Aquinas, *De Trinitate Boethii Commentarium*. The structure of *Divine Science and the Science of God* could be a subject in itself. I think, for example, the first two chapters can be read as an attempt to retrain the readers' habits in order to prepare them for the work done in ch. 3. That Preller began with questions about the "name" of God seems to be the necessary preparation for his overall argument.

14. In *With the Grain of the Universe* I suggested that by attending to Barth's argument in his *Göttingen Dogmatics*, one can conclude that Aquinas is closer to Barth than perhaps

According to Preller the problem is not that reason can establish certain significant things about God but that evidence is lacking for other significant things that may be true of him. Rather, the problem is how we could ever think we might see the significance of any proposition about God, revealed or not. Preller notes that it is misleading to say this is merely a linguistic problem, though it no doubt involves the question of language. Human language is intentional because it is about things and expresses thoughts that are themselves intentional about things. "Successful reference depends upon a meaningful intentionality or conceptual context. 'God,' however, is a name which can never occur within a conceptual context which is meaningful to us" (p. 183).

This means that our speech about God can only be, indeed must be, analogical. But we should not be surprised by this given that any act

---

even Barth recognized. I certainly would not suggest that Preller is providing a Barthian reading of Aquinas, but I think there is no question that his understanding of Aquinas brings Aquinas quite close to Barth. For example, Preller observes that the followers of Barth who try to make him assert that God is finite because of the incarnation fail to see the implications of their claim, that is, either God ceased to be God in the incarnation, or every predicate that applies to Christ applies to God as he always was and will be. Preller observes, I think quite correctly, "Barth's point is that there is no *deus absconditus*, the nature of which is not known by faith, lying behind the *deus revelatus*." *Divine Science and the Science of God*, p. 215.

Preller seldom refers to Barth in *Divine Science and the Science of God*, but it is hard not to read the theological remarks he makes in the last chapter in a Barthian fashion. For example, he quotes Aquinas's claim that "the Mystery of Christ's Incarnation and Passion is the way by which men come to beatitude" in support of his contention that the central empirical referent of sacred doctrine is the humanity of Christ (p. 249). A few pages later he observes, "What is primarily meant by 'the image of God in man' is the imperfect image in the believer. As Karl Rahner remarks, since the Incarnation, all theology has become anthropology—and, we might add, all anthropology has become Christology" (p. 260). Barth's favorite quote from Aquinas was *"Deus est non genre,"* which Preller also highlights (p. 10) and is clearly at the heart of the argument of *Divine Science and the Science of God*. Richard Church, however, rightly reminds me that to read Aquinas in a Barthian fashion remains controversial to say the least.

In *With the Grain of the Universe* I, like Preller, was so intent on showing the "proofs" were not proofs, I failed to suggest why Aquinas discussed them. Of course one answer (and it is too quick an answer) is that they were in the tradition. Just as Aquinas used everything in the tradition to his own ends, so he used the "proofs." For Aquinas, I believe, the proofs were his way of saying, "Given the God of creation we should not be surprised the world looks like this." As Richard Fern puts it, the proofs should be read "as efforts to identify generally accessible features of the world in which religious believers experience the sustaining presence of a sacred reality. What makes these reasons in support of religious belief is that the features identified constitute 'otherwise anomalies,' aspects of our common experience that make good sense, arguably, only on the supposition reality, at rock-bottom, is sacred." *Nature, God, and Humanity: Envisioning an Ethics of Nature* (Cambridge, U.K.: Cambridge University Press, 2002), p. 122. Fern suggests, for example, that the cosmological argument is the attempt to suggest that the existence of anything makes little sense unless something exists necessarily.

of knowing is analogical (p. 52).[15] Accordingly, any attempt to make "being" or "existence" privileged modes of talk about God are doomed to failure. Being and existence after all are also analogical terms,[16] which means at the very least that our talk of God's existence is radically different from speaking of the existence of tables and chairs (p. 152). Moreover, the demand "Give me an explanation of the existence of everything," a demand often assumed to get God-talk off the ground, is a pseudodemand,

> since we cannot conceive of anything which could be such a explanation except in terms of *our* use of "exists." If we grant to Aquinas that existence *must* be "intelligible" and that "intelligibility" means "necessity," and if we further grant to him that "necessity" in this instance means "measured by the free intentional activity of some "intelligent agent," then it follows analytically that there must exist some "intelligent" entity from whose intentional point of view the *esse* of the world is seen to be intelligible *because* it follows from his own immanent powers of "conceiving" reality. (P. 171)

Only God's existence is, therefore, self-evident, because only in God is there no distinction between essence and existence (p. 173). The only reason to apply the term "existence" to God is that the world would remain radically unintelligible if there did not "exist" that from which the world derives its hypothetical necessity. But God's existence does not only mean that God is the source of all other existence. That is why the term "exist" is radically unintelligible when applied to the world. "Exists" is intelligible only when it signifies God himself (pp. 174–75). This led me to claim in *With the Grain of the Universe* that the problem

15. Preller quite rightly, I think, argues that Aquinas had no "doctrine of analogy," because the so-called "doctrine" is not a means of knowing God but "a meta-linguistic analysis of the state of certain words and propositions to *name* God. From God's point of view there is undoubtedly an 'analogy of being'; from our point of view, however, there is only an analogy of 'being.' The proofs for the existence of God are our way of confessing our ignorance of the 'analogy of being.' We do not know the principle which might unify all aspects of our awareness of 'that which is' " (p. 170).

16. I suppose that Preller's account of these matters is sufficient to make him an anti-foundationalist, though I am not sure how such a label helps us better understand him. Given his understanding of analogy, he rightly maintains that reality is "*entirely* reconceivable" (p. 69), but he certainly does not think that all conceptions count equally. He acknowledges that it is quite possible for two necessary and incommensurable language systems to exist, but there is no neutral language available to overcome such incommensurability (p. 60). This is complicated by the fact that to have one concept in a language means, at least if Wilfrid Sellars is right, we must have them all (p. 43). (See Wilfrid Sellars, *Science, Perception, and Reality* (London: International Library of Philosophy and Scientiefic Method, 1963). It is a mark of Preller's good sense he does not try to say more than can be said about these matters.

is not whether God exists, but in what sense it can be said that anything other than God exists. Of course, once it is acknowledged that all that is exists by God's grace, then it is equally true that only God exists necessarily.[17]

But where does that leave us? According to Preller it means "in terms of the natural universe of human discourse, the claims of faith must remain unintelligible, as must also the claim to possess a new mode of understanding in terms of which the claims of faith are intelligible" (p. 225). Was Preller an early representative of Wittgensteinian fideism? I do not think so, but then I do not think anyone is a representative of Wittgensteinian fideism.[18] Rather, I think Wittgenstein provides those who believe in God—a God who, as Preller so carefully demonstrates, cannot be proved—a way to go on that challenges the assumption that if God cannot be proved then belief in God is subjective and not susceptible to being either true or false.

3. WITTGENSTEIN ON ACT AND WONDER

As I suggested above, I believe Preller may well have been far too modest when he suggested that all he has done in *Divine Science and the Science of God* is to show some of the things that must be true of human thought if theological claims are not to be rejected out of hand. Moreover, I am not at all sure he is right that the claims of faith must always remain unintelligible in terms of the "natural universe of human discourse." I do not deny that may often be the case; but I do not see why we must assume in advance that we will know what form the "natural

17. I am grateful to Rob MacSwain for reminding me of this important point.

18. See, for example, the response of D. Z. Phillips to the charge he is a Wittgensteinian fideist in his *Faith after Foundationalism: Critiques and Alternatives* (Boulder, Colo.: Westview, 1995), pp. 236–37. John Berkman has brought to my attention an article by Donald Evans on Preller's book that argues that in developing his argument for the "absolute opaqueness" of God Preller must maintain some minimal understanding of what human language means as applied to God. In particular Evans calls attention to Preller's claim in *Divine Science and the Science of God*, "While the believer does not understand the propositions of Sacred Doctrine, he nevertheless believes that his mind is being conformed by God to himself when he assents to the truth of the propositions in a state of real or infused faith. He not only believes that there exist in the language or Word of God analogical counterparts of the propositions of faith, and that, in the Word of God, those counterparts are intelligible; he also believes that, when he is in a state of real or infused faith, he possess a special sort of 'intention' which gives to his affirmations of the language of faith a real referential and descriptive power that is apparent to God and the *beati*" (p. 262). Donald Evans, "Preller's Analogy of 'Being,'" *The New Scholasticism* 45/1 (winter 1971): 1–37. I am indebted to John Berkman not only for calling attention to Evans's article, but also for helping me see what I am trying to do in this essay.

universe of human discourse" will take. Surely we will simply have to wait and see; or, to draw on Wittgenstein, we will first have to look.[19]

In order to make my case I want to focus on two remarks made by Fergus Kerr in his *Theology after Wittgenstein*. Kerr observes that Wittgenstein's appreciation of William James is a bit odd because Wittgenstein in his later work "strives to show that neither feeling nor reason but *action* is the foundational thing."[20] Second, Kerr suggests that the later Wittgenstein

> moves from wonder at the world as such, in its logical structure, to an attitude of wonder towards particular things, in their individuality—"this blossom, opening!" More to the point, Wittgenstein seems to fear that it is only with difficulty that a mathematician can maintain a sense of awe once he begins to treat a "miracle of nature" as a *problem*.[21]

In the far too brief remarks on Wittgenstein that follow, I want to show that Wittgenstein's discovery that our saying is action, his assertion that Wittgenstein's discovery that our saying is action (that practices are necessary for our ability to understand one another), and what Kerr calls his wonder toward things in particular are interrelated. Moreover, I think their interrelation is an indication of, and a witness to, the created character of all that is. In short I want to suggest that the movement in Wittgenstein's thought from the *Tractatus* to the *Investigations* parallels Preller's account of Aquinas's understanding of the character of our knowledge of God. Put differently, I want to at least suggest that when

19. I am, of course, referring to Wittgenstein's famous remark in the *Investigations* (p. 66), "To repeat: don't think, but look." This command comes in the context of his discussion of games, in which he is trying to admonish us not to develop a theory of games but rather look for family resemblances that help us see not only their similarities, but their differences. His later remark, "One cannot guess how a word functions. One has to *look at* its use and learn from that," is perhaps more relevant to the point I am trying to make. *Investigations*, p. 340. Wittgenstein observes that prejudice stands in the way of our "looking," but he says such a prejudice is not a stupid one. I think he is right to suggest that such a prejudice is not stupid, but rather draws on our hunger to control the variety of objects through theory in order to show that things must be this way or "this is the way things must have happened." Such a desire is not stupid, but I believe is very dangerous.

20. Fergus Kerr, *Theology after Wittgenstein* (2d ed.; London: SPCK, 1997), p. 158. Ray Monk reports that one of the few books Wittgenstein insisted that Drury should read was James's *Varieties of Religious Experience*. "Drury told him that he had already read it: 'I always enjoy reading anything of William James. He is such a human person.' Yes, Wittgenstein replied: 'That is what makes him a good philosopher; he was a real human being.'" Ray Monk, *Ludwig Wittgenstein: The Duty of Genius* (New York: Free Press, 1990), p. 478. Russell Goodman has now shown in his *Wittgenstein and William James* (Cambridge, U.K.: Cambridge University Press, 2002) how deeply Wittgenstein read James, and in particular the *Principles of Psychology*.

21. Kerr, *Theology after Wittgenstein*, p. 204.

Wittgenstein's and Preller's works are read together they each confirm the necessary acknowledgement of what David Burrell, drawing on Robert Sokolowski, calls "the distinction." That is, the distinction between God and the world, which is unlike any other distinction we use "since we mean thereby to distinguish God from everything else that is, in such a way that God is the source of all-that-is."[22]

One might be able to sustain an account of "the distinction" from the perspective of the *Tractatus*, but I hope to show that "the distinction" appears in a quite different light given Wittgenstein's work in the *Investigations*. I am not suggesting that there are not profound continuities between the *Tractatus* and the *Investigations*—indeed, I think the continuities are deeper than the discontinuities. Rather, I want only to suggest that in the *Investigations* Wittgenstein discovered that "the world" could not be comprehended or explained in the mode exemplified by the *Tractatus*.[23] In both the *Tractatus* and the *Investigations* Wittgenstein saw that explanations must come to an end. But, as John Churchill suggests,

> in the *Tractatus* the disembodied pure intellect, picturing the world of facts in the frame of logical form, achieves a pure, will-less wonder at the existence of the world. But in the later philosophy it is not that bare fact of the world's existence that excites our wonder. It is the intricate attunement of human being to the world in all its detail and complexity.[24]

22. David Burrell, *Friendship and Ways to Truth* (Notre Dame, Ind.: University of Notre Dame Press, 2000), pp. 92–93.

23. I am quite frankly not sure whether I can defend this claim or even that it can be defended, depending as it does on how one reads the *Tractatus* as a whole. However, I am thinking of these propositions in the *Tractatus*:

> It is not *how* things are in the world that is mystical, but that it exists (6.44).
> To view the world *sub specie aeterni* is to view it as a whole—a limited whole.
> Feeling the world as a limited whole—it is this that is mystical (6.45).

Ludwig Wittgenstein, *Tractatus Logico-Philosophicus*, trans. D. F. Pears and B. F. McGuinness (London: Routledge & Kegan Paul, 1963).

24. John Churchill, "Wonder and the End of Explanation: Wittgenstein and Religious Sensibility," *Philosophical Investigations* 17/2 (April 1994): 389. Kerr expresses his appreciation for Churchill's fine article in *Theology after Wittgenstein* (p. 204). My dependence on Churchill's article will be apparent. I am not sure why, but I always find it easier to write "about" Wittgenstein by using work that has been written on Wittgenstein rather than making a direct appeal to his work. I think one of the reasons is that I am not sure you can ever write about Wittgenstein because he did not want you to write about him; he wanted you to know how to go on in your own way. I am, of course, not denying that there are quite wonderful books written on his work, such as David Pears's *The False Prison: A Study of the Development of Wittgenstein's Philosophy* (vols. 1–2; Oxford, Mass.: Clarendon, 1997). But even Pears's work tends to betray the character of Wittgenstein's mode of work just to the extent that Pears writes in a traditional philosophical genre. For those inter-

In short, in the *Investigations* we see that "the world" is constituted by making connections between contingencies that make it possible for us to see the beauty of what is.

That Wittgenstein was content in the *Investigations* to do just that—investigate—I think has to do with his recognition that "words are also deeds," or, as he was later to put it in *On Certainty*, quoting Goethe: "In the beginning was the deed."[25] In the *Investigations* he no longer thought his task was to provide an end to philosophical inquiry, but to show why philosophical inquiry can have no end.[26] All of this is but a recognition that neither we, nor the world, nor our relation to the world exists by necessity. To "look behind," to "look inward" are temptations fueled by our desire to secure our existence through the discovery that what exists does so by necessity.[27] The private language argument as well as

ested in how my own work has been shaped by Wittgenstein I can commend no better book than Brad Kallenberg's *Ethics as Grammar: Changing the Postmodern Subject* (Notre Dame, Ind.: University of Notre Dame Press, 2001). I confess I was at first embarrassed even to be compared to Wittgenstein, but then I realized on reading Kallenberg's book for the third or fourth time that Kallenberg just needed me as a stand-in for Christianity. I am indebted to Kallenberg, not only for teaching me much about Wittgenstein, but for teaching me about myself.

25. Wittgenstein, *Philosophical Investigations*, p. 546. The quote from Goethe is found in *On Certainty*, ed. G. E. M. Anscombe and G. H. Wright, trans. Denis Paul and G. E. M. Anscombe (New York: Harper and Row, 1969), p. 402.

26. Many read Wittgenstein's remarks about philosophy in the *Investigations* as a demeaning of the philosophical task. He certainly wanted to help his readers understand when philosophy should come to an end, but I do not think that means he thought the work of philosophy was without importance. "To show the fly the way out of the fly-bottle" (*Investigations*, p. 309) is surely a task worth doing and never ending. Wittgenstein clearly thought most people, or at least people not corrupted by bad philosophy, did not need philosophy in order to live well. But that does not mean that philosophy has no role in helping us avoid the lies that grip our lives. That philosophy "ought really to be written only as *poetic composition*" (Ludwig Wittgenstein, *Culture and Value*, ed. G. H. von Wright, trans. Peter Winch [Chicago: University of Chicago Press, 1977], 24e) suggests he assumed philosophy, like poetry, is to help guard our language from going on a holiday and to extend our ability to see the world. But to write philosophy as poetry is no easy task and explains Wittgenstein's own sense that he cannot quite do what he thinks he should do. At the very least Wittgenstein's attitude toward philosophy embodies the kind of humility exemplified in Aquinas's understanding of the role of the philosopher. Finally, the problem is not with philosophy but, as Wittgenstein well knew, with the prideful use of philosophy. For an account of Wittgenstein's work that stresses the role of learning "to see," see James Edwards, *Ethics without Philosophy: Wittgenstein and the Moral Life* (Tampa: University of South Florida Press, 1985). Few have taught us better how to think with Wittgenstein than James Edwards. However, Kallenberg criticizes Edwards, perhaps rightly, for assuming a self free from all communal, historical, and religious influences, pp. 59–71.

27. Wittgenstein's remarks on "descriptions" in the *Investigations* I think indicate the importance of the movement of his thinking from the *Tractatus* to the *Investigations*. Thus his claim in the *Investigations* (p. 291) that descriptions are instruments for particular uses like the machine drawing that an engineer has before him. Moreover, he is acutely

his contention that intentions are embedded in their situations set by human customs and institutions reflect his recognition that there is no "deeper reality" than that found in the everyday.

In the *Tractatus* language functions to depict facts through a single logical structure. That is, in the *Tractatus* Wittgenstein thinks of language as "a great crystalline structure of sharp logical precision, mirroring a world of facts, at the logical limit of which is a vanishing metaphysical and ethical subject."[28] But in the *Investigations* language is a "logically multifarious jumble of practices thoroughly contingent upon and interpenetrating with human social activities of bewildering variety."[29] Accordingly there is no place for monolithic wonder. Just as Preller helps us understand that the "five ways" cannot "prove" the existence of God, so Wittgenstein helps us see that the ambition of philosophers to comprehend the "world" cannot but fail. Inquiry, investigation, goes all the way down and is never-ending.

Wittgenstein's animosity toward science is at least in part a reflection of how science can dull our sense of the wonder at the particular. "Man has to awaken to wonder—and so perhaps do peoples. Science is a way of sending him to sleep again."[30] His work is the attempt to help us rediscover the particular without providing an explanation or explanations that reduce the particular to an instance of a more general condition. "The insidious thing about the causal point of view is that it leads us to say: 'Of course, it had to happen like that.' Whereas we ought to think: it may have happened *like that*—and also in many other ways."[31]

John Churchill argues that Wittgenstein's understanding of what it means to follow a rule best reveals his understanding in the *Investigations* of what it means for explanation to come to an end. In particular Churchill calls attention to the so called "paradox of rule-following" in the *Investigations*, the paradox quite simply being that anything and nothing can count as a successful following of a rule.[32] The temptation this presents is to believe

---

aware how difficult it is to rightly and exactly describe because, as James noted, "Our vocabulary is inadequate." *Investigations*, p. 610. For an extremely informative article that helps us understand how Wittgenstein's engineering background shaped his understanding of the task of description see Kelly Hamilton's "Wittgenstein and the Mind's Eye," in *Wittgenstein: Biography and Philosophy*, ed. James Klagge (Cambridge, U.K.: Cambridge University Press, 2001), pp. 53–97. For a book that develops in great detail the importance of description for ethics see Charles Pinches, *Theology and Action: After Theory in Christian Ethics* (Grand Rapids: Eerdmans, 2002).

28. John Churchill, "Wonder and the End of Explanation," p. 398.

29. Ibid., p. 399.

30. Wittgenstein, *Culture and Value*, 5e. The hostility expressed in some of Wittgenstein's objections to science can give the impression that he had no use for science, which I do not believe is the case.

31. Ibid., 37e.

32. Wittgenstein, *Investigations*, pp. 198–202.

that an interpretation can help us understand a rule whose application is unclear. But this can only result in endless interpretations. Thus Wittgenstein's conclusion in the *Investigations* is that there must be "a way of grasping a rule which is *not* an *interpretation*, but which is exhibited in what we call 'obeying the rule' and 'going against it' in actual cases."[33]

For every specific rule, Churchill argues, there must be some underlying practices. For Wittgenstein the possibility of rule following, as well as all language and other rational behavior, rests on commonalities of behavior that are not given by necessity. Thus Wittgenstein throughout the *Investigations* conducts thought experiments that explore our understanding or lack of understanding between people and animals, with which we share little or nothing. The point is that "all matters of getting it right and getting it wrong rest finally on shared behavior. Commonality of behavior is the analogue to logical form in the *Tractatus:* it is that upon which the possibility of language depends."[34]

In the *Tractatus* wonder at the existence of the world is inspired by the fact that, absent an explanation, there is a world at all.[35] In the *Investigations*, Churchill suggests, wonder before the unexplained lies in matters of fact about our lives that make rule-governed practices possible. "At the root of every practice is a way of operating that we learn not by having it explained and justified to us, but by simply doing it, or by being trained into it. *This* is how it goes, though there is no reason for that!"[36] The temptation to look for inner processes that allegedly take place in "the mind" is an attempt to avoid the recognition that the way we learn to follow a rule is by training. We crave an explanation to show how a student has of necessity learned to go on, but there can be no explanation more compelling than the training itself.[37]

33. Ibid., p. 201.
34. Churchill, "Wonder and the End of Explanation," p. 401.
35. I am well aware that many who have given up any practice of a faith still find provocative the question "Why is there something, when there could have been nothing?" For example, Jared Diamond in a review article of David Wilson's *Darwin's Cathedral: Evolution, Religion, and the Nature of Society* recalls that as a "hyper-rational" undergraduate at Harvard in 1955 he was challenged by Paul Tillich's use of that question to show that science cannot provide an answer. He ends the article noting that religions will thrive as long as the question has no answer. The problem with the apocalyptic use of the question is that it is not apparent why the question should be asked at all. As a result Christian convictions are distorted because they are made to answer a question that makes little sense. Indeed I suspect such a question is the breeding ground of deism. See Jared Diamond, "The Religious Success Story," *New York Review of Books* 49 (November 7, 2002): 30–32.
36. Churchill, "Wonder and the End of Explanation," p. 401.
37. Churchill makes the nice point, which Kerr obviously thinks interesting, that Wittgenstein's admiration of James's *Principles of Psychology* is puzzling given James's tendency to psychologize verbs such as "think," "interpret," "construe." As Churchill points out, if the function of verbs is not to refer, then there is no arena for an intrinsically intelligible

Churchill summarizes his case:

> In the *Tractatus* what is shown is shown to a vanishing metaphysical subject. In the later philosophy our insight into the end of explanation lies in our discovery of the inclination of humans for seeing *this* as *that*, taking *this* as the natural continuation of a practice, and so on; that is, in our awareness of typical human perceptions and reactions in their role as making possible any rule-governed activity. In the *Tractatus* the talk is of a single, unified and eternal sense of things—a grand ineffable meaning. But in the later philosophy the loci of the possibility of wonder are small, local, various, and mundane. They will lie in such unspectacular facts as the ability humans have to recognize threatening gestures as such, or to respond spontaneously, without training to the expression of others, or to get the hang of this or that practice. The loci of wonder in the later philosophy are the products of time and contingency—how we happen to have evolved, what our cultural practices happen to be like, rather than the grand atemporal necessity of logical form.[38]

Preller's observations in the "Conclusion" of *Divine Science and the Science of God* are therefore all the more interesting. He begins by noting that no language springs full-blown from the head of any human being. Rather, learning to use a language well is an ongoing lesson in pain and frustration. Indeed, ultimately to use a language well we must submit to the "syntactical laws" that make the language a source of intelligibility and light. This means we must often respond without understanding to the "darkly disapproving countenances of those who lay down the pedagogical laws of semantic association. We learn to make the material moves justified by the syntactical laws of our common human language before we learn ourselves to obey those laws" (p. 266). It is hard not to believe that Preller, drawing on what he had learned from Sellars, was thinking with Wittgenstein when he wrote these words. He even gives as his example of how we are constituted by the languages that we speak (and which speak us) the way we learn to make the sound of "red" at certain times and to avoid it at others.

Preller observes that there is a further consequence of this account of language. When a child "makes the leap" forward into the intentional realm of self-consciousness, he becomes something that he was not

---

phenomenon called "mind." "Wonder and the End of Explanation," p. 403. Churchill's point applies equally to Wittgenstein's reading of James's *Varieties of Religious Experience*, which "internalized" religious experience. Surely it is religious behavior on which Wittgenstein should have focused. Of course the puzzle is deeper just to the extent that James's focus on action in the development of his pragmatism put him in tension with the significant role he gave "experience" in the *Varieties*.

38. Churchill, "Wonder and the End of Explanation," pp. 406–7.

previously. Preller then observes that if we ever ceased using the language we now use, we would cease being the same "persons" we now are, which leads him to the claim:

> if our language is distorted—if it does not truly and adequately reflect the intentions of God in creation—then I am not, at the level of conscious self-awareness, what I am intended by God to be, and what I therefore really am as known only to him and expressed only in his Word. It is, I think, a central thesis of the language of faith that I shall only *become* at the level of reflective self-awareness that which I really *am* as a creature of God when my intentional being is constituted by an intelligible "Word" addressed to me and confirmed by my intentional response in kind. (P. 270)

I take Preller's point to parallel the argument I tried to make in the *With Grain of the Universe*, drawing on William James's *The Will to Believe*, that there are some realities that to be "known" require the transformation of the agent.[39] This is why my account of James's understanding of "the will to believe" was shaped by my prior reading of Wittgenstein. The latter, of course, helps us see the role of language in such a transformation that was missing in James.[40] But Preller did see the significance of language. He not only saw the significance of language, but Preller helps us see how Aquinas intended the *Summa* to provide the kind of training necessary for the recognition that we are creatures who must receive our very ability to speak as a gift. Such a recognition does not compel the acknowledgment of a creator, but it does suggest how the failure to live with humility, a failure common to Christian and non-Christian alike, results in a distorted understanding of the way things are.[41]

39. Hauerwas, *With the Grain of the Universe*, pp. 50–61.

40. However, see the footnote on pp. 54–55 of *With the Grain of the Universe*. In that footnote I suggest that James's account of habits could provide a context for understanding the role of language for avoiding the "myth of the given." Wittgenstein's admiration for James is well known, but exactly what he thought he learned from James remains unclear. In *On Certainty* (p. 422) we do find the remark: "So I am trying to say something that sounds like pragmatism. Here I am being thwarted by a kind of *Weltanschauung*." Ludwig Wittgenstein, *On Certainty*, ed. G. E. M. Anscombe and G. H. Wright, trans. Dennis Paul and G. E. M. Anscombe (New York: Harper & Row, 1969).

Edwards provides a very helpful account of Wittgenstein and pragmatism in *Ethics without Philosophy*, pp. 225–30. He concludes that though there are some quite strong similarities between pragmatism and Wittgenstein, Wittgenstein's concern with human understanding "originates in a dissatisfaction with the tradition deeper than that which motivates the pragmaticist" (p. 230).

41. In *Culture and Value* Wittgenstein observes, "The *edifice of your pride* has to be dismantled. And that is terribly hard work" (26e). I do not take this remark to be about "ethics," but rather as an indication that for Wittgenstein pride is one of the factors that

Put in the terms I use in *With the Grain of the Universe*, any account of Christianity that does not make witness constitutive of the practice of the faith cannot be true. Not to be true not only means to be unfaithful to Christian practice, but also means to belie the contingent character of all that is. Witnesses witness our contingency. But Christians believe that God has given us life-forming practices that enable us to live without seeking false comforts in a world of contingency we do not and cannot control. That we must be trained to be human, that we must be trained to communicate with one another so that we make the connections between ourselves, others, and this and that, indicates that the God we worship as Christians is the same God who has created the sun, stars, and this petunia.[42] That Preller helps us in *Divine Science and the Science of God* to recognize why all that is does

---

makes it impossible to see objects as they are. The *Investigations* I think should be read as a form of training in humility. For an account of the *Tractatus* as Wittgenstein's attempt to be "godlike," see Edwards, *Ethics without Philosophy*, pp. 68–73. Anyone familiar with John Bowlin's book, *Contingency and Fortune in Aquinas's Ethics* (Cambridge, U.K.: Cambridge University Press, 1999), will recognize the influence Bowlin's work has had on what I have tried to do in this paper. Bowlin wonderfully illumines the relation between knowledge and the acquisition of virtue by calling attention to the challenge presented in dog training. He observes, "Training dogs well is hard because it is difficult to become the sort of person who can command them with just authority, obey them when appropriate, distinguish false kindness from true respect, and love some thing or activity in a way that will generate a community of common loves with a dog" (p. 156).

42. The kind of training Wittgenstein and Preller gesture toward is wonderfully described in Marjorie Hunt's *The Stone Carvers: Master Craftsmen of the Washington National Cathedral* (Washington, D.C.: Smithsonian, 1999). Her book focuses on Vincent Palumbo and Roger Morigi, who spent a lifetime carving the stone for the National Cathedral. They were each brought up in the "trade." Vincent describes it this way: "When you come from a traditional family you learn from the talking. What happened to me, we was in that trade. We was talking about work anytime; at breakfast, dinner, supper, most of the subject was work. Think about this stone, how we gonna do this, who was gonna do that, we gotta use this trick. So you're growing, and you listen, and you mind, it gets drunk with all those things, and then when it comes time, you remember" (pp. 20–21). Hunt notes that the family was the key institution for this training, laying the crucial foundation early through informal periods of learning. Hunt observes, "Like a child learning language, he [Vincent] begin to acquire a grammar of stone carving; he began to piece together knowledge of the various elements of the craft and the underlying principles that governed them. Sitting around the dinner table listening to his father and grandfather tell stories and discuss work, he became familiar with the names of the tools and the different types of stone. Little by little, he became acquainted with the work processes and specialized terminology of the trade" (p. 21). To "acquire a grammar of stone carving" nicely suggests how the exercises Wittgenstein develops in the *Investigations* are meant to cure the philosophical disease associated with the epistemological presumption we must choose between idealism and realism. A wonderful way to present Wittgenstein's work would be to write a Wittgensteinian commentary on *The Stone Carvers*.

not exist by necessity enables us to see that all that is witnesses to the
God who created what is.

4. CONTINGENCY, CONNECTIONS, AND BEAUTY

I fear I have already tested the patience of any reader who has made
it this far in this essay. Is there any payoff that comes from my attempt
to show a resemblance between Aquinas's and Preller's and Wittgenstein's (and Hauerwas's) understandings of the contingent character of
all that makes up our world? I cannot pretend that what I am about to
suggest amounts to a payoff, but I hope it is at least suggestive. In the
last chapter of *Divine Science and the Science of God*—in which Preller
explores the various attempts to show how the language of faith may
be compatible with "the natural universe of human discourse"—he
has a fascinating discussion of poetry and, in particular, the poetry of
Gerard Manley Hopkins.[43] Preller notes that poets do more than create
new meanings—farmers and bureaucrats do that as well—but poets see
possibilities of interpretation not suggested by straightforward descriptions of the everyday.

Preller uses Hopkins's poetry, noting that Hopkins not only calls
attention to what things do, but to the way things are.[44] According to

43. James Edwards also uses Hopkins's poetry to exemplify Wittgenstein's endeavor to
enable us to "see through" what we see. For example, when Hopkins speaks of the falcon
as "kingdom of daylight's dauphin," Edwards suggests he is trying to help us see through
what we ordinarily see. "If we suddenly see the dauphin of the kingdom of daylight sail-
ing there in the heavens, if that image takes hold of us and for a moment disappears as a
'mere' image, then upon our return to our everyday conceptions we become newly aware
of *their* status. By means of the extraordinary image, we are forcefully reminded of the
role of those everyday conceptions in determining what we see; thus we can see through
the ordinary objects of our sight. The temporary appropriation of the poetic image delit-
eralizes all our seeing, at least for a time. And in that deliteralization is a corresponding
expansion. Once it is brought home to us that the world is much richer than our everyday
conceptions of it, we can never be quite so complacent in our ordinary ways of seeing,
feeling and acting. There are words yet unconceived in our familiar forms of life." *Ethics
without Philosophy*, p. 212.

44. I am indebted to Brad Kallenberg for his critical reading of this paper. He has
saved me from a number of mistakes that are the result of a lazy mind. Too often I let my
language be captured by a dualism Wittgenstein tried to help us overcome. For example,
in my effort to suggest how the language of faith tells us about "the way the world is," I
may give the impression that language is something that "depicts" "reality" "out there."
The language of faith does convey the way the world is for those whose lives are shaped
by that language, but that it does so only makes it possible for the way the world is to be
exemplified in their lives. Kallenberg rightly notes that Hopkins's claim that each thing
"is what it does" is at the heart of the attempt by Wittgenstein to overcome the "realism-
skepticism" problem. In a letter to me Kallenberg observes, "we inhabit a world that is

Preller, Hopkins suggests each thing *is* what it *does:* "What a thing does constitutes its 'self'—it is its 'selving forth.' Hopkins sees the *esse-operatio* of nature as a mode of self-expenditure. What things *do* in the world is to blaze forth in a more or less lavish and expensive display of their potency, and then die out in a brilliant trail of 'blue-bleak embers' which 'fall, gall themselves, and gash gold-vermilion'" (pp. 222–23).

Preller observes that Hopkins introduces no new "facts" into his description of reality, and another poet might even disagree with him. But they would not be disagreeing about the empirical fact that objects come into being and disintegrate. Rather they would be disagreeing about the proper mode of *taking* that fact. Moreover, how "that fact" is taken by the reader of Hopkins's poem tells us something about how the world is—e.g., we learn why "the reader" and "the fact" are not two independent entities. Rather, as Preller suggests, just as Hopkins thinks the world is saying something to our longing for the permanence of beauty, so also Aquinas believes the contingency of the world says something to our desire for the good.[45] "Our desire" is constitutive of the way things are.

Preller, however, thinks that Hopkins's use of religious language in his poetry confirms his contention that the language of faith cannot share the same form of other human language. Preller notes that Hopkins

can *assert* that self-expenditure is sacrifice—a yielding by nature of beauty back to God—to be understood only in the light of Christ ("my chevalier!"). Hopkins suggests that the flux of the world can only be understood, that is, in the light of faith. He cannot produce that faith or exhibit the meaning of religious language—he must depend upon the meaning of the language of faith when he uses it in his poetry. (P. 224)

Yet again I wonder if Preller has done justice to the significance of his own analysis of Hopkins's poetry. That the world can only be understood "in the light of faith" does not in itself tell you that language of faith fails to tell you anything about the way the world is. Indeed Preller's account of Hopkins's poetry suggests that as readers of Hopkins we would know less about the world than we do if his poetry did not exist. Of course

internally related to language/form-of-life/communal practices." Accordingly the claims Christians make about the way things are do not draw on representational accounts of how we know, but rather such claims are meant to help us discover how the language we speak creates conditions for its own felicity. But those conditions also provide the context for conversations with those who do not speak our language of faith.

45. I note that Preller says that Aquinas believes the contingency of the world says something to our longing for "complete intelligibility." *Divine Science and the Science of God*, p. 223. I substituted "good" for "complete intelligibility" because I think it closer to Aquinas's own understanding.

even if such is the case, given the low epistemological status generally given to poetry in our time, to compare the language of faith to poetry may not seem to many to be doing the language of faith any favors.[46]

There is, however, a remarkable passage in *Culture and Value*, which I believe supports my suggestion that Preller's remarks about Hopkins advance the case for the way the language of faith can tell something about the way the world is. Wittgenstein reports that one of his friends, Engelmann, told him that when he discovers a drawer full of his old manuscripts, he first thinks they are splendid and that he should make them available to other people. But when he imagines publishing some of them, the whole business loses its charm and becomes impossible. Wittgenstein comments that when Engelmann looks at his work and finds it good, but cannot publish it,

> he is seeing his life as a work of art created by God, and, as such, it is cer-
> tainly worth contemplating, as is every life and everything whatever. But
> only an artist can so represent an individual thing as to make it appear to us
> like a work of art; it is *right* that those manuscripts should lose their value
> when looked at singly and especially when regarded *disinterestedly*, i.e., by
> someone who doesn't feel enthusiastic about them in advance. A work of
> art forces us—as one might say—to see it in the right perspective but, in the
> absence of art, the object is just a fragment of nature like any other.[47]

Wittgenstein's work I believe to be the ongoing attempt to help rediscover the frightening beauty of the particular. That is why he thought philosophy must finally be a form of poetry. In the *Investigations* he asks, "Could there be human beings lacking in the capacity to see something *as something*—and what would that be like? What sort of consequences would it have?—Would this defect be comparable to colour-blindness or to not having absolute pitch?—We will call it 'as-pect-blindness.'"[48] "Aspect-blindness" turns out to name our normal condition. Faced by the sheer variety of the world, we seek to control the variety through theory, that is, we try to demonstrate that the way

46. For an attempt to help us see the interrelation between the "signatured" character of artistic truth and the kind of truth characteristic of religious speech see George Dennis O'Brien, *The Idea of a Catholic University* (Chicago: University of Chicago Press, 2002), pp. 33–45, 80–87.

47. Wittgenstein, *Culture and Value*, 4e. I do not believe Wittgenstein had a theory of art because I do not think Wittgenstein had a theory about anything. It is certainly the case, however, that he had fascinating remarks about art and aesthetics throughout his work. In particular see *Lectures and Conversations on Aesthetics, Psychology, and Religious Belief*, ed. Cyril Barrett (Berkeley: University of California Press, 1997). The "motto" Wittgenstein liked so much— "Everything is what it is and not another thing"—appears in his "Lecture on Aesthetics," p. 27.

48. Wittgenstein, *Investigations*, p. 213e.

things are is the way things have to be. That is why it is so frightening for us to see "the object" as a fragment of nature, which can only be related to other fragments of nature by narratives that help us see the connections between contingent things and events without losing their contingent and particular beauty.[49]

I think we have no way to know whether Wittgenstein was or was not a Christian. I certainly do not think much hangs on whether he was or was not in terms of his significance for theology.[50] What I do think is that the kind of exercises he developed to help us see the particular are not unlike the kind of exercises Christians must go through—the

49. This sentence obviously has resonances I have learned from the work of Iris Murdoch, who may well have learned them from Wittgenstein. In his biography of Murdoch, *Iris Murdoch: A Life* (New York: Norton, 2001), Peter Conradi tells us Murdoch never had the opportunity to listen to Wittgenstein lecture, but she was in constant conversation with people who had studied with Wittgenstein. In what manner Murdoch's increasing Platonism may or may not have transformed what is clearly Wittgenstein's influence on her would make a fascinating study. However, Charles Pinches has anticipated what such a comparison might look like when he says, commenting on Murdoch's Platonism: "Platonism pulls us, finally, beyond this world to a god above it. Christianity, while terribly attracted by this upward motion, must resist it. It must reenter the world—which it can never see as in some sense 'unreal.' I do not know if there is such a thing as distinctly Christian art, but if there is, it must include this return. Great art must always challenge our lived perceptions of what is real. In addition to this challenge, Christian art may need to include a re-representation of the lived world, as real." *Theology and Action: After Theory in Christian Ethics*, p. 187. Earlier (p. 185) Pinches suggests that my later work is not as determined by my earlier emphasis on how art can provide the way to see truthfully. That may be the case, but if it is, all it means is that I have failed to say what I should have been saying.

50. I, therefore, differ from my good friend, James McClendon, who argues that Wittgenstein was a Christian. See his *Systematic Theology: Witness* (vol. 3; Nashville: Abingdon, 2000), pp. 227–70. Norman Malcolm certainly makes a strong case that, whether Wittgenstein was or was not a Christian, the point of view he develops in the *Investigations* is analogous to a religious point of view. Malcolm argues that there are "four analogies between Wittgenstein's conception of the grammar of language, and his view of what is paramount in a religious life. First, in both there is an end to explanation; second, in both there is an inclination to be amazed at the existence of something; third, into both there enters the notion of an 'illness'; fourth, in both, *doing, acting*, takes priority over intellectual understanding and reasoning." See Norman Malcolm, *Wittgenstein: A Religious Point of View*, ed. and with a response by Peter Winch (Ithaca, N.Y.: Cornell University Press, 1993), p. 92. Winch rightly questions whether Malcolm's analogies are as revealing as Malcolm thinks, but obviously the case I have tried to make in this essay shares some features of Malcolm's account. Winch observes that Malcolm's argument that explanations have to stop does not mean we are required to regard acceptance of things as they are as a gift (pp. 113–14). Winch, for example, calls attention to Wittgenstein's remarks in *Culture and Value* (71e) about the sheer "cussedness of things," which he thinks describes an attitude diametrically opposed to gratitude. Winch observes, however, that the significance of such expressions for Wittgenstein depends not on the words used but on the difference their use

kind of exercise that Preller rediscovers in Aquinas—to see in the sheer "thereness" of what is: God's work. In 1947 Wittgenstein wrote a set of remarks that now appear on the same page of *Culture and Value*. Though I am sure it is sheer contingency that they appear on the same page, I am equally convinced that they are interrelated:

> The truly apocalyptic view of the world is that things do *not* repeat themselves. It isn't absurd, e.g., to believe that the age of science and technology is the beginning of the end for humanity; that the idea of great progress is a delusion, along with the idea that the truth will ultimately be known; that there is nothing good or desirable about scientific knowledge and that mankind, in seeking it, is falling into a trap. It is by no means obvious that this is not how things are.
>
> The miracles of nature.
> One might say: art *shows* us the miracles of nature. It is based on the *concept* of the miracles of nature. (The blossom, just opening out. What is *marvellous* about it?) We say: "Just look at it opening out!"[51]

makes in the lives of users. But that seems to be Malcolm's point, namely, that Wittgenstein thought the failure to live with gratitude is a failure to recognize the way things are.

Unlike Malcolm, however, I am less confident that I know what I am talking about when I talk about a "religious point of view." I have also refrained from appealing to Wittgenstein's well-known remarks on religion, Christianity, and theology. I think his remarks on these matters are, like everything else he said, well worth pondering, but I do not think they add or subtract from the position I have tried to develop in this essay. I do think, however, that the remarks in *Culture and Value* concerning the resurrection are among his most important: "Perhaps we can say: Only *love* can believe the Resurrection. Or: It is *love* that believes the Resurrection. We might say: Redeeming love believes even in the Resurrection; hold fast even to the Resurrection. What combats doubt is, as it were, *redemption*" (33e).

51. Wittgenstein, *Culture and Value*, 56e. Another way of approaching what I have tried to do in this essay is through an account of "negative theology." Alex Sider, for example, in an essay commenting on Denys's account of our knowledge of God stresses the importance of Denys's understanding of hierarchy as the necessary context for his account of negative theology. Sider notes, "For Denys, all creation is ordered with respect to and by God, so that it is harmoniously structured and reflective of God's glory. Much of Denys' work is devoted to detailing how God can be accurately reflected by a harmony of parts. Because for Denys, God is the sole single principle, no one aspect of created reality could approach an adequate manifestation of God. Creation, therefore, witnesses to God's glories precisely in virtue of its multiplicity. Aspects of creation are divided and subdivided into parts that, when taken in concert, tell us something about what God is like. For example, we can infer from Denys that the differentiation of the virtues is an instance of this: by cultivating the virtues in their variety, we come to see how courage requires temperance, justice, prudence, and so on. Moreover, in seeing how the virtues are interconnected we come to know something about their unity in God. This goes as well for the basic structure and order of material things. One basic task for theology is therefore to reflect on the interconnections among objects in creation in order to begin to see how God's glory

---

surpasses the wonderful intricacy of the world. Thus, on Denys' view, the life of stones as such is less revelatory of God than that of humans, but both are necessary—because we must reflect on how stones are like and unlike humans and vice versa—to approach more fully our knowledge of God. The importance of hierarchy for Denys lies not in the ranking of humans above stones, but in the way that the created hierarchy as a whole displays how creation is intrinsically ordered to reflect God." "The Hiddenness of God and the Justice of God: Negative Theology as Social Ethical Resource" (unpublished), pp. 5–6. I am indebted to Sider for a critical reading of an earlier version of this paper. His criticism has made it a much better paper. I am also indebted to Jeff Stout for his close reading and editing of this paper.

5

THE NARRATIVE TURN

Thirty Years Later

1. WHY NOT ALL WHO CRY "NARRATIVE" ARE BLESSED

My first position was in the Department of Bible and Christianity at Augustana College in Rock Island, Illinois, in 1968. I had never lived in the Midwest, much less in a Mississippi river town. One of the first things I noticed about Rock Island is no one drank at home. They drank at the local bar that was usually right around the corner. To walk into any of those bars after work in the late afternoon was to discover a community of people who had been drinking at the same bar for the last thirty years. Anyone who might wander into one of these bars who was not a regular was immediately identified as not belonging.

If you lived in the Quad Cities area you often heard a story that nicely suggests the sociology of these bars. It seems a stranger, probably someone from Saint Louis, wandered into one of these bars. He walked up to the bar, ordered a beer, but then was struck by the fact that no one in the bar was talking to one another. He stood there staring into his beer when suddenly one of the men shouted out, "43!" The place erupted in a gale of laughter. Then it got quiet again. After some minutes another patron shouted, "16!" with the same uproarious result. This pattern continued for some time, which led the stranger to ask the bartender what was going on.

He explained that this group of folk had been coming to this bar for so long, they had come to know one another so well that rather than tell the same story over and over again, they had just numbered them one through a hundred. It was explained that this saved a lot of time and in no way inhibited the pleasure they found in hearing an oft-told tale. The stranger allowed (in the Midwest they "allow") he thought this was a terrific idea and desiring to join in, asked if he could tell one. The bartender shrugged, gesturing, "Why not?" The stranger waited a few minutes and then shouted, "36!" No response at all. Chagrined, he turned to the bartender, who said, "Boy, you sure can't tell them."

I begin with this story because you probably ought to begin a lecture about stories with a story. But more important, I fear that the current celebration of the importance of narrative may lead us to believe that every time we shout, "Story!" we can assume we know how to tell one another stories or why stories are important. Moreover, I fear that if in fact we speak and act as if we know more about the significance of stories than we do, I am partly to blame. I was there, so to speak, at the beginning. I published my first article with "story" in the title in 1973 in the *Journal of Religious Ethics*. That article, "The Self as Story: A Reconsideration of Religion and Morality from the Agent's Perspective," became the fourth chapter in my first book, *Vision and Virtue: Essays in Christian Ethical Reflection*, which was published in 1974.[1] The rest, so to speak, is history: which means I am often identified as a "narrative theologian."

I hate the idea I am a "narrative theologian." I hate all qualifiers to theology other than "Christian." Any qualifier other than "Christian" suggests that someone is trying to highjack Christian theology for their peculiar set of interests or that they are trying to provide a theory about theology that is more determinative than first-order theological claims. As I will explain below, I also dislike the description "narrative theology" because it can suggest that theology is more concerned with narrative than with God. So I am going to use this opportunity to say what the role of narrative should be in theology by calling attention to how I understand the connections between the various ways I used appeals to the importance of narrative in my own work.

However, I first want to indicate what I regard as some of the unfortunate developments that the return to narrative has had. I am particu-

---

1. Stanley Hauerwas, *Vision and Virtue: Essays in Christian Ethical Reflection* (Notre Dame, Ind.: University of Notre Dame Press, 1981). The 1974 edition was published by the small South Bend press called Fides Press. I like very much that my first published book was published by a press that needed all the faith it could muster just to stay in business.

larly concerned with how some have used the rediscovery of narrative to further an apologetic strategy on behalf of Christianity, that is, the attempt to make Christianity intelligible in modernity. I am thinking of those who like to quote Elie Wiesel's "God made man because God is a lover of stories" in the interest of calling attention to the unavoidability of stories.[2] The suggestion is then made that as long as stories are unavoidable, why not try the story Christians tell about our understanding of ourselves? We need all the stories we can get, and some of the best stories can be found in religious traditions. This way of selling the importance of stories is sometimes accompanied by a disdain for doctrine or theology because those activities allegedly kill the liveliness of stories through conceptual and analytical investigation.

What bothers me about this way of calling attention to the importance of stories is that it is but a disguised form of the well-known strategy of Protestant liberalism that tries to find some "connection" in human experience that can make sense of Christian claims. The result is usually some reductive account of the Christian faith that identifies a "core" or "essence" of what is really important about what we believe as Christians. Appeals to narrative become a way to say that everyone, whether they know it or not, has some faith perspective, that is, a fundamental attitude to the world that cannot be shown to be true or false, but that we cannot be without. That apologetic strategy, a strategy that remains an ongoing temptation particularly in a time when Christianity is in decline, is ironically one I had hoped might be challenged by calling attention to the narrative character of Christian convictions about the way things are. I did so because good stories defy summary.

At least one of the difficulties I had with the appeal to narrative in service to an apologetic task is that in an odd way it resulted in an underwriting of the modern stress on the sovereign self. It did so because what became important is that you become the teller of the tale you need. So the focus, often unacknowledged or recognized, was on the agent prior to the story. So the sovereign self still reigned, only now that self took the form of a story. In this respect I think it is not unimportant that many, such as George Lindbeck and Hans Frei, who were among the first to direct our attention to the narrative character of existence, had been influenced by Wittgenstein. From Wittgenstein they had learned that we are spoken before we speak. This means that to call attention to the significance of words and stories is just the beginning not the end

2. I use this quote in an essay in honor of Hans Frei called "The Church as God's New Language," which now appears in my book *Christian Existence Today: Essays on Church, World, and Living in Between* (Grand Rapids: Brazos, 2001), pp. 47–66. This book was originally published by the Durham, N.C., press, Labyrinth, in 1988.

of the work that must be done if we are to investigate the world that is opened to us through the stories that tell us.

It is not clear to me that any of us know what we are talking about when we describe the time in which we allegedly live as "postmodern." But if "postmodernity" names the time, as Gerard Loughlin suggests, when people recognize they are "not the sovereign of their stories," then there is some connection between the emphasis on narrative and postmodernism.[3] But unlike many who are said to represent postmodernism, those like Lindbeck and Frei have no intention of giving up questions of whether stories are truthful or untruthful. As Loughlin puts it:

> Christian truth has never been a matter of matching stories against reality. It has always been a matter of matching reality-stories against the truth: Jesus Christ. For the Christian Church it has always been a life-story that comes first, against which all other things are to be matched. This life-story is what "truth" means in Christianity. Nor is this a matter of making up the truth, because it is the truth that makes up the story. The story is imagined for us before it is re-imagined by us: the story is *given* to us.[4]

Those attracted to narrative theology as an apologetic strategy may seem to agree with Loughlin because they often emphasize the importance of stories in the Bible. There is no question that much of the content of the Bible is in the form of stories. Moreover, I think it is true that the Bible is best understood as a complex story with many subplots that resist any overly simple telling.[5] It is, of course, also the case that the

3. Gerard Loughlin, *Telling God's Story: Bible, Church, and Narrative Theology* (Cambridge, U.K.: Cambridge University Press, 1996), p. 32.

4. Ibid., p. 23.

5. A. Katherine Grieb uses the helpful metaphor of "nesting" when she suggests that Paul's argument in Romans "in defense of God's righteousness is constructed on a series of stories nested within the one great story of what God has done for Israel and for the Gentiles in Jesus Christ." *The Story of Romans: A Narrative Defense of God's Righteousness* (Louisville: Westminster John Knox, 2002), p. ix. Grieb argues that "Romans is not a theological treatise on either faith and works or predestination. Instead it is a sweeping defense of the righteousness of God, the covenant faithfulness of God 'to the Jew first and also to the Greek,' a phrase Paul repeats several times at the beginning of the letter and demonstrates in the logic of his argument. . . . The story of God's righteousness in Jesus Christ is at once the story of (1) God's sovereign renewal of the created cosmos, (2) God's redemption of humanity from universal bondage to Sin and Death, and (3) God's reconciliation of Jews and Gentiles (which involves both God's faithfulness to Israel and the keeping of God's promise for the Gentiles). It is critical to discern the *apocalyptic* framework in which the story appears: creation groans with expectation (Rom. 8:22) as Paul and his communities live out the script of the end time; they are players in the last act of God's apocalyptic drama of salvation, a story that began with creation and the fall and continues through Israel's history up to the present moment" (p. xxiii). Nothing has been quite as important as the freeing of Paul from the terms set by debates in the Reformation.

Bible contains material that is not primarily narrative in form. I would want to argue, though (and I think it undeniable) that those forms of literature in the Bible—e.g., the Psalms, the wisdom literature, and the more discursive books of the New Testament—are unintelligible apart from the story of God's call and care of Israel and the life, death, and resurrection of Christ.

So I do not in any way mean to demean the significance of the narrative character of the Bible, but I think it is a mistake to try to do theology by basing the work theology is meant to do on a literary type.[6] Again the problem is how such a move reproduces the habits of Protestant liberalism. The narrative character of the Bible, for example, is used to underwrite a generalized anthropology that delivers insights about the human condition. Of course there is nothing wrong with having insights about the human condition. But insights, even about the human condition, are a dime a dozen. People seldom, and rightly so, are willing to risk their lives or even make a small sacrifice on the basis of an "insight."

Because these apologetic strategies became so identified with the appeal to narrative, I simply quit writing about the importance of narrative for theology.[7] That I did so does not mean I thought what I had said about the importance of narrative in my earlier work was mistaken. Of course I think I now could provide a clearer account than I did then of

6. Too often I fear appeals to narrative as the characteristic of the Bible ironically have the effect of separating the stories of the Bible from the text of the Bible. This has the effect of spiritualizing the Bible by failing to see the significance of the bodily character of the text. David Dawson has written brilliantly about this by showing how "in Origen's view salvation requires a radical transformation of body, but it cannot entail its replacement, even as an allegorical reading requires deepening and extending, but not replacing the text's literal sense. Transforming the body through reading the literal sense can be compared to transforming the body through ingesting food." *Christian Figural Reading and the Fashioning of Identity* (Los Angeles: University of California Press, 2002), p. 65. Dawson notes that Origin will argue that Scripture is "itself a sacrament like the Eucharist. Christ the lamb is still the Word, that Word is found in Scripture, and eating the Word refers to the interpretation of Scripture. In his *Treatise on the Passover,* he writes 'If the lamb is Christ and Christ is the Logos, what is the flesh of the divine words if not the divine Scripture?' " (p. 71). For a systematic account of this understanding of Scripture, see Telford Work, *Living and Active: Scripture in the Economy of Salvation* (Grand Rapids: Eerdmans, 2002).

7. I think the last thing I wrote on narrative qua narrative is the "Introduction" to the book I edited with Greg Jones called *Why Narrative? Readings in Narrative Theology* (Grand Rapids: Eerdmans, 1989). Actually, to say the "Introduction" is the last thing I wrote on narrative would be stretching the truth. Greg wrote most of what appears there. My "writing" basically consisted of our conversations about what the "Introduction" should say. I still think the essays in this collection remain the best available and certainly anyone wanting to begin to think about these issues should begin with this book. The book continues to be available through Wipf and Stock Publishers in Eugene, Oregon.

why I think it important to call attention to the narrative character of Christian convictions. But I have increasingly become convinced that rather than talking about narrative as a category in itself, we are better advised to do theology in a manner that displays what we have learned by discovering the unavoidability of the narrative character of Christian convictions. After *The Peaceable Kingdom,* which I believe is my most complete account of why it is important to recognize the narrative grammar of Christian convictions, I seldom have written directly about narrative qua narrative.[8] Rather I have thought it more important to do theology in a manner that displays the narrative form of the gospel. After all, recognition of the necessity of narration for any account of our lives does not save. God saves.

I think I know why I no longer call attention to the "importance of stories" or attempt any endeavor that might be called "theorizing about narrative"; but I wish I knew why another thinker who is responsible for calling attention to the importance of "narrative" for practical reasons no longer writes about narrative. I am, of course, referring to Alasdair Mac-Intyre. In *After Virtue* narrative was the crucial category in MacIntyre's account of the moral life. In his work after *After Virtue,* tradition seems to have replaced narrative as the hub around which MacIntyre's position revolved. In *After Virtue* MacIntyre had argued that narrative is required for any account of our actions that attempts to show the connection between shorter- and longer-term intentions.[9] MacIntyre argued that narratives provide the linkage between our actions because our very concept of an intelligible action is more fundamental than the concept of an action. Accordingly he argued that human actions in general are but enacted narratives in which agents are at best but coauthors of their own narratives. The narrative of my life is but part of an interlocking set of narratives embedded in the story of those communities from which I derive my identity.[10] Accordingly there is a close correlation between personal identity and practical reason. Both are finally best displayed as the enactment of ongoing narrative(s).

MacIntyre's account of action and why narratives are required to make connections between what we do and do not do was very similar to the kind of analysis I had tried to develop in *Character and the Christian Life,* which was originally published in 1975. Indeed for reasons very much like those given by MacIntyre, I was led to see why the account I had given of human action in *Character and the Christian Life* was

8. Stanley Hauerwas, *The Peaceable Kingdom: A Primer in Christian Ethics* (Notre Dame, Ind.: University of Notre Dame Press, 1983).

9. Alasdair MacIntyre, *After Virtue* (Notre Dame, Ind.: University of Notre Dame Press, 1984), p. 208.

10. Ibid., pp. 218 and 221.

inadequate exactly because at that time I did not have the concept of narrative, and in particular MacIntyre's account of an intelligible action, as part of my repertoire.[11] So it was extraordinarily important for me to see MacIntyre confirm some of the hunches I had begun to have about the importance of narrative. But then MacIntyre has not returned to this account of the importance of narrative in his latter work.

I am not suggesting that simply because he does not develop this account of narrative in his subsequent work MacIntyre has changed his mind about what he had to say about narrative in *After Virtue*. Yet it is interesting that in *Whose Justice? Which Rationality?* as well as *Three Rival Versions of Moral Enquiry* he seems to think it much more important to develop an account of tradition. Of course, in *After Virtue* he had already begun to explore why any account of rationality requires a tradition understood as a "historically extended, socially embodied argument" about the goods that constitute that tradition.[12] It may well be that MacIntyre's intellectual agenda in his later work simply does not require him to return to his earlier account of narrative; but it nonetheless remains quite interesting that narrative no longer has the central focus for him it had in *After Virtue*.

I have wondered if one of the reasons for MacIntyre's reticence to draw attention even to the narrative character of tradition might be that if MacIntyre were to develop his account of the importance of narrative, he would not be able to talk about the importance of narrative qua narrative. Instead he would have to talk about *a* narrative, which might well force him to develop his thought in ways that would require him to do something more than philosophy. That "something else" I think is theology, which is the subject that MacIntyre has spent a lifetime avoiding. But I am a theologian. Moreover, I think it is not accidental that if we are to understand the significance of narrative, such an understanding is only available through theological reflection.

2. IN THE BEGINNING

"In the beginning" is where any account of the narrative character of Christian convictions must begin. Actually that is not quite a strong enough claim. "In the beginning" is where any display of "why narrative" must begin to show why a narrative is constitutive of any claims that would tell us the way the world is. This is the heart of the

11. I discuss this in a new "Introduction" to *Character and the Christian Life: A Study in Theological Ethics* (Notre Dame, Ind.: University of Notre Dame Press, 2001). The "Introduction" originally appeared in the 1985 second edition of the book.

12. MacIntyre, *After Virtue*, p. 222.

argument I developed in my Gifford Lectures, *With the Grain of the Universe: The Church's Witness and Natural Theology*.[13] There I argue that if it were possible to prove the existence of God, then we would have evidence that the God Christians worship does not exist. If we could prove God, then a necessary relation between God and God's creation must exist; but that is exactly the kind of relation that cannot be shown to exist.

Christian theology insists that there is never a question about God's existence. Only God exists, which means only in God are existence and essence one. Only God, therefore, can act without loss. That only in God are essence and existence one Aquinas thought to be the metaphysical implication of "In the beginning when God created the heavens and the earth" (Gen. 1:1). The Christian claim, therefore, that God created *ex nihilo* is the metaphysical expression necessary to account for why we know ourselves and our world by the story told about ourselves and our world in the Bible.[14] It is contingency all the way down, which means the only way we have to know God and ourselves is by the connections made possible by truthful stories and, in particular, the story that begins, "In the beginning."[15]

Accordingly, David Burrell argues that the distinction between God and the world is unlike any other distinction we might employ because we distinguish God from everything else in a way that God is the source of all there is. This means that God cannot be placed over against the universe as though God were on par with those things in the universe we need to distinguish from other things. God cannot be so situated because God did not create from lack, but rather creation manifests the gratuity of God's love—a love that cannot be used up. So we cannot distinguish the creator from creation as if God were one item among others. Accordingly God alone exists by necessity, but the necessity is not the Aristotelian "could not be otherwise" but rather God "could

---

13. Stanley Hauerwas, *With the Grain of the Universe: The Church's Witness and Natural Theology* (Grand Rapids: Brazos, 2001).

14. For my exploration of the theme of *creatio ex nihilo* see the essay on Iris Murdoch, "Murdochian Muddles: Can We Get Through Them If God Does Not Exist?" in my book *Wilderness Wanderings: Probing Twentieth-Century Theology and Philosophy* (Boulder, Colo.: Westview, 1997), pp. 155–70.

15. Richard Rorty is quite right to maintain the "contingent" character of language, selfhood, and community in his *Contingency, Irony, and Solidarity* (Cambridge, U.K.: Cambridge University Press, 1989). Christians have no reason to deny that "our language and our culture are as much a contingency, as much a result of thousands of small mutations finding niches (and millions of others finding no niches), as are the orchids and the anthropoids" (p. 16). But there is the question whether the description "contingent" can do much work on Rorty-like grounds. Thus one can always ask, "Contingent to what?" If it is all contingent, do we learn anything by calling it all contingent?

not not be." "God alone exists 'by right,' as it were, being 'necessarily existent in itself,' whereas existence 'comes to' everything else."[16] This is why our knowledge of God and ourselves is analogical, so that the analogies are tested and extended through the stories we are taught by those who have learned to worship God rightly.

Though this understanding of God is usually put in ontological terms of "being," it is crucial to see that Aquinas's understanding of being is about action. God's being is his activity.[17] Which means we, perhaps, understand better what Aquinas is about when he makes the ontological point in terms of happiness. He says,

> Since happiness signifies some final perfection; according as various things capable of happiness can attain to various degrees of perfection, so must there be various meanings applied to happiness. For in God there is happiness essentially; since His very Being is His operation, whereby He enjoys no other than Himself. In the happy angels the final perfection is in respect of some operation, by which they are united to the Uncreated Good: and this operation of theirs is one only and everlasting. But in men, according to their present state of life, the final perfection is in respect of an operation whereby man is united to God: but this operation neither can be continual, nor consequently, is it one only, because operation is multiplied by being discontinued. And for this reason in the present state of life, perfect happiness cannot be attained by man.[18]

Thus, as John Milbank has insisted, "in the beginning" was an act of "original peace." As I noted above, only God can act without loss, which means creation is not an alien act. In Milbank's terms, "Christianity recognizes no original violence." Accordingly, peace is not the suppression of difference, but rather is the "sociality of harmonious difference."[19] We were created by peace, making it impossible for us not to long for peace. But such a peace is not that secured by ensuring that change does not threaten order, but rather by our being made participants in a community in which our activity matches our desires. Accordingly "peace" is but the name given to a life of virtue in which what we do

16. David Burrell, *Friendship and Ways to Truth* (Notre Dame, Ind.: University of Notre Dame Press, 2000), p. 94.

17. This is Burrell's central contention in his *Aquinas: God and Action* (London: Routledge & Kegan Paul, 1979).

18. Thomas Aquinas, *Summa Theologica*, I–II, 3, 2.4, trans. Fathers of the English Dominican Province (Westminster, Md.: Christian Classics, 1981). This is, I think, Thomas's way to say that in this life we will never get the story of our lives straight.

19. John Milbank, *Theology and Social Theory: Beyond Secular Reason* (Oxford, U.K.: Basil Blackwell, 1990), p. 5. As Milbank puts it late in *Theology and Social Theory*, "creation is therefore not a finished product in space, but is continuously generated *ex nihilo* in time" (p. 425).

is not different than what we are. Such a life in this life, of course, is known only through hope.

Milbank draws an implication from this understanding of creation that I think has not been appropriately appreciated for its importance. He argues that narrative is a more basic category than either explanation or understanding, because narrative is the mode of comprehension that allows us to understand not only ourselves but all that is. Explanation—the mode of science that assumes the material sphere of our lives is only governed by efficient causation—turns out to be unable to account for itself on its own terms.[20] Understanding—the attempt to account for ourselves by positing a spiritual domain of meaning—results in endless deferment that hovers "like ectoplasm above the surface of material reality."[21] When explanation and understanding are assumed to be the only modes of comprehension, the result cannot help but finally be nihilism, in which all that remains is the will to power.[22] Please note Milbank is not denying that explanation and understanding may have an appropriate use in particular contexts. What is being denied is that explanation and understanding are our only or primary modes of rationality.

20. Milbank, *Theology and Social Theory*, p. 264. For an account and critique of science quite similar to Milbank's, see John Lukacs, *At the End of an Age* (New Haven: Yale University Press, 2002). Lukacs argues that science itself confirms that reality cannot be comprehended in terms of cause to effect for no other reason than that subatomic particles cannot be described by "essence" or "matter" but rather exist only as an event (p. 110). Lukacs notes the "fundament" of science is "mechanical causation," which means three things: "First: that the same causes must—always and everywhere—have the same effects. Second: that there must be an equivalence between the force of cause and that of its effect. Third: that the cause must always and everywhere precede its effect" (p. 113). Yet Lukacs observes that this kind of causality cannot make sense of human life nor the lives of the most complex organism of the universe (p. 114).

21. Milbank, *Theology and Social Theory*, p. 267. Dawson underscores Milbank's point in an analysis of Eric Auerbach's work. Dawson notes that Auerbach did not think a figural reader needs to invoke the term "meaning," that is, he wanted to resist the notion of doubleness the search for meaning seems to imply. To ask for the meaning of a word too often implies that the existence of the word is inadequate. In contrast Auerbach "underscores the reality of figure and fulfillment as entities in the world of space and time, and by 'meaning' he refers to the interrelationship of such real things, rather than some strange mental 'thing' with an existence all its own apart from that relationship. Auerbach is suspicious of meaning precisely because it so easily claims for itself a right of independent existence that belongs only to historical persons and events." David Dawson, *Christian Figural Reading and the Fashioning of Identity*, p. 87.

22. Though there is no necessary relation between the critique of foundational epistemologies and an emphasis on the importance of narrative, I think it is not accidental that many who find they cannot avoid some account of the narrative character of practical rationality also tend to be antifoundationist. They do so because they realize there is no place to start to think or to ground what we think in some place different from what we think. Rather they come to realize we can only begin and end in the middle.

The alternative to explanation and understanding is descriptions made possible by truthful stories. Descriptions, however, turn out to be extraordinary discoveries that demand constant reappropriation if we are not to be misled by our speech. For example, Christians are tempted to turn the description "sin" into an explanation or understanding that makes sin but a manifestation of a "deeper reality." In like manner we often assume that fundamental moral descriptions, e.g., "courage" or "murder," require a theory to sustain their meaning. But descriptions do not require a theory. Rather, we learn how they work and the kind of people we ought to be to sustain such descriptions by the practices and correlative narratives for a people to explain their way of life to themselves and others.[23]

The Christian narrative stands in contrast to explanation and understanding just to the extent that Christians offer descriptions that are unintelligible if our very existence does not come as a gift. Such an account cannot pretend to offer a noncontextual "universality," a universality that only hides the violence necessarily perpetrated in its name, but can only offer the reality of a people who have learned to live peaceably in a world of violence. In Milbank's words, "instead of a peace 'achieved' through the abandonment of the losers, the subordination of potential rivals and resistance to enemies, the Church provides a genuine peace by its memory of all the victims, its equal concern for all its citizens and its self-exposed offering of reconciliation of enemies."[24]

That the church is able to offer such a peace has been made possible by the life of the one we call Jesus. For it is in his life we believe we rightly see the end that was "in the beginning." That story, the story of Jesus, we also believe is the story of the church. Again as Gerard Loughlin puts it:

> the story of Jesus Christ continues in the story of the Church, and is thus not ended; or as Frei has it, that the stories of all are included in the story of Christ, so that the end of his story is the end of all stories. The story of Christ continues in the story of the Church because the Church is precisely constituted as the continuation of Christ's story. Christ leaves so that the Spirit may come to lead the Church in "a little while" to Christ. Everything

23. For the best account we have of description, see Charles Pinches, *Theology and Action: After Theory in Christian Ethics* (Grand Rapids: Eerdmans, 2002). As Pinches puts it, "*any* act, in virtue of being a human act, already has a narrative home, which means that any description of a human action already has begun the process of embedding the thing done in a narrative" (p. 218). Of course some acts take many years to discover their appropriate description or descriptions. For example, the recent destruction of the World Trade Center may well have been an act of terrorism, but whether that description will be adequate remains to be determined.

24. Milbank, *Theology and Social Theory*, p. 302.

given to Christ is given to the Church (John 17:7–8); and the Church is sent out "into the world" (John 16:7–24). The Church is the community that tells Christ's story by being itself the continuing story of Christ; embodying the story of Christ in the circumstances of its day.[25]

That is the story that Christians believe is not only true but also saving. Indeed without that story we believe that the world could not have a story. For there is no world if there is no church. So our very ability to say "In the beginning" is made possible because we are able to say "We have seen the end." That is what it means to say that the universe is adequately understood only if it is understood eschatologically. There was a beginning because there is an end. We were not created for no purpose, but rather for the glory of God. That alone is the story of stories.

3. TELLING THE STORY IN MODERNITY

The argument to this point (if that is not to give what I have tried to do a far too exalted complement) has tried to show why the attempt to show the unavoidability of narrative entails massive theological and metaphysical claims. Perhaps better put: the appeal to narrative is the primary expression of a theological metaphysics and is, therefore, an unembarrassed claim about the way things are.[26] If it could be shown, for example, that there could be a satisfactory account of existence that did not entail a narrative, then we might have evidence that what Christians (and, I suspect, Jews and Muslims) believe about the way things are is false. Accordingly we are some distance from those who would emphasize the importance of stories because of the charms of some stories. I do not think charming stories are to be despised, but charm, as is well known, can be a hiding place for the most destructive vices, not the least being the inability to distinguish between truthfulness and lies.

25. Loughlin, *Telling God's Story*, p. 84. The importance of narrative for christological reflection is simply beyond the focus of this chapter. Barth's refusal to separate the person and work of Christ set the stage for christological reflection that takes seriously Jesus' life and teaching as constitutive of the kingdom of God he was. Loughlin's claim that the story of Christ is the end of all stories does not mean that it brings to an end any other stories but that other stories find their *telos* in the story of Christ.

26. I think it is no accident that three of the most compelling accounts of Christian theology in recent time stress the significance of narrative. See, for example, James McClendon, *Systematic Theology* (vols. 1–3; Nashville: Abingdon, 1986, 1994, 2000, respectively); Robert Jenson, *Systematic Theology* (vols. 1–2; New York: Oxford University Press, 1997); and Joe R. Jones, *A Grammar of Christian Faith: Systematic Explorations in Christian Life and Doctrine* (New York: Rowman & Littlefield, 2002).

However, I suspect the significance of the return to narrative is best appreciated in ethical and political terms and, in particular, the peculiar challenges of modernity. I have a well-deserved reputation for "modernity bashing," but often those who criticize me for using a hammer when a scalpel is called for fail to attend to my central concerns. Those concerns have been quite simple. It has been my contention that "modernity" names the time that tried to forget we are timeful beings.[27] In other words modernity was the attempt to "start over" in a manner that left behind the gifts of the past. Interestingly enough, the development of the modern discipline of history was one of the ways modernity specialized in a determined mode of forgetfulness. The past could be forgotten through history by the attempt to show that "what happened" was explained by antecedent conditions. History, in short, too often is our attempt to turn the past into a number.

The forms of thought often associated with the Enlightenment are usually identified as the source as well as justification of this attempt to begin anew. Immanuel Kant is, I think, rightly seen as the most articulate thinker of this extraordinary project. Kant's work, like that of most of those associated with the Enlightenment project, is complex—making any generalization about what ways he does and does not suggest a decisive break with the past hard to determine. However, my primary interest has never been in laying blame at the feet of any one figure, but rather to understand the stories that are living through us that are difficult to name because to name them means we are already in a transition to other stories.[28]

"America" names for me sets of some of the most powerful stories that grip our lives. If you ask, "Why America?" my only answer is that

27. I put together the essays in *Wilderness Wanderings: Probing Twentieth-Century Theology and Philosophy* because I thought they provided an interesting investigation of timefulness. Of course that exploration was primarily undertaken through analysis of others, which meant what I thought I was trying to do was not as evident to my readers as it was to me.

28. John Lukacs suggests that we are at the end of modernity in his *At the End of an Age*. In a wonderful paragraph that begins his account of modernity, he observes "modernity" is a shorthand for "the Bourgeois Age[, which] was the Age of the State; the Age of Money; the Age of Industry; the Age of Cities; the Age of Privacy; the Age of the Family; the Age of Schooling; the Age of the Book; the Age of Representation; the Age of Science; and the age of an evolving historical consciousness." He then observes that except for the last two "all of these primacies are now fading and declining fast" (p. 15). Lukacs by no means thinks that everything about the modern age is bad. He notes we are healthier than ever before, large populations live in relative comfort, and every state proclaims it is a democracy. Yet he thinks that the contradictions within the modern project have led to its own demise. Lukacs argues that the way forward will require historical thinking, by which he means not the work that historians do, but rather the recognition of the historicity of all our knowledge. Yet he notes the historian Dante or Shakespeare is not yet among us (p. 83).

is where I am stuck. Yet it is also the case that America, perhaps more than any other country, exemplifies the ambitions of the Enlightenment. It does so for complex reasons, not the least being the assumption that "America" names a virgin land in which people could begin anew no longer encumbered by the hierarchial habits of the Old World. I have always thought no better example of the American ambition could be found than John Rawls's account of the original position.[29] Equally important, of course, is that America is a capitalist country. No system is more antithetical to memory than capitalism. As Milbank observes, "the capitalist system is, in itself, indifferent to attachment to location and to the content of particular customs and traditions; it imparts no sacrality either to place or to hierarchical modes of rule."[30] Liberal political arrangements coupled with capitalist systems conspire to produce a timeless people whose memories are at best formed by nostalgic sentimentalities.

Thus my oft-made claim that "modernity" names the time that produces people who believe they should have no story except the story they chose when they had no story. This story is, of course, a creation story, but now we become self-creators. The self, however, that is so created is one incapable of being habituated in the practices necessary to sustain a life of virtue. I am not suggesting that liberal political theory or practice is devoid of any account of the virtues, but rather that any such account but replicates an account of human action shaped by explanatory paradigms that make "me" different from what I do.[31] Thus cynicism becomes the central virtue of modernity, insuring that I can

29. It is a story in itself to document how Rawls's account of the original position in *A Theory of Justice* (Cambridge, Mass.: Harvard University Press, 1971) has mutated through his subsequent work. Yet I think it is not hard to see how the device of the original position continues to inform his understanding of international relations in *The Law of Peoples* (Cambridge, Mass.: Harvard University Press, 2002). In that book Rawls denies that his account of a "realistic utopia" is ahistorical. Thus people will "depend on the facts of social conduct as historical knowledge and reflection establish them: for example, the facts that, historically, political and social unity do not depend on religious unity, and that well-ordered democratic peoples do not engage in war with one another" (p. 16). Rawls's animus against religion is nowhere more evident than in this book. For example, he observes, "not to be overlooked is the fact that Hitler's demonic conception of the world was, in some perverse sense, religious" (p. 20).

30. Milbank, *Theology and Social Theory*, p. 273.

31. For example, John Rawls suggests that liberal conceptions of politics "require virtuous conduct of citizens, the necessary (political) virtues are those of political cooperation, such as a sense of fairness and tolerance and a willingness to meet others half-way." *The Law of Peoples*, p. 15. Rawls no doubt thinks other virtues might well be important, but they are not "political." Yet the very distinction between political and nonpolitical virtues begs the question of whether any polity does not require, for example, the virtue of honesty or courage if the political system is to have any chance of being at once truthful and

always stand back from my activity in order to make it possible for me to disavow who I am.

If the church is in fact a community determined by a counterstory to the story that we story ourselves, I have suggested the church cannot help but appear as a counterpolitics to the politics of the world. I am, therefore, accused of tempting Christians to withdraw from the world and abandon their responsibility to work for relative justice. I confess I often am tempted to withdraw, but there is no place to which we can withdraw. Christians are, after all, surrounded. However, we can in the meantime draw on God's good patience to be a patient people in the world so that the world may know that the story goes on.

Christians trained by such a patience might well discover that in this or that place and in this or that time they share much with their non-Christian brothers and sisters. The world may well try to live as if there are no stories, or at least as if there are no true stories, but such a life is impossible. Indeed the problem for most in our time and place is not that they have no story, but that too many stories—stories reduced to numbered shorthand—possess our lives, making it impossible to live out any story well. Therefore I suspect Christians can do nothing more important than take the time in a world that believes time is in short supply to listen to the stories others tell and in so hearing gain fresh ears to hear and live the story we believe makes us participants in God's life.

---

nonviolent. Certainly Aristotle would have found Rawls's distinction between political and nonpolitical virtues incoherent. Even on his own grounds one wonders if Rawls's extraordinarily "thin" account of the virtues necessary to sustain his liberal polity would be sufficient.

6

SUFFERING BEAUTY
The Liturgical Formation of Christ's Body

1. LESSONS FROM A NUN

La Crosse, Wisconsin, is not the kind of place where you expect to be forced to rethink what you thought you thought. But I learned an important lesson in La Crosse relevant to questions surrounding the subject of this conference,[1] that is, the liturgical formation of Christians. I was in La Crosse because I taught summer school at Notre Dame. It was during the time—that is, the early seventies—that many of the women's orders were sending some of their numbers back to summer school to learn the "new morality" they associated with Vatican II. Accordingly I met wonderful women who, for example, had given their lives to teaching seventh-graders in Muscatine, Iowa. I also learned at that time that I would never be able to remember the names of what seemed to me innumerable orders of Catholic sisters. Thus my claim that the only thing the pope does not know is how many different kinds of Mennonites and orders of Catholic sisters there are.

1. This chapter was written for the annual meeting (2001) of the Society for Catholic Liturgy. The theme of the conference was liturgy and ethics.

The Franciscan Sisters of the Perpetual Adoration, however, I remember very well. Not only did I teach several of their numbers, but they invited me to give a series of lectures at their summer meeting at Viterbo College in La Crosse. The sisters founded Viterbo College, naming it after the town in Italy that had given the order a relic of St. Francis. The summer I was there was the hundredth anniversary of these wonderful sisters' adoration of the Eucharist. For a hundred years at least, two sisters (two in case one fell asleep) had prayed before the Eucharist.

These lovely women wanted me to share something of their life in La Crosse. So they organized a tour of La Crosse for Father Maly, an Old Testament scholar from Cincinnati who was also lecturing to their gathering, and me. One of our stops was at the abbey of the Benedictine Sisters of the Perpetual Rosary. It was a huge building but there were only eight sisters left and five of them were above seventy years old. One of the younger sisters came out to visit with us. She knew who Father Maly was and was honored by his visit. She gave us a sense of the history of these sisters, noting that due to their small numbers they were no longer able to keep the perpetual rosary. They supported themselves by baking the altar bread for the diocese.

As we stood up to leave, this sister leaned over the low wall separating us, grasped Father Maly's hand, and with tears in her eyes said, "Oh Father Maly, please pray for vocations. I know the young, shaped as they are by civil rights and the protest against the Vietnam war, think they need to be out in the world acting on behalf of justice. It is good that many feel that way. But God needs our prayers. So please pray that God will send us vocations so that we may continue to pray for God's world." I thought, "That has got to be right." Worship is not what we do to motivate the passion for justice. Worship, which from beginning to end is prayer, is justice.

In his beautiful book on prayer, Cardinal Danielou observes:

> The diversity of the Church's functions within the unity of the body of Christ is something very beautiful. It is important that we hold to the task that is entrusted to us by the others: the apostle must concern himself with souls, the monk recite the Office, the nun care for the elderly. By not fulfilling our function, we betray the trust of all the others. A monk who would leave his monastery too often, even for an authentic apostolate, would nevertheless be spiritually deluded, because the entire Church needs him to recite the Divine Office. As St. Paul says, "If one member is sick, the whole body is sick." (1 Cor. 12:26)[2]

2. Jean Danielou, *Prayer: The Mission of the Church*, trans. David Schindler (Grand Rapids: Eerdmans, 1996), pp. 12–13.

Yet it is not just the church that needs the monk's prayers, but the whole world. In *The City of God* Augustine maintains that "Justice is to be found where God, the one supreme God, rules an obedient City according to his grace, forbidding sacrifice to any being save himself alone."[3] For Christians prayer is sacrifice, because we pray in the name of Christ. Just as Jesus is the Father's prayer for the world, so God's church, through the miracle of the Spirit's work, makes us God's continuing prayer for the world. This means quite literally that there is nothing more important for Christians to do than to pray, in particular, for our enemies.

Drawing on what I learned from the Benedictine sister in La Crosse, Wisconsin, I have been unsympathetic with attempts to explore what, if any, relation may exist between liturgy and ethics. Elsewhere I have argued that the politics that creates the "and" between liturgy and ethics reproduces the politics of modernity that privatizes what makes the church the church, namely, the worship of God.[4] That Christians now must try to understand, for example, how prayer may or may not be related to the moral life indicates something has gone profoundly wrong with the practices that are meant to shape the Christian community.

Once the "and" becomes a standard feature of the way we think about these matters, we fail to notice that we also assume a moral psychology that makes the Christian moral life unintelligible. The liturgy becomes the "motivation" for the achievement of justice in this or that area of human life. As a result, as I argue below, an account of moral behavior is assumed that makes the acquisition of virtue impossible. The habits necessary for the formation of the virtues must be those acquired by agents for whom what they do is not different than who they are. When liturgy becomes a motivation for action that does not require the liturgy for the intelligibility of the description of what we have done, then we lose the means as Christians to make our lives our own.

That there now exists a Society for Catholic Liturgy (which I have no reason to believe is a "bad thing") may be but an indication of the challenge before us if we are to reclaim how liturgy should or may form Christians. That a separate society exists to take care of liturgy can be a permission for Catholic moral theologians to ignore the importance of liturgy for moral formation and reflection. Even worse, because you exist Christian educators may fear wandering into what appears to them an academic area that is beyond their competency. So in the interest

3. Augustine, *The City of God*, trans. David Knowles (Harmondsworth, U.K.: Penguin, 1972), p. 890 (19.23).

4. See, for example, ch. 10, "Worship, Evangelism, Ethics: On Eliminating the 'And,'" in my *A Better Hope: Resources for a Church Confronting Capitalism, Democracy, and Postmodernity* (Grand Rapids: Brazos, 2000), pp. 155–61.

of securing academic respectability among the guilds, the life of the church becomes divided into specializations in which each specialization becomes an end in itself. As a result, the fragmentation of our lives in modernity—a fragmentation that affects Christians no less than it affects anyone in social orders like America—is hidden from us by the fragmentation of the knowledges characteristic of the modern university as well as the theological disciplines.

Fragmentation is the social condition that creates the politics that makes intelligible the question: "What is the relation between liturgy and ethics?" To challenge that question, therefore, presents an extraordinary challenge for anyone today who desires to think as a Christian about the world in which we live. This is particularly true for the kind of theological project I represent. This was brought home to me by a comment made by Jody Bottum about the argument I make in my Gifford Lectures, *With the Grain of the Universe: The Church's Witness and Natural Theology.*[5] Commenting on the last chapter of my book, in which I hold up the lives and work of John Howard Yoder and John Paul II as truthful witnesses to the true God, Bottum observed what my position requires is not just the existence of such witness but an entire poetics.

Some may think, given my avowed anti-Constantianism, that I could not welcome Bottum's suggestion. Yet I believe he is right to challenge not just me, but all of us who seek to reclaim the central role of the Christian worship of God for the material practices that form Christian bodies in the world in which we find ourselves. For by "poetics" Bottum means the material conditions to shape the imagination of a community necessary not only to produce the crafts and art that express our faith, but also to enact a politics that is counter to the politics of this world.[6] To even begin to think, to imagine, what such a poetics means for Christians must begin and end with the liturgy.

5. Stanley Hauerwas, *With the Grain of the Universe: The Church's Witness and Natural Theology* (Grand Rapids: Brazos, 2001). Dr. Bottum made his comment at a meeting of the Dulles Colloquium, where the first and last chapters of my book were read.

6. An indication of the poverty of our politics as Christians is the paucity of the Christian artistic imagination. I am not suggesting that all art that serves to witness to our God must be done by Christians, but certainly Christianity requires explicit artistic expression in music, architecture, and the plastic crafts of the stories that make us Christian. Cardinal Ratzinger observes that we are experiencing a crisis not only in sacred art, but in art. That Christians have been schooled to think they must first be artists before they are Christians but reflects the politics that results in the trivializing of art. Ratzinger rightly maintains, however, that Christians cannot live without material embodiments of our faith. "The complete absence of images is incompatible with faith in the Incarnation of God. God has acted in history and entered into our sensible world, so that it may become transparent to him. Images of beauty, in which the mystery of the invisible God become visible, are an essential part of Christian worship." *The Spirit of the Liturgy*, trans. John Saward (San Francisco: Ignatius, 2000), pp. 130–31. One of the indications of the

I do not pretend that I know how to meet the challenge Bottum's comment presents, but I know I want to meet his challenge. Indeed, I believe in many ways everything I have tried to do to reclaim the distinctive character of the Christian moral tradition to be an attempt to begin to imagine what a Christian poetics might look like in our time.[7] I have done so by trying to recover the significance of the virtues as a way to understand the formation of our lives as Christians. What I now must do is try to explain why I think an account of the virtues offers a particularly constructive way to understand the liturgical formation of our lives as Christians.

2. PRACTICAL REASON, LITURGY, AND FORMATION

I cannot presume those who planned this program on the liturgical formation of Christians assumed that formation necessarily means "moral formation." However, since you asked me to keynote the conference, and because my primary professional identification is as an ethicist, it is not beyond reason to assume you expected me to say something about how the liturgy may have a role in the moral formation of Christians. This is not an unreasonable expectation since elsewhere I have reported on the course I have taught in Christian ethics in the Divinity School at Duke, which is shaped by the liturgy.[8]

The significance of the liturgy for the way I think about moral formation is not, as some may think, the result of a "high church" bias. I certainly do have a high church bias, though I am not sure why such an orientation should be described as a "bias." But I think the reason liturgy is so important to me is not only because of how I understand

---

trouble in which artists find themselves today is the strong distinction between art and craft. Without denying that some useful distinctions may be made between some modes of art and some crafts, the strong distinction between art and craft serves to make art isolated from the practices of any determinative community. Art for art's sake turns out to be the expression that serves the empty heart of liberal social orders.

7. In a wonderful letter to me, Rusty Reno, who had the onerous task of writing an article on my "political theory," says, "I have a pretty clear idea of what I want to say: Hauerwas argues that Christianity has political significance if and only if the Christian form of life has the density of a brick, something that puts the hurt on worldly powers. Not only is this descriptively accurate—all the Hauerwas buzz words denote density (story, memory, virtue, character, narrative, community, church)—it also strikes a nice biographical note." Reno's last comment refers to my being raised a bricklayer. I cannot pretend I have done well what Reno suggests I have done, but it has been an animating center of my work. More important, Reno's comment reminds us that "poetics" names the formation of a material culture across time.

8. I give a brief account of the course in ch. 10, "The Liturgical Shape of the Christian Life: Teaching Christian Ethics as Worship," in my *In Good Company: The Church as Polis* (Notre Dame, Ind.: University of Notre Dame Press, 1995), pp. 153–68.

liturgy but because of the way I understand ethics. A focus on the virtues and the narrative necessary for the virtues to be individuated as well as related to one another begs for the kind of enactment the liturgy names. Moreover, just as the liturgy is the work of the whole community, so the virtues reflect the practices of a community, making possible the virtuous formation of the lives that are constituted by that work. It is from the essential practices of a community, practices that name the ongoing habits that make it possible for the community to sustain a history, that liturgy forms and reforms our lives.

So it is my hope that the way I have tried to return ethics to a focus on the virtues has also invited a reclaiming of the significance of the liturgy for formation of our lives morally. I want to use this occasion, however, to make candid and explore a set of conceptual relations I think crucial if we are to rightly understand the liturgical formation of our lives. I want to show that ethics and liturgy cannot be abstracted one from the other because they are activities shaped by the common reason of the church. I use the description "common reason" in both senses of common—i.e., common reason is constituted by the judgments Christians share in common about matters that constitute their common good. Ethics and liturgy but name different ways of specifying the practical wisdom of the church about the everyday practices necessary to constitute the life of the church across time. The virtues are the way Christians talk about the moral formation necessary for our being a timeful people.

Aristotle and Aquinas rightly argued that the virtues are acquired through habituation and, in particular for Aquinas, the habituation of the passions. The habits we acquire necessary to make us not only do what justice requires but to become just in the doing are complex responses learned over time. Therefore to become just means acting as the just act; but you cannot become just by slavishly imitating what the just do. Rather, you must feel what the just feel when they act justly. The virtues, therefore, can only be acquired through our actions if what we do is not different from what we are. The virtues can be learned through doing, but the "doing" cannot be a product separate from the agent. Aristotle observes, "men become builders by building houses, and harpists by playing the harp. Similarly, we become just by the practice of just actions, self-controlled by exercising self-control, and courageous by performing acts of courage."[9]

Yet according to Aristotle, there is a crucial difference between building houses or playing the harp and becoming self-controlled. To

9. Aristotle, *Nicomachean Ethics*, trans. Martin Ostwald (Indianapolis: Bobbs-Merrill, 1962), 1103a30–1103b1.

be sure, the arts and the virtues share common features. Both require apprenticeship to a master; both require attention to detail; both require practice.[10] There is, however, one essential difference between the arts and the virtues. In the arts the product may be separated from the agent; but such a separation is impossible for those who would be virtuous.[11] According to Aristotle, characteristics (*hexis*, which I think is best translated as skilled, or complex, habits) develop from corresponding activities. That is the reason "we must see to it that our activities are of a certain kind, since any variations in them will be reflected in our characteristics. Hence it is no small matter whether one habit or another is inculcated in us from early childhood; on the contrary, it makes a considerable difference, or, rather, all the difference."[12]

For our actions to be actions that make us virtuous, we must act according to right reason. "Right reason" is distinguished from theoretical reason because it deals with the contingent—that is, matters that can be other—rather than necessary relations. Accordingly, inquiry into practi-

10. Aquinas observes, "man has a natural aptitude for virtue; but the perfection of virtue must be acquired by man by means of some kind of training. Thus we observe that man is helped by industry in his necessities, for instance, in food and clothing. Certain beginnings of these he has from nature, viz., his reason and his hands; but he has not the full complement, as other animals have, to whom nature has given sufficiency of clothing and food. Now it is difficult to see how man could suffice for himself in matters of this training: since the perfection of virtue consists chiefly in withdrawing man from undue pleasures, to which alone all man is inclined, and especially the young, who are more capable of being trained. Consequently a man needs to receive this training from another, whereby to arrive at the perfection of virtue." *Summa Theologica*, I–II, 95, 1, trans. Fathers of the English Dominican Province (Westminster, Md.: Christian Classics, 1981).

11. Aristotle's distinction between the virtues and the crafts is not the same as the distinction in modernity between art and crafts. Aristotle no more has an account of art for art's sake than he has an understanding of the virtues for virtue's sake. The virtues for Aristotle, indeed for all the ancients with the possible exception of some of the Stoics, entail teleological understanding of human action. That they do so suggests that Aristotle might find the kind of habits necessary to achieve the status of a skilled craftsperson to be quite close to his understanding of what it means to become virtuous.

Aquinas explicitly says that art requires the developing of virtue, noting: "In order that man may make good use of the art he has, he needs a good will, which is perfected by moral virtue; and for this reason the Philosopher says that there is a virtue of art; namely a moral virtue, in so far as the good use of art requires a moral virtue. For it is evident that a craftsman is inclined by justice, which rectifies his will, to do his work faithfully." *Summa Theologica*, I–II, 57, 3, 2. For an extremely important account of Thomas's understanding of the relation of virtue and beauty see Thomas Hibbs, *Virtue's Splendor: Wisdom, Prudence, and the Human Good* (New York: Fordham University Press, 2001).

12. Aristotle, *Nicomachean Ethics*, 1103b20–25. As early as *Character and the Christian Life: A Study in Theological Ethics* (Notre Dame, Ind.: University of Notre Dame Press, 1985), I suggested that Aristotle's and Aquinas's understanding of the kind of habituation the virtues entail was best understood as "skills for action" (pp. 78–79). *Character and the Christian Life* was originally published in 1975.

cal reason cannot be an end in itself, because it is concerned not just with knowing what virtue is, but with becoming virtuous.[13] Therefore, unlike the arts, where excellence usually is perceived in the result, the virtuous must not only act rightly, but for the act to be virtuous the agent must have certain characteristics as they perform the action:

> first of all, he must know what he is doing; secondly, he must choose to act the way he does, and he must choose it for its own sake; and in the third place, the act must spring from a firm and unchangeable character. With the exception of knowing what one is about, these considerations do not enter into the mastery of the arts; for the mastery of the virtues, however, knowledge is of little or no importance, whereas the other two conditions count not for a little but are all-decisive, since repeated acts of justice and self-control result in the possession of these virtues. In other words, acts are called just and self-controlled when they are the kind of acts which a just or self-controlled man would perform; but the just and self-controlled man is not he who performs these acts, but he who also performs them in the way just and self-controlled men do.[14]

This means that someone may "copy" the actions of a just person, but the action quite literally is not the same action if the habits that make the agent just are absent. That is why attempts to understand the relation between liturgy and ethics as motivation to action, as cause to effect, are so disastrous for an account of the moral life as the life of virtue. If what we are and do morally as Christians is intelligible abstracted from liturgical action, then we have, perhaps with the best intentions, reproduced the modern assumption that action descriptions can be divorced from agents.[15]

But action descriptions can be divorced from agents. Thus we think it important that we are able to name wrongs and goods independent of their role in a well-lived life. Aristotle is clear that some names of actions denote a baseness—adultery, theft, and murder—that cannot be made good by being done in the right manner, at the right time, to the right person, and with the appropriate emotion.[16] Yet this did not lead Aristotle or Aquinas to conclude that someone could be considered, for example, to have the virtue of fidelity as long as they did not commit adultery. That refraining from or doing certain actions does not develop a virtue creates

---

13. Aristotle, *Nicomachean Ethics*, 1103b26–30. The *Nicomachean Ethics* must, therefore, be read not as a book about "ethics," but rather as a training manual to make us good.

14. Ibid., 1105a31–1105b9.

15. For a more detailed investigation of these issues, see "Gay Friendship: A Thought Experiment in Catholic Moral Theology," in my *Sanctify Them in the Truth: Holiness Exemplified* (Nashville: Abingdon, 1998), pp. 105–21.

16. Aristotle, *Nicomachean Ethics*, 1107a10–20.

the problem of how to think about moral formation once it is realized that doing the right thing will not be sufficient to make us good and, even more important, to have those virtues constitute a coherent life.[17]

In order for a community to form us to understand why adultery is incompatible with fidelity requires the ongoing exercise of practical wisdom. Practical wisdom is the continuing analogical testing of the descriptions of our actions in the light of the virtues so we rightly understand the connection (a contingent connection to be sure) why, for example, adultery is incompatible with fidelity. Often such testing is not necessary, as the relation between the virtues and the description of our behavior is carried by communal habits. That is why, if a community is in good working order, for someone to question why adultery is incompatible with marriage may seem an unanswerable question; or the only answer is "That is the way we have always done things."

"That is the way we have always done things," moreover, is not a bad answer. But that answer may hide from the community the importance of being able to explain to ourselves as well as to our children the connections that make the way we do things make sense. Casuistry was one of the ways the church developed a tradition to help us remember the connections as well as face new challenges. That casuistry sometimes threatened to become an end in itself, to be nothing more than the application of the law, and as a result lost the importance of the virtues, does not mean casuistry can ever be left behind. It just needs to be done better.

My complete lack of knowledge of liturgical history and theology makes it possible for me to suggest that theological reflection on the liturgy may be analogous to the kind of practical wisdom I am suggesting is constitutive of the church's moral tradition. There is no one way to worship God, and the elements of the liturgy may appear differently in different times and cultures.[18] The connections are contingent, but

17. This may indicate one of the decisive differences between prayer and virtues. In this life—in Aquinas's terms the life of the wayfarer—the virtues are always "broken." Not only are the virtues insufficiently formed in us, so that we do not do what we ought to do, but the virtues' lack of unity that comes from charity means that our virtues are just as likely to be the occasion of sin as righteousness. The perfect activity, our acting in such a manner that we are not different than what we do, is an ongoing challenge. Prayer, however, through the aid of the Holy Spirit, may be as close as we can get to perfect activity; for prayer requires the receptivity necessary for our prayers to be complete.

18. Cardinal Ratzinger, for example, observes, "every age must discover and express the essence of the liturgy anew. The point is to discover this essence amid all the changing appearances. It would surely be a mistake to reject all the reforms of our century wholesale. When the altar was very remote from the faithful, it was right to move it back to the people." *Spirit of the Liturgy*, p. 81. A few pages later, however, Cardinal Ratzinger suggests, I must say rightly, that "nothing is more harmful to the liturgy than a constant activism, even if it seems to be for the sake of genuine renewal" (p. 83).

that does not mean that good and less good reasons can be developed for why the prayer of confession should follow the hearing of the word rather than after the greeting. The rationality of liturgical order is a matter of wisdom governed by the shape of the story of Jesus Christ and how that story makes possible the location of the church's life as part of God's trinitarian life.[19]

This explains why, when asked by parents how they should raise their children to be "moral," I usually recommend baseball. We rarely become good by trying to be good, but rather goodness "rides on the back" of worthwhile activity. I can think of few practices as morally compelling as baseball. Once young persons are rightly initiated into baseball, it does not occur to them to ask why they only get three strikes. Once a young person is initiated into the life of the family, it should not occur to her or him to ask why their mother and father only sleep with each other. If the game of baseball is to remain the beautiful game it is, you only get three strikes. If the family is to remain the wonderful and complex life it is, then husbands and wives only sleep with one another.

If what I have tried to say is close to being right, perhaps all we need to do is substitute liturgy for baseball and we will be able to say how liturgy in good working order forms the moral life of Christians. Even though there are few practices I think more important that baseball and liturgy, I think the matter is a good deal more complex than suggesting that we might become good through baseball and/or the liturgy. To be a good and even great baseball player does not necessarily mean that such a player will be a good person. In a similar fashion, to participate in well-enacted liturgies does not mean a participant will be virtuous. So in spite of my attempt to suggest how the liturgical formation of Christ's body can be understood, we still seem stuck with the question of what kind of relation there may be between liturgy and ethics. Perhaps all that can be said is that the liturgy is the necessary but not sufficient condition for the virtuous formation of our lives as Christians.

19. I am not taking sides in the debate Catherine Pickstock has begun with her spirited defense of the Roman Rite against the reforms of Vatican II. I would like to take sides, but I clearly do not know enough about the Roman Rite to defend or criticize it. I am quite sympathetic, however, with Pickstock's suggestion that "the haphazard structure of the Rite can be seen as predicated upon a need for a constant re-beginning of liturgy because the true eschatological liturgy is in time endlessly postponed." See her *After Writing: On the Liturgical Consummation of Philosophy* (Oxford, U.K.: Blackwell, 1998), p. 173. Her account of the "liturgical subject," moreover, is I believe very similar to that which I have tried to develop in terms of the virtues. For a defense of Pickstock, see Aidan Nichols, O.P., *Looking at the Liturgy: A Critical View of Its Contemporary Form* (San Francisco: Ignatius, 1998), pp. 82–86.

3. ON THE BEAUTY OF GOODNESS AND THE GOODNESS OF BEAUTY

Yet I think there is more to be said than this rather lame conclusion. What needs to be said, however, takes us into deep metaphysical waters that involve nothing less than the "transcendentals"—that is, the relation of truth, beauty, and goodness. I think it no accident that the thin character of much of mainline Protestant worship reflects as well as reproduces the superficial lives associated with Protestantism in America. No matter how well meant the efforts are to turn worship into entertainment, the result is the sentimental perversion of worship that fails to provide any resistance to the ugliness of our surrounding culture—an ugliness, perhaps, nowhere more apparent than in the unbridled licentiousness of people unashamed of their greed.

Of course, it may be objected that to suggest that tacky worship produces tacky people or tacky people produce tacky worship comes dangerously close to suggesting that moral and liturgical practice is a matter of taste. So let me be as clear as I can be. Moral and liturgical practice is a matter of taste. The problem is not that they are matters of taste, but rather the modern assumption that taste is but a matter of subjective opinion.[20] Nothing tells us quite as much about people's moral convictions as their taste. Nothing tells us quite as much about a church as how it worships. Goodness and beauty are rightly matters of taste, but a taste that has been learned from a people trained to worship the true God truly.[21]

20. To call attention to the importance of taste risks making certain class characteristics normative for worship. The rich often appear to have "developed taste" not because they can distinguish the beautiful from the pretty, but because they can afford to hire people who can distinguish the beautiful from the pretty to decorate their lives. Yet it must also be remembered that the poor often are saved from the pretensions that underwrite current social conventions that define the beautiful. What needs to be said is that no class is free from the temptation of the sentimental that so often is the breeding ground of the ugly. One of the worst forms of class prejudice, however, is the assumption that the "poor" do not desire the church's full liturgy. That Roman Catholicism remains the church of the poor has everything to do with the confidence that the poor desire to have their desires shaped by the prayers of the church.

There is also the problem of the material culture that sustains worship. Again the rich often can afford to decorate the church in a manner that the poor cannot. Too often such decorations, exactly because no expense was spared, turn out to be quite ugly. In this respect it is interesting to reflect on the building as well as the existence of the great medieval cathedrals. They may have been built by the wealthy, but they were enjoyed by the poor. The beauty of poor churches, however, is often in the faces of the worshipers.

21. Wittgenstein makes the fascinating observation that "the words we call expressions of aesthetic judgements play a very complicated role, but a very definite role, in what we call a culture of a period. To describe their use or to describe what you mean by a cultured taste, you have to describe a culture. What we now call a cultured taste perhaps didn't exist in the Middle Ages. An entirely different game is played in different ages." Ludwig Wittgenstein,

I am not suggesting, however, that the goodness of the life of virtue must be sustained by the beauty of the liturgy. Indeed such a correlation would be a disaster in modernity. Josef Pieper observes that in a desperate attempt to reclaim room for leisure from the forces aimed at a world in which nothing exists but work, some attempted to shield the realm of art from such a world by developing the doctrine of "art for art's sake."[22] Accordingly, art is distinguished from craft exactly because art can only be art if it has no use to anyone. The museum becomes the cathedral to this new creation, existing for no reason except to allow us to gaze on that which we are confident must be beautiful, for otherwise it would not be in the museum.[23] Thus the presumption by many that whatever salvation this life may have, it will be mediated through what Charles Taylor describes as the epiphanies produced by art.[24] When the liturgy becomes art understood in this modern sense, the church cannot help but be a museum of a beautiful but exotic past.[25]

Lectures and Conversations on Aesthetics, Psychology, and Religious Belief, ed. Cyril Barrett (Berkeley: University of California Press, 1997), paragraph 25.

22. Josef Pieper, *Leisure: The Basis of Culture,* trans. Gerald Malsbary (South Bend, Ind.: St. Augustine's Press, 1998), pp. 37–38.

23. Terry Eagleton provides an extraordinary account of the category of the aesthetic in modernity, arguing that the indeterminacy of the definition of the aesthetic allows it to figure in a range of preoccupations such as freedom and equality, spontaneity and necessity, self-definition, autonomy, particularity, and universality. He argues that the "category of the aesthetic assumes the importance it does in modern Europe because in speaking of art it speaks of these other matters too, which are at the heart of the middle class's struggle for political hegemony. The construction of the modern notion of the aesthetic artifact is thus inseparable from the construction of the dominant ideological forms of modern class-society, and indeed from a whole new form of human subjectivity appropriate to that social order." *The Ideology of the Aesthetic* (Oxford, U.K.: Blackwell, 1990), p. 3.

24. Charles Taylor, *Sources of the Self: The Making of the Modern Identity* (Cambridge, Mass.: Harvard University Press, 1989), pp. 419–93. Taylor describes his use of "epiphany" as the "notion of a work of art as the locus of a manifestation which brings us into the presence of something which is otherwise inaccessible, and which is of the highest moral significance; a manifestation, moreover, which also defines or completes something, even as it reveals" (p. 419). Taylor notes that for many of our contemporaries art has become their religion so the artist is endowed with exceptional sensibilities (pp. 422–23).

25. John Saward observes that for St. Thomas religion was the virtue that renders due honor to God who alone is the God of infinite beauty. "If a man does not exercise that virtue, at least to the extent of recognizing the order of God's creation he is incapable of art. An atheistic art is a self-contradiction. Human making has no meaning if there is no divine Maker to give man meaning. If there is no God, there is no truth, beauty, or goodness; nature has no order or harmony, and art has no foundation." *The Beauty of Holiness and the Holiness of Beauty: Art, Sanctity, and the Truth of Catholicism* (San Francisco: Ignatius, 1996), pp. 75–76. Elaine Scarry, who as far as I know is not a Christian, in an interesting way supports Saward's judgment in *On Beauty and Being Just* (Princeton, N.J.: Princeton University Press, 1999). She says, "One can see why beauty has been perceived to be bound up with the immortal, for it prompts a search for a precedent, which in turn prompts a search for a still earlier precedent, and the mind keeps tripping backward until

That is why it is crucial, particularly in light of the challenges of modernity, that the beauty of the liturgy not be separated from the goodness of the One worshiped; nor can the goodness of lives of virtue be devoid of the beauty endowed by the Holy Spirit. The lives formed through the liturgy must at once be beautiful and good, reflecting the beauty and goodness of the One alone who is perfectly beautiful and good. The beauty and goodness of such lives have an end not as some further accomplishment but constitutive of lives well lived. There is no hard edge between service and prayer, nor can there be. Duty for duty's sake is not the way Christians are called to serve God and one another. Rather, the unselfing worship makes possible makes the heedless character of Christian service beautiful exactly because the virtues so constituted witness to the goodness of God.

Perhaps no place are beauty and goodness more united than in the truthful speech liturgy requires. The language of prayer is exacting, an exactness that fosters over time—elegance. The prayers of the church, unlike our prayers, have been honed to say no more and no less than what must be said to confess sin, to praise God, to respond with thanksgiving to the gift of Eucharist. Liturgy is the source of the word-care necessary for our lives to be beautiful and good—beautiful and good because by constant repetition we have learned the habits necessary to speak truthfully.[26] To learn to speak truthfully is a skill never finished if we are to resist the lies that lay in the languages that speak us. To be free, therefore, from the lies of the world requires that we be pulled into a community that submits our speaking to the discipline of prayer.

We dare not forget, however, that God's brilliant beauty and goodness are more than we can comprehend. Cardinal Danielou calls attention to these remarkable lines from Rilke: "If one of them [an angel] took me suddenly upon his heart, I would succumb to death from his overwhelming existence, because beauty is nothing but the beginning of terror."[27] Through God's beauty we are unselfed, thus formed, making possible our reception of charity, the form of all the virtues. It is surely no accident that the cross of Christ is often the center of Christian wor-

---

it at last reaches something that has no precedent, which may very well be immortal. And one can see why beauty—by those same artists, philosophers, and theologians of the Old World and the New—has been perceived to be bound up with truth. What is beautiful is in league with what is true because truth abides in the immortal sphere. . . . The beautiful person or thing incites in us the longing for truth because it provides by its compelling 'clear discernability' an introduction to the state of certainty yet does not satiate our desire for certainty since beauty, sooner or later, brings us into contact with our own capacity for making errors" (pp. 30–31).

26. For a wonderful account of "word-care" see Stephen Fowl's *Engaging Scripture: A Model for Theological Interpretation* (Oxford, U.K.: Blackwell, 1998), pp. 161–69.

27. Danielou, *Prayer,* p. 4.

ship.[28] The cross, the epitome of human cruelty and ugliness, is quite literally the manifestation of God's beauty[29]—a beauty that we cannot possess but only suffer. By suffering such a beauty, a beauty that hides not its suffering, we are possessed and thus saved from the ugliness of our sin. In short we are made holy.

Nathan Mitchell observes that from birth "we humans are addicts, and our deepest addiction is to a mistaken identity, to a false self. We insist on living someone else's life, not our own."[30] The problem, of course, is that we cannot will our way out of our addictions, but rather we must be attracted by a beauty and goodness that is so compelling we discover that our lives are not our own. Such a discovery comes through suffering and takes time, because we do not give up our illusions easily. Liturgy is quite literally where we learn to suffer God's beauty and so suffering discover we are made in God's image. Through worship we discover the truth about ourselves, making possible lives of goodness otherwise impossible.

The beauty, the goodness, and the truth of our liturgy is tested by our being sent forth. If we are not jarred by the world to which we return, then something has gone wrong. The feeling of being out of place need not last long or even occur after every Eucharist, but the beauty we have beheld in the gift of God's Son leaves its mark. Formed by such beauty we no longer desire to live by the lies that would have us call lies true, evil good, and ugliness beautiful. Through prayer, prayers that often we

28. For an extraordinary account of the role of Grunewald's great painting of the crucifixion see Andre Hayum, *The Isenheim Altarpiece: God's Medicine and the Painter's Vision* (Princeton, N.J.: Princeton University Press, 1989). Hayum conclusively argues that Grunewald's remarkable work was done specifically for the hospital dedicated to those suffering from the terrible disease called St. Anthony's fire. That the sufferers received comfort from the altarpiece surely suggests that suffering and beauty are closely related. At least they are closely related in Christianity. Karl Barth kept a copy of Grunewald's painting over his desk I think in an effort to remind himself that his work, like the elongated finger pointing to the crucified that Grunewald gave to John the Baptist, was to do nothing more than to point to Christ. I am indebted to Rosalee Velloso Ewell for calling attention to Hayum's book as well as her paper "Aesthetic Subversions: The Theology of Resistance in the Works of Matthias Grunewald and Paul Hindemith" (unpublished).

29. The inspiration for this essay came as a gift. Bill Moore is an artist and a good friend. Paula Gilbert, my wife, and I have bought many of Bill's marble and wood sculptures. We usually prefer his abstract forms. Recently, however, Bill sculpted a bronze crucifix mounted on a cross of hickory and gave it to me. It is rather large and hangs alone on one wall of my office. I find the crucifix at once beautiful and frightening. It is the first thing I see when I begin work and the last thing I see when I leave. The crucifix stands as a constant reminder that theology at once is serious work but ill done when the work of theology lacks humility. My words lack the beauty of Bill's gift, but they are all I have to give to say, "Thank you for a gift that I had not known I so desperately needed."

30. Nathan D. Mitchell, *Liturgy and the Social Sciences* (Collegeville, Minn.: Liturgical Press, 1999), p. 76.

know not what we pray, we become incorporated into God's prayer for the world. I do not remember the name of the Benedictine sister who asked Father Maly to pray for vocations. I do remember, however, I thought she glowed with a beauty I have seldom seen. It was the beauty that comes from effortless goodness. Such beauty surely was born from daily praying the rosary. Without such beauty and goodness we are surely lost. So by all means may we join her prayer for vocations.[31]

31. I am indebted to Jana Bennett and Charlie Collier for their remarks on this paper.

III

PERFORMING NONVIOLENCE

7

EXPLAINING CHRISTIAN NONVIOLENCE

Notes for a Conversation with John Milbank and John Howard Yoder

1. WHY JOHN HOWARD YODER WAS NOT A PACIFIST

The souls of the organizers of this conference are in deep trouble.[1] If Protestant evangelicals had anyone to whom they could confess, they would need to seek out such people, because they certainly have sinned. Their sin is to have put me in a situation that tempts me to sin, that is, they have put this weak soul, as Catholics say, "in the near occasion of sin." I have been so placed because events have conspired to make it necessary for me to give my paper knowing that it will be followed by a paper by Milbank. Which means that Milbank has to listen to me tell him why I am right and he is wrong about most things but more importantly why he should be an advocate of Christian nonviolence. This is an occasion of sin, at least for a pacifist, just to the extent that I

---

1. This chapter was written for a conference at Wheaton College on Christianity and violence. A version of it also appears in Kenneth R. Chase and Alan Jacobs, eds., *Must Christianity Be Violent?* (Grand Rapids: Brazos, 2003), pp. 172–82.

am tempted to use this favorable, but coercive, turn of events to frame the issues in a manner favorable to me before Milbank gets to speak. If this is but the outworking of metaphysical violence, I intend to make the most of it.

It may seem odd for me to use this occasion to pick a fight with Milbank. I suspect that many people assume that John and I are more or less on the same side. That assumption I think, given the cultural options of the day, is correct. However, as Michael Hanby, my former student who wrote his dissertation with John, has observed: "That people think Hauerwas and Milbank are on the same side is only an indication of how dumb a time it is in which we live. In another cultural situation Hauerwas and Milbank would be sworn enemies." Hanby, I think, may well be right—in another time Milbank might make the case that my kind should be burned at the stake. After all I represent the anarchical anabaptist[2] who the orthodox, whether they be radical or not, usually think threatens the presumptive unity claimed by Christendom. From the orthodox point of view, pacifist readings of Scripture cannot help but appear heretical, and heretics are rightly regarded as the worst sort of criminals. If you are serious, and Milbank is serious, you ought to be willing to kill people like me.

I am, of course, having fun, but I begin this way to illustrate the argument I want to make in this paper. My argument quite simply, and it is a simple point, is that pacifists cannot let their understanding of Christian nonviolence be determined by what we are against. We do not know what violence is or may be if we do not know violence against the background of a more profound peaceableness. Accordingly, I cannot let Milbank determine what I need to say about Christian nonviolence. But it is not easy for pacifists to display peaceableness because violence seems to be far more interesting and entertaining. For example, any attempt to develop a defense of "Christian nonviolence" but reproduces the problem I am trying to avoid. The very phrase, "Christian nonviolence" cannot help but suggest that peace is "not violence." Yet a peace that is no more than "not violence" surely cannot be the peace that is ours in Christ.

This is not just a terminological problem. It is an ontological and moral problem that makes clear why the modern attempt to separate ontological and ethical questions could not but distort the character of our lives. In the Christian tradition Augustine, rightly I think, maintained that sin is literally nothing. Just as the lie lives parasitically off the truth, so violence cannot be named or identified unless our lives

---

2. I use the lowercase "anabaptist" the way James McClendon used the lowercase "baptist," that is, to indicate that what anabaptists stand for is not to be found only in those officially identified as Anabaptist.

are constituted by more determinative practices of peace.[3] I hesitate to acknowledge the ontological questions at the heart of any attempt to develop and/or defend Christian pacifism, because Milbank is a much more adept metaphysician than I can even pretend to be. I will never understand, much less be able to argue, as Milbank does, with Deleuze.[4] Yet I think I have said enough to make clear why I think it would be a mistake to try to convince anyone, even Milbank, to become a pacifist by pretending to know what violence is to be avoided.

This is one of the reasons I have always felt something of a fraud when I claim to be a pacifist. My sense of being fraudulent is not simply because—Texan that I am—I am a violent person. That I do not know how to be nonviolent is, of course, a problem, but even more troubling is my sense that I do not know what I am claiming when I claim to be a pacifist. I assume, however, that my declaration at least means I create expectations in others who can and should call me to account for living in a manner that belies my conviction that, if I am to live a truthful life, I must be nonviolent. In other words, nonviolence is at least a declaration that should make me vulnerable to others in a manner that hopefully can put me on the way to being at peace in a world of violence.

If peace is ontologically the character of our existence, then I think it is a mistake to describe John Howard Yoder as a pacifist. He could not be a pacifist because, as he never failed to emphasize, "there is no such thing as a single position called pacifism, to which one clear definition can be given and which is held by all pacifists."[5] What made, and continues to make, Yoder's work so significant for me was his refusal to make "pacifism" a position, an implication, derived from more determinative theological claims. You simply cannot find in Yoder any account of "pacifism" that can be abstracted from his Christology, eschatology, ecclesiology, or understanding of the Christian life. Yoder did not find it necessary to provide an ontological account of his understanding of Christian nonviolence, but I think the way he worked exhibits why peace is metaphysically more determinative than violence. Yoder's understanding of Christian nonviolence is constitutive of his understanding of God and how God has, through the work of the Holy Spirit, made us participants in God's salvation.

3. See, for example, Robert Jenson's wonderful "Introduction: Much Ado About Nothingness," in *Sin, Death, and the Devil*, ed. Carl Braaten and Robert Jenson (Grand Rapids: Eerdmans, 2000), pp. 1–6.

4. For Milbank's remarks on Deleuze, see Milbank, *Theology and Social Theory* (Oxford, U. K.: Basil Blackwell, 1990), pp. 278–80, 294–96, 302–6.

5. John Howard Yoder, *Nevertheless: Varieties of Religious Pacifism* (Scottdale, Pa.: Herald Press, 1992), p. 12.

After surveying other forms of pacifism in *Nevertheless,* Yoder identified his own position as "The Pacifism of the Messianic Community."[6] This is a stance of nonviolence that is unintelligible without the confession that Jesus is the Christ and that Jesus Christ is Lord. "In the person and work of Jesus, in his teachings and his passion, this kind of pacifism finds its rootage, and in his resurrection it finds its enablement."[7] Christian nonviolence can, therefore, not be a position about violence abstracted from discipleship to this One as God's anointed. Discipleship, moreover, is not a heroic endeavor of individuals, but rather the way of life of a community that finds in its shared life a foretaste of God's kingdom.

Christian nonviolence, therefore, does not name for Yoder a position or even a principled stance that works from a predetermined understanding of what counts as violence or nonviolence. Rather Christian nonviolence names the present reality of a community that refuses to be determined by the very "world" it creates by its own existence. In his extraordinary but never published book, *Christian Attitudes to War, Peace, and Revolution: A Companion to Bainton,*[8] Yoder does not even discuss what he takes to be the most defensible account of Christian pacifism until the end of the book. He rightly, I think, understood that our Christians forebears were not pacifist if we mean by that a position they could identify in distinction from their understanding of what it means to worship and be disciples of Jesus Christ.

Yoder, therefore, has no reason to deny that in the early centuries some Christians were in the Roman army or that the reason other Christians did not serve had more to do with idolatry than the avoidance of violence. For Yoder, pacifism did not and does not stand by itself.[9] Christians found themselves in tension with the authority structure of the day for numerous reasons. The objection to the shedding of blood was just one part of a polar whole. Accordingly the question "Did the early Christians reject the state *as such?*" cannot be answered. It cannot be answered because there was no "state as such."[10] Therefore where it

6. Ibid., pp. 133–38.

7. Ibid., p. 134.

8. Copies of Yoder's book, which were his lectures in his course on Christian attitudes to war and peace at Goshen Biblical Seminary, can be obtained from Cokesbury Book Store at the Divinity School, Duke University.

9. It is amazing how critics of Yoder's pacifism fail to "get" this crucial aspect of Yoder's account of pacifism. The whole point of Yoder's work is to show that nonviolence is not a position you can or should take prior to or subsequent to the answer given to Jesus' question, "But who do you say that I am?" (Luke 9:20). *The Politics of Jesus: Vicit Agnus Noster* (Grand Rapids: Eerdmans, 1995) was written to show that nonviolence and Christology cannot be separated.

10. Yoder notes that the assumption that there is a state "as such" is an intellectual construct that "we can't help using for later purposes" even if it is not there for the early

was possible for early Christians, at some times and places, to qualify their polarization with authority structures, they did so without feeling any unfaithfulness. For example "by the end of the second century Christians could and did use the civil courts to define property law, e.g., to protect the legal status of a Christian cemetery. Christians didn't feel that such 'involvement' was a moral sell-out."[11]

That Christians could use the legal structure to protect the graves of their dead was not a problem for Christians because it was clear that law did not constitute their lives—the church did that. In similar fashion Christians in the fourth century could find themselves in the Roman army even though they still did not think they could kill or swear oaths of loyalty to Caesar. They could do so, Yoder observes, because the Roman soldiers were often simply bureaucrats. They carried the mail, administered the roads, enforced the laws and the prison system. In short they were not violent at all, "except in the global sense that they were 'part of the system,' or in the political sense that such a person has the status of an officer. Yet he doesn't kill anybody, he doesn't persecute anybody, he doesn't throw anybody to the lions. He probably even is dispensed from the oath and the ceremonies."[12] So grew what Yoder calls "creeping empire loyalty." Such loyalty clearly results in "Constantianism," which Yoder, I think, rightly deplores. But it is crucial to see that he does so for reasons that are not that different from Augustine—namely, with Constantianism the true church becomes invisible because now it is assumed that God is governing the world through Constantine. As a result peace is turned into an ideal rather than a practice constitutive

---

Christians (*Christian Attitudes to War, Peace, and Revolution,* p. 26). Yoder does not explain why we cannot refrain from asking about the "state as such" for "later purposes." In *The Christian Witness to the State* (Newton, Kans.: Faith and Life Press, 1964), Yoder rightly, I think, refuses to provide any account of the state as such. He understands such accounts cannot help but be ideological legitimations that too easily result in making the state more than it needs to be. As he puts it, "the Christian witness does not provide any foundations for government, either practically or philosophically, but . . . the Christian rather accepts the powers that be and speaks to them in a corrective way. It is when we speak to those in power and to the dominant majority groups in the population that we plead the case of the minorities and the absent; this does not mean that if we were speaking to the minority groups themselves we should be uncritical or flattering" (p.41).

11. Yoder, *Christian Attitudes to War, Peace, and Revolution,* p. 26. I have no idea why Yoder chose the example of Christians seeking to protect their graves but he could not have found a better example in light of later scholarship. I am thinking, for instance, of Peter Brown's account of the importance of graves for Christians in his *The Cult of the Saints: Its Rise and Function in Latin Christianity* (Chicago: University of Chicago Press, 1981), as well as Robert Wilken's *The Christians as the Romans Saw Them* (New Haven: Yale University Press, 1984). Wilken provides a wonderful account of Pliny's attempt to understand Christians as a burial society.

12. Yoder, *Christian Attitudes to War, Peace, and Revolution,* p. 31.

of the church.[13] Correlatively, Christians now look for sources of moral knowledge other than the Scriptures and, in particular, the teachings of Jesus. Christians begin to think the primary moral question is "What would happen if everyone acted like that?" no longer remembering that Christians should ask, "How must we act as disciples of Christ?"

I cannot pretend that this is an adequate account of Yoder's pacifism, but I hope I have at least convinced you that Yoder's pacifism does not name a position separable from his overall theological stance. For Yoder, pacifism is what he takes to be "the politics of Jesus," that is, the church. In Yoder's words:

> The cross was the effect of the fact that his new regime was a *kingdom:* he talked about it in political terms, in connection with righteousness, decision making, money and power and offenders and all the other things that politics deals with. Yet it was non-coercive. So the way he lived it was to die for it, and he told his disciples that they would have to do the same. But if the new order in its newness is characterized by non-coerciveness, then the community which is the bearer of this order will have to be a voluntary community. That means in turn that the community that bears this new order will have to be for the time being a minority community. This option is what came later to be called "church." The word *ecclesia* in the Greek of the time was not a religious term. It means town meeting, assembly, a group of people gathered to do business of public concern. That's what Jesus created; directly by gathering people around him during his earthly ministry, indirectly by the fact that his message after the resurrection and pentecost produced that new kind of body within society.[14]

So Yoder is not a pacifist if by that you mean someone who assumes that pacifists know in advance what may and may not be violence. Of course Yoder assumes that Christians do not kill, but that is only to state what it means to be a pacifist in the most minimal fashion. The practice of peace among Christians requires constant care of our lives together, through which we discover the violence that grips our lives and compromises our witness to the world. If the church is not peace, then the world does not

---

13. Yoder, *Christian Attitudes to War, Peace, and Revolution*, pp. 45–46. Yoder's characterization and critique of "Constantinianism" has been analyzed and criticized by Alex Sider in his "Constantinianism before and after Nicea: Issues in Restitutionist Historiography," in *A Mind Patient and Untamed: Assessing John Howard Yoder's Contribution to Theology, Ethics, and Peacemaking,* ed. Gayle Gerber Koontz and Ben Ollenburger, with an introduction by Stanley Hauerwas (Philadelphia: Cascade Press, 2003).

I realize this account of Augustine is controversial, but it is so only if one reads Augustine through Niebuhrian eyes. For a quite different account that suggests Augustine held a quite robust account of the church, see Rowan Williams's "Politics and the Soul: A Reading of *The City of God*," *Milltown Studies* 19/20 (1987): 55–72.

14. Yoder, *Christian Attitudes to War, Peace, and Revolution,* p. 428.

have an alternative to violence. But if the church is not such an alternative, then what we believe as Christians is clearly false. For when all is said and done, the question of peace is the question of truth and why the truth that is ours in Christ makes possible a joyfulness otherwise unobtainable.

2. WHY MILBANK SHOULD DECLARE HE IS A PACIFIST

Now that I have convinced you that Yoder is not a pacifist, I want to argue that Milbank should be forced to declare that he is a pacifist. At least he is a pacifist just to the degree that Yoder is not a pacifist. Put in the terms made immortal by that preeminent American politician, George Wallace, I hope to show when all is said and done there is not a dime's worth of difference between Yoder and Milbank on matters that matter about peace. What difference there is, moreover, is one about which Yoder is right and Milbank is wrong. In more friendly terms: it is not that Milbank is wrong, but rather an indication that sometimes Milbank does ontology when he ought to be listening to Jesus.

Milbank is, of course, rightly famous for his contention that in contrast to the *mythos* that shapes modernity, a *mythos* that assumes "in the beginning there was chaos and violence," Christianity

> recognizes no original violence. It construes the infinite not as chaos, but as a harmonic peace which is yet beyond the circumscribing power of any totalizing reason. Peace no longer depends upon the reduction to the self-identical, but is the *sociality* of harmonious difference. Violence, by contrast, is always a secondary willed intrusion upon this possible infinite order (which is actual for God). Such a Christian logic is *not* deconstructible by modern secular reason; rather, it is Christianity which exposes the non-necessity of supposing, like the Nietzscheans, that difference, non-totalization and indeterminacy of meaning *necessarily* imply arbitrariness and violence. To suppose that they do is merely to subscribe to a particular encoding of reality. Christianity, by contrast, is the coding of transcendental difference as peace.[15]

Milbank supports these claims by providing a rich account of the Trinity that I think has yet to be appreciated for its quite extraordinary power.[16] As interesting as Milbank's trinitarian reflections are, however,

---

15. John Milbank, *Theology and Social Theory: Beyond Secular Reason* (Oxford, U.K.: Basil Blackwell, 1990), pp. 5–6.

16. Milbank begins to develop his trinitarian reflections in *Theology and Social Theory* (pp. 422–30), but his most complete account is in his essay "The Second Difference," which is now to be found in his *The Word Made Strange: Theology, Language, Culture* (Oxford, U.K.: Blackwell, 1997), pp. 171–93.

more important—at least for the subject before us—is his account of Augustine's two cities in the last chapter of *Theology and Social Theory*. His account of Augustine is important exactly because Milbank uses an account of Augustine to help us see why the ontological presumption of "In the beginning there was peace" does not entail pacifism. Augustine is crucial for Milbank because Augustine rightly saw why Christian theology entails the presumption of the ontological priority of peace over conflict; a presumption, moreover, anchored not in universal reason, but in a narrative, a practice, and a dogmatic faith.[17] That is why, finally, Christians cannot defeat narratives of violence in principle. Finally we can only out-narrate them.[18]

Milbank interrupts his account of Augustine in order to provide an analysis of the work of René Girard. Milbank does so I think because his criticism of Girard allows him to challenge not just Girard's account of atonement, but all accounts of the atonement that offer an "explanation of violence." Milbank thinks Girard is right to stress Jesus' refusal of violence, but he does not provide a sufficient account of the concrete "form" taken by Jesus' nonviolent practice. Girard's (and Anselm's) "satisfaction theory of the atonement" makes sense only to the extent "they remind us that Jesus is significant *as* the way, the kingdom, *autobasileia*. One can rescue Girard's argument for Jesus's finality and divinity if one links it with the idea that the exemplary narratives of Jesus show us the 'shape,' and the concrete possibility of a non-violent practice."[19] Accordingly an abstract attachment to nonviolence is not sufficient to be nonviolent. We need to practice nonviolence as a skill, a skill honed through the idiom of the Bible, which reaches its consummation in Jesus and the church.

I call attention to Milbank's criticisms of Girard because they sound very much like what Yoder might have said. Yet I hope to show that Milbank's own account of the necessity of violence comes very close to making the same mistake he finds in Girard. Milbank's ontology of violence leads him to believe he knows more about violence than he should if Christology precedes ontology. Milbank may object that his is

---

17. Milbank, *Theology and Social Theory*, p. 390.

18. Since *Theology and Social Theory*, Milbank has increasingly turned in a neoplatonic direction. As a result I am not clear if he still believes that all Christian theology can do is to "out-narrate" other alternatives. In his more recent work there is at least a hint that he thinks he now has at his disposal ontological moves that can in principle defeat all other alternatives. I take it that is why he wishes to distance himself from all "pragmatic" justifications of Christian convictions. See, for example, his "Intensities," *Modern Theology* 15/4 (October 1999): 445–97. A revised form of this article now constitutes the second chapter of Milbank's and Catherine Pickstock's book, *Truth in Aquinas* (London: Routledge, 2001), pp. 19–59.

19. Milbank, *Theology and Social Theory*, p. 396.

an ontology of peace, but if that is the case I find it difficult to understand why he assumes we must make peace with violence.

Milbank quite rightly, and again in a manner similar to Yoder, objects to any interpretation of *The City of God* that thinks Augustine is providing a theory of the state to which the church must then be related. Augustine criticizes the Roman commonwealth exactly because it is not a polity, but rather grounded in the individualism of antique ethics and politics. In contrast, the church is a polis, a political reality, extended through time.[20] The bounds between the church and whatever may pass as the state are, therefore, best kept "hazy." For the church is to make *usus* of the peace of the world, that is, of slavery, "excessive" coercion, and competing economic interests, but the church can never try to derive these things from her own life. Therefore "a Christian" ruler must use the earthly peace by subordinating such a peace to the ecclesial purpose of charity. In short, after Christ the "Christian emperor" is just only to the extent he or she understands the ruler's function to be an exercise of pastoral care.[21]

For Augustine, as well as the early church in general, the division between coercion and noncoercion was the crucial criterion for separating the political from the ecclesial. Augustine came to see, however, that the church as well as the *imperium* must of necessity use coercive methods, the justification of which depends on the purpose "that coercion has in mind." The purpose of ecclesial coercion can only be peace, which can only be attained "in the long-term" by "non-coercive persuasion" because the free consent of the will is necessary for peace to be achieved. However, according to Milbank, and this is the crucial move, Augustine correctly saw

the need for some measures of coercion, in some circumstances, because freedom of the will in itself is not the goal, and sometimes people can be temporarily blind and will only be prevented from permanent self-damage when they are forced into some course of action, or prevented from another. Such coercive action remains in itself dangerous, as it risks promoting resentment, but this risk is offset by the possibility that the recipient can later come to understand and retrospectively consent to the means

20. Ibid., p. 403.
21. Ibid., p. 407. Milbank even suggests that Augustine thought that a "Christian emperor will make the empire recede into the Church." Such a view may seem quite foreign to Yoder's account of Christian nonviolence, but I believe that Yoder would not in principle rule out the possibility of such a rule. See in particular Yoder's "The Christian Case for Democracy," in *The Priestly Kingdom: Social Ethics as Gospel* (Notre Dame, Ind.: University of Notre Dame Press, 1984), pp. 151–71. Yoder observes that what we call government cannot be identified only by the sword. Accordingly, there are many "styles of involvement for the Christian which is not dominated by the sword."

taken. Such action may not be "peaceable," yet can still be "redeemed" by retrospective acceptance, and so contribute to the final goal of peace. And Christianity has traditionally seen peace as the comprehensive eschatological goal, and *not* as the name of a virtue.[22]

According to Milbank, however, the coercion used by the earthly city does not have true peace in view but rather seeks no more than the compromise of wills that cannot help but become an end in itself. Insofar as the *imperium* lies outside *ekklesia* it remains a *tragic* reality, disciplining sin, in which the punishment itself is nearer to sin than the peace of God. Augustine's fundamental mistake, therefore, in legitimating the coercion of the Donatist was in the realm of ontology.[23] His account of nonsinful, "pedagogic," coercion tried to justify a positive account of punishment that was inconsistent with his best ontological presumptions. It was so "because in any coercion, however mild and benignly motivated, there is still present a moment of 'pure' violence, externally and arbitrarily related to the end one has in mind, just as the schoolmaster's beating with canes has no intrinsic connection with the lesson he seeks to teach."[24]

All punishment cannot help but be a tragic risk because punishment by its very nature has a privative relationship to being and, therefore, cannot escape the taint of sin. That is why God cannot be said to punish. We are not punished for our sin, but rather sin is our punishment. At the most basic level punishment is self-inflicted. The church must seek to reduce the sphere of the operation of punishment while recognizing the tragic "necessity" of "alien" punishment. To be sure the trial and crucifixion of Jesus calls into question all forms of alien discipline, which means that the church must be an *asylum*, a refuge, in which forgiving and restitutionary practice is possible.[25] But we cannot hope for this practice to be extended into the state because the state, "by its very nature," can only be committed to the formal goals of *dominium*.

I confess it is not at all clear to me why Milbank wants to begin talking about the "very nature" of the state or, more importantly, describing that nature in terms reminiscent of Max Weber and Reinhold Niebuhr. Milbank, in a review of my book *Against the Nations*, quite rightly called me to account for underwriting a "residual Niebuhrianism" in my defense of pacifism.[26] Yet I cannot help but hear Niebuhrian themes in his

22. Milbank, *Theology and Social Theory*, p. 418.
23. Augustine, according to Garry Wills, was actually very patient with the Donatists. See for example Garry Wills, *Saint Augustine* (New York: Penguin, 1999), pp. 105–26.
24. Milbank, *Theology and Social Theory*, p. 420.
25. Ibid., p. 422.
26. Milbank's review appears in *Modern Theology* 4 (January 1988), pp. 211–16. I respond to Milbank's criticism in my "Epilogue" to Paul Ramsey's *Speak Up for Just War or Pacifism* (University Park: Pennsylvania State University Press, 1988), pp. 176–177.

account of the unavoidability of violence. More important, it is by no means clear to me why Milbank's account of punishment—even if we accept his view that punishment always entails an "alien moment"—does not in fact commit him, particularly given the state formation characteristic of modernity, to what amounts to a pacifist position. After all, it is hard to see how the liberal state has the legitimacy necessary to punish. Moreover if Milbank is trying to argue that violence is unavoidable because we cannot avoid the necessity of punishment, it is by no means clear how he can move from his defense of punishment to, for example, a defense of war.

As far as I know Milbank only addresses how war might be understood and/or justified in one brief paragraph in *Theology and Social Theory.* Drawing on Rowan Williams, Milbank characterizes Augustine's view that a war in defense of the state, or any form of excessive coercion, can be justified only when what is being defended is "fundamentally unjust."[27] I am not at all sure what point Milbank is making, but I take him to mean that the punishment "war" names cannot even retrospectively be consented to by those who suffer such violence. But then I must ask: does Milbank thereby think that attempts to limit war in the name of justice are impossible? Moreover, if he does so, then why should we not think he is a pacifist?

Of course, Milbank may want to argue that it is by no means clear that we know what "war" is. As I have argued elsewhere, too often those who would appeal to a "just war" assume that they know what a war is and then ask if this or that war conforms or not to just war criteria. Such a view fails to understand that the just war "theory" at its best is the attempt to discipline the violence of the state in a manner that certain forms of that violence can bear the honorific description of war.[28] If the violence just war practices seek to discipline comes only after the

27. Milbank, *Theology and Social Theory,* p. 419. Milbank's reference is to Rowan Williams's article, "Politics and the Soul: A Reading of *The City of God,*" *Milltown Studies* 19/20 (1987), pp. 55–92. I also admire Rowan Williams's article and used it in the first chapter of my *After Christendom?* (Nashville: Abingdon, 1999). I cannot, however, find in Williams's article Milbank's suggestion that what is being defended by war must be "fundamentally unjust" if a Christian can engage in it. Rather Williams says war cannot be fought on behalf of the City of God. As he puts it, "So we arrive at the paradox that the only reliable political leader, the only ruler who can be guaranteed to safeguard authentically *political* values (order, equity, and the nurture of souls in these things) is the man who is, at the end of the day, indifferent to their survival in the relative shape of the existing order, because he knows them to be safeguarded at the level of God's eternal and immutable providence, vindicated in the eternal *civitas dei*" (p. 67).

28. For my reflections on these matters, see my "Can a Pacifist Think about War?" in *Dispatches from the Front: Theological Engagements with the Secular* (Durham, N.C.: Duke University Press, 1994), pp. 116–35.

so-called war has begun, then it is too late for the war to be "just." At this point I am simply asking Milbank to clarify his understanding of attempts to discipline war in the name of justice.[29] I assume he would argue that war must be fought to secure justice; but it is not clear what account of justice he assumes can justify war.

Milbank also owes us a richer account of violence than the ontological moves he makes provide. I am not sure what to make of the claim that every form of coercion and punishment involves a moment of "pure violence," that is, an arbitrary association of pain with a particular lesson. Is this an ontological or empirical claim? If it is the latter, it is clearly not sustainable.[30] Indeed it seems to me the very concept of a moment of "pure violence" is the kind of abstraction Milbank found doubtful in Girard. Violence is an analogical term that depends on paradigmatic narratives if we are to understand the different kinds of violence that enable us to make meaningful distinctions. That process is never-ending, particularly when the narrative that determines our discernment of violence is the life and death of Jesus. Attempts to find the one feature that makes violence violence, that shortcuts the process of analogical reasoning, must be resisted as a premature if not violent attempt to get a handle on history.

Yoder does not pretend that Christians can be free of the violence that comes from being "part of the system." To be so involved, however, does not mean that we cannot make distinctions between violence and coercion as well as between various kinds of violence that tempt us to live less than nonviolent lives. Indeed I assume that is why Christians rightly declare that our worship as well as our desire to follow Jesus require, as well as make possible, nonviolence. Such a declaration is a promissory note: Christians must always be ready to discover how our lives may be implicated in violence that we have failed to notice.

29. James Childress has pointed out that there is a substantial difference between those who think that just war is an attempt to develop a theory of exception to the general Christian prohibition against violence and those who assume that the aim of just war is to achieve justice. The latter position does not presume that we live in a world of peace to which war is some kind of interruption, but rather we must live in a world in which war can be and must be disciplined for just means and ends. These two positions require quite different accounts of how the various just war "criteria" are derived as well as justified. James Childress, "Nonviolent Resistance: Trust and Risk-Taking Twenty-five Years Later," *Journal of Religious Ethics* 25/2 (fall 1997): 213–20.

30. There is, after all, no one thing called punishment. Excommunication and the ban are interesting examples of a community pronouncing judgment that is meant to help the person understand that they are not being punished further but rather are being offered a way to return to the community. How would they know they have estranged themselves and need to be reunited unless they are told that is the state they are in whether they know it or not? Of course, excommunication and the ban may be wrongly used, but that does not invalidate them as forms of "punishment" by nonviolent communities.

That is why the nonviolent have such a stake in truthful speech. For we often learn that our failure to acknowledge the violence we do to one another as well to ourselves is the result of our inability to name our engagements. Christians committed to nonviolence can therefore never assume we know we are nonviolent. Rather, our nonviolence is a declaration that renders our lives vulnerable to challenges that may reveal that we are implicated in forms of violence we have not recognized or have chosen to ignore. By discovering the violence in our lives we hope we may witness to those that do not follow Christ the violence that may grip all our lives.

3. A WORD ON MY BEHALF

I want to end by saying a word on my behalf. Put differently, I want to make candid some of the presuppositions that have shaped the way I have tried to provide an account of Christian nonviolence. I have, of course, never pretended that I have anything to say about nonviolence that Yoder has not said and said better than any of my efforts. I have, however, attempted to develop some conceptual machinery that I hope may be of some use for helping us, as the original title of the paper for this conference promised, to "live peacefully in a violent society." For I continue to think that Christian nonviolence is necessary not because it promises us a world free of war, but because in a world of war as faithful followers of Christ we cannot be anything other than nonviolent.

I therefore think Milbank is wrong when he observes that "Christianity has traditionally seen peace as the comprehensive eschatological goal, and *not* as the name of a virtue."[31] To be sure, Milbank's judgment that peace is not a virtue is supported by Aquinas. Aquinas, quoting Augustine, observed that virtue is not of the last end because virtue is the way to the end. Therefore peace cannot be a virtue because it is of the last end.[32] Yet the matter is more complex (which is almost always the case in Aquinas) because peace is the work of charity, which no one denies is a virtue. Peace is not a virtue only in the sense that it is encompassed in charity—which is at once a virtue and an activity—through which we love God and our neighbor. And we must remember that in Aquinas charity is nothing less than our friendship with God.

Peace and friendship, moreover, share similar characteristics to the extent that they are interdependent virtues. They are odd virtues because

31. Milbank, *Theology and Social Theory*, p. 418.
32. Thomas Aquinas, *Summa Theologica*, II–II, 29, trans. Fathers of the English Dominican Province (Westminster, Md.: Christian Classics, 1981).

they first qualify a relationship rather than a passion. Years ago I wrote an essay called "Peacemaking: The Virtue of the Church" in which I tried to develop, on the basis of Matthew 18:15–22, how peacemaking names an activity intrinsic to the church that requires a community of people capable of telling one another the truth.[33] I have no intention of boring you by rehearsing the argument I tried to make in that essay, but I call attention to it because that essay exemplifies my conviction that peacemaking, just as friendship was for Aristotle and Aquinas, is necessary for any account of the Christian virtues. Indeed I believe that peacemaking is like friendship, at least the kind of friendship Aristotle defends—that is, "some sort of excellence or virtue, or involves virtue, and it is, moreover, most indispensable for life."[34]

I raise the question of whether peace can be considered to be a virtue only because I think exploration of this issue helps us understand why Christian nonviolence cannot be determined or justified if we think all that is required is for us to be "not violent." This is the same point with which I began this essay, but I hope the importance of this suggestion is clearer in light of the questions raised by Milbank about nonviolence. Advocates of Christian nonviolence betray the very activity about which we care when we direct attention primarily to what we are against. Such a strategy cannot help but give the impression that most of our life is gripped by violence, from which we must try to rescue some small shards of peace. But I believe that our existence is one constituted by peace, God's peace, and that violence is the exception. That is why it is so important for those of us committed to Christian nonviolence to work to name for ourselves and our neighbors the peace, the friendships, without which we cannot live.

I believe the best essay I have written on peace is called "Taking Time for Peace: The Moral Significance of the Trivial."[35] It is a modest little essay in which I tried to counter the survivalism associated with the work of Jonathan Schell and Gordon Kaufman by calling attention to peaceable activities such as raising lemurs, sustaining universities,

---

33. Stanley Hauerwas, *Christian Existence Today: Essays on Church, World, and Living in Between* (Grand Rapids: Brazos, 2001), pp. 89–97. This book was originally published by Labyrinth Press of Durham, N.C., in 1988.

34. Aristotle, *Nicomachean Ethics*, trans. Martin Ostwald (Indianapolis: Bobbs-Merrill, 1962), 1155a, 1–5. I am on record expressing agreement with Milbank's arguments against MacIntyre's account of the virtues. I think, however, that his case would have been stronger if Milbank had shown how MacIntyre's account requires not only charity but peace. See Stanley Hauerwas and Charles Pinches, *Christians among the Virtues: Theological Conversations with Ancient and Modern Ethics* (Notre Dame, Ind.: University of Notre Dame Press, 1997), pp. 55–69.

35. Hauerwas, *Christian Existence Today*, pp. 253–66.

having children, and, of course, playing baseball. To be sure, in the face of alleged nuclear destruction these appear trivial or inconsequential activities; but I believe that without them and many other such examples, we have no hold on what it means to be nonviolent. If we are as Christians to survive the violent societies that threaten to engulf us, we will do so just to the extent that we discover such worthwhile activities through which we learn not just to be at peace but that we love peace. That is why, contrary to the title of this essay, nonviolence cannot be explained. It can only be shown by the attractiveness of the friendships that constitute our lives.

8

PUNISHING CHRISTIANS

1. HOW NOT TO BEGIN THINKING ABOUT PUNISHMENT

John Howard Yoder begins his contribution to a book entitled *The Death Penalty Debate* observing that "it has not been my privilege to be vocationally involved in ministries of witness related to 'corrections,' nor in the social sciences which study these matters, but my conviction as to the importance of the matter has not diminished."[1] That the question of punishment was never far from Yoder's attention is indicated by his early pamphlet entitled "The Christian and Capital Punishment" as well as the book, *You Have It Coming: Good Punishment—The Legitimate Social Function of Punitive Behavior,* he was preparing when he died.[2] Some may think it strange or odd that Yoder, the pacifist, took

1. John Howard Yoder, "Against the Death Penalty," in H. Wayne House and John Howard Yoder, *The Death Penalty Debate: Two Opposing Views of Capital Punishment* (Dallas: Word, 1991), p. 107.

2. John Howard Yoder, "The Christian and Capital Punishment" (Institute of Mennonite Studies Series 1; Newton, Kans.: Faith & Life Press, 1961); and John Howard Yoder, *You Have It Coming: Good Punishment—The Legitimate Social Function of Punitive Behavior.* Yoder prepared and "published" the latter book for his Internet site in 1995. I have a downloaded copy of the book, which indicates that in spite of Yoder's claim that he had not kept up in the social science literature surrounding issues of punishment, in fact he had. He was particularly interested in the work of René Girard.

punishment so seriously; but Yoder rightly thought those committed to Christian nonviolence cannot avoid providing an account—or even more important, alternative practices—of and for punishment.

I suspect one of the reasons many do not think that pacifism deserves serious consideration is not because they think war is a "good thing." Rather they sense that pacifism simply cannot give an account of how our daily lives depend on violent forms of behavior. How could we live if we had no understanding of crime and/or were unwilling to punish those who engage in crime? I began to explore this kind of challenge in an essay entitled, "McInerny Did It: or, Should a Pacifist Read Murder Mysteries?"[3] That essay was written in honor of my friend Ralph McInerny, a philosopher and writer of murder mysteries. In this essay, which is written to honor another friend, Duncan Forrester, I will try to extend the argument I began in that essay in the hope that I can convince those who think of themselves as almost pacifist to drop the "almost."

It is my hope that the focus on punishment will provide a way to explore what some, including Duncan himself, may think to be differences between us on matters concerning the responsibility of Christians to the societies in which they find themselves. Duncan has graciously expressed appreciation for the kind of questions I have been pressing against Christian accommodation to liberal social arrangements. Yet he is a good Scot. He has worked tirelessly as a representative of the Church of Scotland to help Scotland be a more just society. Contrary to what some may think I should think as a representative of Christian nonviolence, I applaud Duncan for the work he has done for social reforms in Scotland. For example, he has thought hard about, as well as helped encourage, prison reform in Scotland.[4]

The work Duncan and his colleagues have done for reform of Scottish prisons is the kind of work Yoder would encourage. For example, Yoder observes that neither Jesus nor Paul rose up against capital punishment. They did not do so because the gospel cannot eliminate such practices "from secular society, since, being non-coercive, the gospel cannot 'rule the world' in that way. Yet, to condone the way things stand is not approval: 'from the beginning it was not so' (Matt. 19:8)."[5] According to

3. This essay was originally published in *Recovering Nature: Essays in Natural Philosophy, Ethics, and Metaphysics in Honor of Ralph McInerny*, ed. John O'Callaghan and Thomas Hibbs (Notre Dame, Ind.: University of Notre Dame Press, 1999), pp. 163–75. It can also be found in my book *A Better Hope: Resources for a Church Confronting Capitalism, Democracy, and Postmodernity* (Grand Rapids: Brazos, 2000), pp. 201–10.

4. I know of this work primarily through conversations with Duncan, but he discusses the work of the penal policy group in his essay "Priorities for Social Theology Today," in *Vision and Prophecy: The Tasks of Social Theology Today*, ed. Michael Northcott (Edinburgh, U.K.: Centre for Theology and Public Issues, 1991), pp. 29–31.

5. Yoder, "Against the Death Penalty," p. 141.

Yoder, though Jesus said this about the Mosaic provision for divorce, this is the way early Christians thought about other areas where the world was ruled by pagan powers. Yet the Christians also thought that the new level of love and forgiveness made possible by the Holy Spirit is good news for the "real world" because such love will work as salt and light for those who are not Christians. Yoder continues:

> This should be true anywhere; even more evidently should it be the case in the Anglo-Saxon world, where a large number of citizens claim some kind of Christian sanction for society's values. If Christ is not only prophet and priest but also king, the border between church and the world cannot be impermeable to moral truth. Something of the cross-bearing, forgiving love, and dignity which Jesus' life, death, and resurrection revealed to be the normative way to be human, must be the norm for all humans, whether they know it or not. We cannot *expect* of anyone, not even of believers, that that norm be lived out perfectly. Yet, [there] is the calling of the followers of Jesus to testify that there is no other norm. The one strategy which will not serve that calling, which could not be done in the first century, and cannot be done in our century, is to claim to possess, and to impose on society, a body of civil rules independent of the faith of the persons called to respect them. The alternative is to work with the acceptance of the others' unbelief which is what I call "condoning" the lesser moral level of the civil order.[6]

Yoder's understanding of the permeable boundaries between church and world does not in itself, however, suggest how Christians ought to think about punishment in general and/or, in particular, capital punishment. He observes that watching the debate between advocates and opponents of capital punishment over the years has taught him that there is no one right place to begin.[7] That there is no place to begin seems to me to be right, but it is a hard lesson learned. For our temptation is to once again roll out the various theories of punishment—rehabilitation, defense against the criminal (deterrence), retribution—and then to grade the practice of punishment against these theories of punishment.[8]

The problem is not that these theories are "wrong" (though I think they often give us a false sense that we know what we are talking about

6. Ibid., p. 141.
7. Ibid., p. 107.
8. The examples of this strategy are legion, but for a recent display of how this kind of analysis works see Avery Cardinal Dulles, "Catholicism and Capital Punishment," *First Things* 112 (April 2001): 30–35. I am not suggesting that the various theories of punishment are not useful ways of exploring the conceptual issues entailed in various claims about punishment. Rather I am calling into question the temptation for the theories to take on a life of their own irrespective of the thick practices that surround punishment in different historical periods and in various cultural locations.

when we talk about punishment); but it is by no means clear what work the theories are meant to do. In particular the theories give the impression that how Christians punish is but an instance of a more general practice of punishment shared by all societies. It is that presumption I want to challenge in this essay by calling attention to the way Christians have punished and should punish.

Of course the strategy of beginning with general theories of punishment is often an attempt to show that capital punishment fails to be justified on grounds of this or that theory. For example, it is suggested that capital punishment cannot pass muster if we believe that rehabilitation or the protection of society is the primary purpose of punishment. You certainly cannot rehabilitate someone you have killed nor does it seem that the use of capital punishment protects society by deterring others from killing. It is often pointed out, for example, that murderers are seldom repeat offenders, unless they are professional killers, so capital punishment does little to deter. Professionals after all will not be deterred exactly because they are professionals.

One response to the attempt to defeat capital punishment by showing it does not deter is to observe that capital punishment is associated with the wrong crime. If we killed people for stock fraud, for example, there is every reason to believe that capital punishment would deter. Erect a gallows or a guillotine on Wall Street, televise the execution of those guilty of stock fraud, and I think there is every reason to believe that stock fraud would be a much less common crime. That most people today recoil against killing people for theft indicates that questions of punishment involve more than the various abstract theories of punishment suggest in and of themselves.

For example, Duncan Forrester reports that the Penal Policy Group that took as their assignment an attempt to understand how the penal system worked and should work in Scotland began by looking at the various theories of punishment. However, he reports it soon became apparent that none of the theories, or even all the theories used together, explained what actually happens in the penal system in Scotland. He observes his group increasingly became convinced "that theories often disguise, mystify, and subtly justify what is really happening."[9] It was only when the group began to go more deeply into the experience of being and surviving as a prisoner did theological themes begin to emerge to illumine the practice of punishment. Forrester observes,

> We discovered the necessity of *hope*. We noted that although offence involves *guilt*, this is not today recognized as something with which the penal

9. Forrester, "Priorities for Social Theology Today," p. 30.

system can or should engage. And, most important of all, we noted that in the Christian tradition offence, crime and sin are met with *forgiveness* which wipes away the guilt and the memory, while our society remains highly punitive and former prisoners rarely experience real forgiveness and reconciliation at the hands of their neighbors and colleagues. We concluded that any Christian account of punishment must see it as *discipline* directed to the good of society and of the offender. Most of those working in the system or in academic criminology found the notion of forgiveness a fresh and exciting and challenging idea. In Christian theology it is of course rooted deeply in the understanding of God, and theologians would wish to affirm that it is a universal truth that God is a God who forgives.[10]

I am sure that Forrester and his colleagues are on the right track for helping us think as Christians about punishment. Too often attempts to think through the practice of punishment using the standard theories means theological considerations are absent or used to support positions determined on other grounds. I am, moreover, sure that Forrester and his colleagues are right that the *telos* of punishment must be reconciliation and forgiveness. As he observes, the absence of the hope of forgiveness means "prisons become human warehouses and both offenders and those who operate the criminal justice system have great difficulty in seeing their experience and their work as significant and meaningful."[11]

Yet I am equally sure that we must be careful not to let appeals to forgiveness and reconciliation hide from us the seriousness of punishment and the proper role punishment has, not only for any society but in particular in the church. It is not enough for Christians to say

10. Forrester, "Priorities for Social Theology Today," p. 30. I think it wrong to suggest that the Christian practice of forgiveness "wipes out memory." On the contrary, forgiveness makes memory possible. For an argument along these lines see my *A Better Hope*, pp. 139–54.

11. Forrester, "Priorities for Social Theology Today," p. 30. For a careful analysis of the moral arguments for capital punishment see Lloyd Steffen, *Executing Justice: The Moral Meaning of the Death Penalty* (Cleveland: Pilgrim, 1998). I am convinced by Steffen that the moral arguments against capital punishment are persuasive. That the arguments have not resulted in the abolition of capital punishment certainly makes his claim that capital punishment gains its support from the presumption that the state must exert power—i.e., capital punishment has a symbolic role of legitimation—is, to say the least, interesting. Steffen's theological reflections in the last chapter of the book, however, seem to me far too captured by deficient atonement theories. For an extraordinary account of how satisfaction theories of the atonement have shaped the practice of capital punishment, see Timothy Gorringe, *God's Just Vengeance* (Cambridge, U.K.: Cambridge University Press, 1996). Gorringe's book not only forces one to rethink the usual justifications for punishment, but just as important Gorringe challenges atonement theories not governed by more determinative christological claims. After reading Gorringe, the appropriate question is *why anyone* has assumed Christians need a "doctrine" of the atonement.

"forgiveness" if they do not exemplify in their own lives why punishment is a necessary practice if the church is to be the church. Appeals to forgiveness are too easy if we have not first made clear why we think it is wrong to execute people for stock fraud. After all the church at one time thought those convicted of heresy should be killed—a position we may find extreme, but one justified if you believe that heresy is a more serious crime than murder. A murderer after all only robs us of our life; a heretic robs us of our salvation.

In order to explore the theological issues at the heart of punishment I want to introduce Oliver O'Donovan's compelling justification of capital punishment. His account, moreover, is all the more important because it emerges in the process of his critique of John Paul II's praise in *Evangelium Vitae* for the growing tendency in our time for the limited use or abolishment of capital punishment. O'Donovan, I think, rightly fears that the pope on this matter may have succumbed to the sentimental humanism of our time. However, before such a judgment can be sustained I need to attend to the details of O'Donovan's analysis and critique of the pope's position.

2. O'DONOVAN'S ANALYSIS OF *EVANGELIUM VITAE*

O'Donovan's critique involves a close reading of the passage in *Evangelium Vitae* that deals with capital punishment. That passage reads:

> This is the context in which to place the problem of the *death penalty*. On this matter there is a growing tendency, both in the Church and in civil society, to demand that it be applied in a very limited way or even that it be abolished completely. The problem must be viewed in the context of a system of penal justice ever more in line with human dignity and thus, in the end, with God's plan for man and society. The primary purpose of the punishment which society inflicts is "to redress the disorder caused by the offense." Public authority must redress the violation of personal and social rights by imposing on the offender an adequate punishment for the crime, as a condition for the offender to regain the exercise of his or her freedom. In this way authority also fulfills the purpose of defending public order and ensuring people's safety, while at the same time offering an incentive and help to change his or her behavior and be rehabilitated.
>
> It is clear that for these purposes to be achieved, *the nature and extent of the punishment* must be carefully evaluated and decided upon, and ought not go to the extreme of executing the offender except in cases of absolute necessity: in other words, when it would not be possible otherwise to defend society. Today, however, as a result of steady improvements

in the organization of the penal system, such cases are very rare, if not practically nonexistent.

In any event, the principle set forth in the new *Catechism of the Catholic Church* remains valid: "If bloodless means are sufficient to defend human lives against an aggressor and to protect public order and the safety of persons, public authority must limit itself to such means, because they better correspond to the concrete conditions of the common good and are more in conformity to the dignity of the human person."[12]

O'Donovan begins his criticism of the pope's position noting that three points in particular are in need of clarification—(1) What characteristics of a society are presupposed by the "steady improvements" to which the pope refers? (2) What kind of situation would count as an "absolute necessity"? (3) Why does the pope justify capital punishment in classical retributive categories, but make the possibility for the lessening use of capital punishment turn on remedial considerations?[13] Though the first two questions of clarification are important, O'Donovan's most important challenge to the pope's position involves the third challenge.

12. I am using the text as it appears in *The Encyclicals of John Paul II*, ed. with introductions by J. Michael Miller, C.S.B. (Huntington, Ind.: Our Sunday Visitor, 1996), paragraph 56.

John Paul II's claim that "this is the context" to discuss capital punishment is fascinating. Paragraph 55 deals with the "paradox" that occurs when the right to protect one's own life and the duty not to harm someone else's life cannot be reconciled in practice. John Paul II observes that the "intrinsic value of life and the duty to love oneself not less than others are the basis of a *true right* to self-defense." He then notes that the commandment to love the neighbor presupposes love of self as set forth in the great commandment. Therefore, "no one can renounce the right to self-defense out of lack of love for life or for self. This can only be done in virtue of a heroic love which deepens and transfigures the love of self into a radical self-offering, according to the spirit of the Gospel Beatitudes. The sublime example of this self-offering is the Lord Jesus Christ."

I confess I find the pope's defense of self-love as the basis for self-defense puzzling. If our self-love is to be formed by charity, what could it possibly mean to suggest that Christians have a right to self-defense? Our love for life and self only makes sense if the "self" is shaped by the love of God found in the cross. To suggest that such a love is "heroic" seems to accept the natural, if not sinful, self as normative.

This is extremely important for the issue of capital punishment, for the pope goes on to suggest that legitimate defense is not only a right but a "grave duty" for those responsible for the common good of the family or the state. Accordingly it happens that there is a need to render an aggressor incapable of causing harm, which may even require the taking of the aggressor's life. In such cases the "fatal outcome" is not murder because the loss of life is attributable to the aggressor's action. As we shall see this justification makes the pope's judgments about capital punishment the harder to understand.

13. Oliver O'Donovan, "The Death Penalty in *Evangelium Vitae*," in *Ecumenical Ventures in Ethics: Protestants Engage Pope John Paul II's Moral Encyclicals*, ed. Reinhard Hütter and Theodor Dieter (Grand Rapids: Eerdmans, 1998), pp. 220–23.

O'Donovan observes that in the late eighteenth and nineteenth centuries a consensus developed that retributive appropriateness was the final criterion for means of punishment.[14] Accordingly, the death penalty was required since only life could witness to the sanctity of life. O'Donovan accordingly observes: the pope simply gives no reason why we should believe that rehabilitation should count more than public safety. But even more important, the pope does not adequately explore what is at stake in his praise for societies that have abandoned retribution as the primary purpose of punishment. In order to clarify what the pope needs to say, O'Donovan offers an account of why retribution can never be disavowed by the public authorities.

Punishment is expressive act, according to O'Donovan, just to the extent that "punishment must pronounce judgment on the offense, describing it, disowning it, and refounding the moral basis for the common life which the offense has challenged."[15] Punishment, so to speak, "gives back" the offense, not simply as vengeance, but in the sense that a true statement is made about what has happened. Retribution is the primary end of punishment, which means that is what punishment *is* in the same way that telling the truth is the primary end of making a statement. Retribution is the alternative to vengeance because vengeance is "private" and, therefore, arbitrary.[16]

So understood, punishment is not a means to some other end—even the end of making the offender good—but rather the end of punishment

14. O'Donovan does not explain how or why this "consensus" developed or whether it is a development Christians should applaud. I should think the "reformative" account of punishment was and is the justification most modern people assume justifies punishment.

15. O'Donovan, "The Death Penalty," p. 224.

16. I understand the distinction O'Donovan is making between retribution and vengeance, but I confess I find it a bit forced. If vengeance is the symbolic way people gesture that order is deeper than disorder, it seems appropriate that retribution serve to provide the vengeance those directly involved in a crime feel they need. That those who have someone close to them violated so often express the need to have the perpetrator of the violence killed and even to see them executed cannot be easily dismissed as "a primitive attitude." That a "public authority" should perform the execution is important, but the execution remains the working out of vengeance.

Yoder, in his early pamphlet "The Christian and Capital Punishment," maintained that vengeance shapes capital punishment. His position in this regard does not necessarily make his view of capital punishment different from O'Donovan's stress on justice because Yoder also observes that "vengeance is happening; the necessity is that it be controlled. Thus the significance of civil order is that it *limit* vengeance to a level equivalent to the offense. . . . Vengeance was never God's highest intent for men's relations with one another; permitting it within the limits of justice, i.e., of equivalent injury, was never really his purpose" (p. 7). According to Yoder, what God wants to do with evil, what he wants us to do with evil, is "to swallow it up, drown it in the bottomless sea of His crucified love" (p. 7). Yoder's account of how the civil order "limits vengeance" has at least resemblance to O'Donovan's understanding of justice.

is justice. To be sure there may be secondary goods associated with punishment, but such goods should not qualify that the end of punishment is justice. As O'Donovan puts it, "punishment is a kind of enacted language" reminding us that the equivalence of punishment to crime is a "symbolic construct" that "evolves as the symbolic meaning of certain acts with the context of social expectation changes."[17] Thus it may be, as Montesquieu observed, that in countries with mild laws inhabitants are as much affected by slight penalties as inhabitants of countries with more severe laws. O'Donovan hopes that the pope's understanding of the "improvements in the penal system" simply means that the influence of the Christian message makes it possible for those in authority to follow Ambrose's message concerning the use of capital punishment—"You will be excused if you use it, admired if you refrain."[18]

Yet O'Donovan fears John Paul II may in fact come close to recommending the abolition of capital punishment in principle. For example, O'Donovan calls attention to paragraph 40 of *Evangelium Vitae*, in which the pope seems to be moving to a position that would not require capital punishment to be considered a necessary part of a humane justice system. In paragraph 40 the pope in commenting on the prohibition of murder in the Decalogue says: "Of course we must recognize that in the Old Testament this sense of the value of life, though already quite marked, does not yet reach the refinement found in the Sermon on the Mount. This is apparent in some aspects of the current (i.e., *then* current) penal legislation, which provided for severe forms of corporal punishment and even the death-penalty."[19]

O'Donovan thinks this account of capital punishment breaks the link between public safety and the system of retributive justice. As a result capital punishment becomes but an emergency provision that allegedly is no longer required in modern, economically developed, and well-governed states. Accordingly the coercive powers of the state in criminal justice are derived and justified from a just war perspective of "legitimate defense."[20] From O'Donovan's perspective this is a terrible mistake because

17. O'Donovan, "The Death Penalty," p. 225.
18. Ibid., p. 227.
19. Ibid., p. 229.
20. I confess I am not quite sure what point O'Donovan is making by suggesting that the pope is making a mistake when he seemingly justifies capital punishment in terms of the just war logic of "legitimate defense." I assume he must mean that "legitimate defense" is a "last resort," which makes capital punishment justified only if the survival of the society is at stake. But that would rob capital punishment of its "normality." In other words capital punishment is not like just war if it is required by justice. That said, I think the relation between just war reflection and capital punishment has not been sufficiently spelled out either by those who support just war and capital punishment or by those who

one should never attempt such a thing. The right of the state to impose coercive measures against wrongdoers arises not from its need to defend itself but from its office of *judgment*. . . . For if the death penalty is never at home in ordinary penal practice, then it is never invoked for purposes germane to penology but only to shore up the institution upon which all penal practice depends, that is, the state. The idea of an "emergency provision," whether we meet it in John Paul or in some well-known Protestant exemplars, implies an inevitable drift towards statism; for once the power of the sword is notionally set free from the constraints of justice *in extremis*, there can be no function for the sword but to enforce the state's grip. We should hardly be surprised if the state that is refused the just use of force in ordinary operations but is promised a *carte blanche* in emergency, sets about creating one.[21]

To make capital punishment morally discontinuous from other forms of coercive punishment not only invites a loss of constraint on when states may declare their very existence is at stake, but, even more disturbing theologically, severs death from God's judgment. According to O'Donovan all Christians have to say that death is not part of God's "original" created order. Death is not just death, but judgment on sin. Without such a view of the linkage between judgment and death Christ becomes but another victim of injustice rather than the one who bore

---

support neither. In particular I think O'Donovan's analysis opens up the question of what "justice" a just war is meant to serve. This is particularly important if just war is understood not as an exception to nonviolence, but rather is required because justice always requires us to defend the neighbor. It is, therefore, wrong to try to rid the world of war if war is a necessity for the realization of justice. If such is the case, then capital punishment and war are analogous but it remains a question in what ways the justice that is the end of each is similar and different.

21. O'Donovan, "The Death Penalty," pp. 232–33. For O'Donovan's extended account of the importance of judgment, see *The Desire of the Nations: Rediscovering the Roots of Political Theology* (Cambridge, U.K.: Cambridge University Press, 1996), pp. 37–41, 147–51. O'Donovan explicitly criticizes Yoder's account of Matthew 18:15–20. O'Donovan thinks Yoder, at least in *The Original Revolution*, gives the state a role in judgment. Unfortunately, according to O'Donovan, Yoder did not continue that line of analysis in *The Politics of Jesus*. I am not convinced. O'Donovan, I think, fails to appreciate Yoder's refusal to give a "theory" of state action. For Yoder "vengeance happens"; it does not need a justifying theory.

By some "well-known Protestant exemplars," O'Donovan means Barth. In *Church Dogmatics*, III/4, trans. A. T. Mackay, et al. (Edinburgh, U.K.: T & T Clark, 1961), Barth argued that capital punishment "must be put on the far edge of what can be commanded." According to Barth there is a place for killing of those "whose existence threatens the state and its stability in such a way that a choice has to be made between their existence and that of the state" (p. 446). Barth thinks, for example, the treasonous giving of secrets to the enemy might be grounds for capital punishment. O'Donovan quite rightly observes that Barth-like justifications put the ordinary operations of penal justice in an idealized light. Such justifications hide from us the coercive character of all punishment that draws its power over us through our mortality.

our sins and suffered our death. That is why, as happy as it may be to be rid of the ordinary uses of the death penalty, we "cannot be rid of the symbolic role that the death penalty plays in relating death to judgment. There will always be a death penalty in the mind—if, that is, we are all to learn to 'die with Christ,' understanding our own deaths as a kind of capital punishment."[22]

So runs O'Donovan's justification of capital punishment. I admire O'Donovan's argument because he makes candid the moral and theological presuppositions associated with retributive accounts of punishment. Christological questions are rightly at the center and O'Donovan rightly puts them where they should be. Moreover O'Donovan makes clear that capital punishment cannot be separated from why and how we punish in other aspects of our lives. Accordingly any alternative account to O'Donovan's understanding of punishment requires if not forces us to leave behind the sentimentalities so characteristic of compassionate responses to punishment.

3. THE CHRISTIAN PRACTICE OF PUNISHMENT

O'Donovan rightly calls into question the sentimental humanism that currently dominates discussions surrounding capital punishment in liberal social orders. Moreover, O'Donovan helps us see why it is extremely unwise for Christians to identify with the call for an end to capital punishment just to the extent our understanding of punishment is confused with humanist ideologies and practices. Yet I do want capital punishment to come to an end because I think the end of punishment has been transformed by the cross and resurrection of Christ. Moreover, I think that transformation is a possibility not only for the practice of the church but for any society and the public authorities (what is sometimes identified as the state) who have responsibilities to serve the goods in common, which include punishment.

By distinguishing "public authorities" from the "state" I mean to do no more than to call into question the assumption that the "state as

22. O'Donovan, "The Death Penalty," p. 235. O'Donovan suggests that to the extent John Paul II leaves this understanding of capital punishment behind, he becomes a modernist in spite of his otherwise attack on "the culture of death." O'Donovan notes that at the heart of the "culture of death" rests a culture of life. "Precisely because our brief span must (it seems to us) carry the whole meaning of existence, offering all the reconciliation we can ever hope to find; precisely because death (whether Christ's or ours) is allowed no role in this reconciliation; we become greedy of life, demanding to live each moment to the full, snatching from others opportunities to live that could compete with our own, making calculated sacrifices of the 'worthless' lives to enrich the 'worthwhile,' and so on" (p. 236).

such" is a known entity. I assume peoples can exist with structures of authority that are not the same as "a state" particularly when the state in modernity is identified with the locus of hegemonic power. This may seem an unimportant distinction, but too often the "state" is simply accepted as a given in a manner that makes it impervious to the gospel. For example, Avery Cardinal Dulles observes that while the church can and does punish, she is also indulgent toward offenders. For example, he observes "it would be clearly inappropriate for the Church, as a spiritual society, to execute criminals, but the State is a different type of society. It cannot be expected to act as a Church."[23]

Far be it from me to suggest that a cardinal of the Church of Rome has gone over to the Lutherans, but to claim that something called the "state" exists that has not been transformed by Christ could be interpreted as accepting the Lutheran understanding of the distinction between the orders of creation and redemption. For example it is quite interesting to contrast Dulles's (and O'Donovan's) understanding of the state with that of John Howard Yoder.[24] Responding to the assumption shared by many that to call for the end of capital punishment is to destroy all government, Yoder observes that for the Christian to accept the question "But where will this lead?" is to distort the whole problem. Of course Christians know the world does not share our faith, that the world cannot be expected to live as Christians should live, but that does not mean there is some line drawn in the sand that determines what Christians cannot ask of the societies in which we find ourselves.

The resurrection and ascension of Christ mean there is no situation in which Christians think nothing can be done.

---

23. Avery Cardinal Dulles, "Catholicism and Capital Punishment," p. 34. Dulles, like O'Donovan, thinks in predominately Christian societies the state can lean toward leniency as long as such leniency does not violate the demands of justice. Dulles, also like O'Donovan, thinks the state must believe in a transcendent order of justice, which it has an obligation to protect. Such an order of justice is but a "symbolic anticipation of God's perfect justice" (p. 33). Dulles quite rightly distinguishes this view of the state from the general view in our time that sees the state as but the instrument of the will of the governed, in which the death penalty becomes but an expression of the collective anger of the group. When this happens, punishment is no longer an analog of the divine judgment on objective evil but simply the self-assertive act of vengeance. I share Dulles's view of the transformation of the state in modernity, but I wonder why he does not conclude from that change that in such social orders capital punishment should be ended exactly because the end of capital punishment has been lost. I often wonder why the same line of reasoning does not lead advocates of just war, which again is dependent on some account of justice, to call for an end to war. Liberal societies simply lack an account of justice that would make just war intelligible.

24. My suggesting that Dulles and O'Donovan may have a similar view of this matter may be mistaken. O'Donovan may well believe that the church can and should execute criminals.

The world can be challenged, one point at a time, to take one step in the right direction, to move up one modest notch in approximation of the righteousness of love. To challenge capital punishment no more undermines government than does the rejection of the oath (Matthew 5:33–37, James 5:12) undermine truth telling; no more than does the consent of the governed destroy the authority of the state. The civil order is a fact. That it might be done away with by pushing the critique of love "too far" is inconceivable. Thus the Christian (and any believer in democracy) will be concerned to restrain the violent, vengeful potential of the state. That potential for violence does not need our advocacy; it is already there.[25]

Of course, Dulles and O'Donovan may object that Yoder fails to understand that the issue is not whether the state exists or, even, whether we have a justification to sustain the legitimacy of the state. The issue is justice. Yet just as he challenges the assumption that there is any one thing called the "state," so Yoder questions the assumption that there is any univocal "concept of justice, having the same meaning in all times and places, consisting in an exact logical or mathematical equivalence of offense and retribution, and that such 'justice' must (or can) be either wholly respected or fundamentally rejected."[26] There is, therefore, no culturally invariant understanding of what equivalent punishment should or does entail. The presumption that "retributive justice" requires the murderer's life in return is not written in stone.[27] For Yoder justice is a direction not an achievement. I take this claim to mean no more than what is emphasized in all classical accounts of justice, namely, that justice depends on the practices of a people that embodies the hard-won wisdom of the past tested by the challenges of the present in the hope of a better future.

Yoder has no reason to deny O'Donovan's account of punishment as an "enacted language." O'Donovan, moreover, rightly suggests that as a language punishment can and should evolve; the symbolic meaning of certain acts changes, given the context of social expectation.[28]

25. Yoder, "Against the Death Penalty," p. 142. Yoder observes that "anarchy" is a grammatical abstraction with no reality. There are varied forms of government, from tyranny to constitutional democracy, but given the many possibilities there is always authority. Even in cases where authority is functioning too little for the welfare and stability of the society, the reason for such dysfunctioning is never due to Christian love being too effective.

26. Ibid., p. 143.

27. Yoder observes that if life for life is required by justice, then there is no reason why the mentally handicapped should be spared the death penalty. The character or "freedom" of the murderer should not be taken into account if all that matters is that justice be served. Yoder rightly uses all the anomalies created by capital punishment—it can result in killing the innocent, it falls disproportionately on the poor and African-American, its infrequency ironically makes it more arbitrary—to call into quesiton its use.

28. O'Donovan, "The Death Penalty," p. 225.

Rather Yoder is trying to force questions about the "context of social expectation" that Christ's cross and resurrection have made possible. For Yoder is sure that if it is inappropriate for the church to execute criminals, this is equally the case for the public officials of any society. If the shedding of blood is meant to expose the killer to killing in expiation in the name of justice or the cosmic order, it is Yoder's contention that Christ is the end of expiation.[29] At the very least this means that Christians cannot help but challenge accounts of justice that assume the only way to restore the injustice murder names is by taking the life of the murderer.[30]

That Christ is the end of expiation does not mean, however, that Christians do not reach out to one another in a manner that some may call punishment. Yet the Christian understanding of punishment must begin with the recognition that we are not punished for our sins, but sin is our punishment. John Howard Yoder and John Milbank are not usually considered allies, but I believe they share this understanding of sin. In *Theology and Social Theory* Milbank observes that God does not will to punish sin, because "punishment is not an act of a real nature upon another nature, and God always remains within his nature. Punishment is ontologically 'self-inflicted,' the only punishment is the deleterious effect of sin upon nature, and the torment of knowing reality only in terms of one's estrangement from it."[31]

According to Milbank the trial and punishment of Jesus judges all other trials and punishments just to the extent that the latter cannot help but be "alien." It is, therefore, not adequate to say, as O'Donovan seems to do, that such "alien punishment" is a symbolic language. The

29. Yoder, "Against the Death Penalty," p. 128.

30. The refusal to kill those who kill can be seen as a kind of cruelty just to the extent such a refusal refuses to allow those that kill to determine their own self-understanding. To kill another human being can be the ultimate act of self-assertion, the claim of ultimate autonomy, and thus an act that creates an extraordinary loneliness. Murder is not an act to be shared. The refusal to kill others is the refusal to let them determine the meaning of their lives. The refusal to punish them for murder is the refusal to let their loneliness determine who they are.

31. John Milbank, *Theology and Social Theory: Beyond Secular Reason* (Oxford, U.K.: Basil Blackwell, 1990), p. 420. In an extraordinary essay on the book of Job, Herbert Fingarette argues that "the Book of Job shatters, by a combination of challenge and ridicule and ultimately by direct experiential demonstration, the idea that the law known to human beings reflects law rooted in the divine or ultimate nature of being, and the idea that the divine or ultimate nature of being is in its essence lawlike." Fingarette argues that if God were required to punish us for disobedience to God's law, then we could control God by forcing God to punish us. That is a bargain decisively rejected in Job. "The Meaning of Law in the Book of Job," in *Revisions: Changing Perspectives in Moral Philosophy*, ed. Stanley Hauerwas and Alasdair MacIntyre (Notre Dame, Ind.: University of Notre Dame Press, 1983), pp. 249–86. The quote comes from p. 269.

tragic necessity of such punishment cannot be a sign of God's justice if God's justice is the cross. So the only

> tolerable, and non-sinful punishment, for Christians, must be the self-punishment inherent in sin. When a person commits an evil act, he cuts himself off from social peace, and this nearly always means that he is visited with social anger. But the aim should be to reduce this anger to a calm fury against the sin, and to offer the sinner nothing but good will, so bringing him to the point of realizing that his isolation is self-imposed.[32]

Milbank's position does not commit him to the absurd position that we know that we are being punished for our sin. Indeed one of the most frightening realities is that we may appear to be quite happy in our unrighteousness—happiness can be a form of punishment. To suffer for our sins is a great gift that makes possible the identification as well as the appropriate penance for our sin. Penance is the means we hope makes possible reconciliation with God, the neighbor against whom we have sinned, and even ourselves. Milbank is quite right that the effect of sin estranges us from ourselves creating a loneliness that cannot be overcome. To be punished as a Christian is to be called home so that we may be reunited with the community of forgiven sinners called church and, thus, reconciled with our own life.

Christian punishment is properly understood to be excommunication or binding and loosing. To be confronted by our brothers and sisters because of our sin is a call to reconciliation. Not to hear the call is to condemn ourselves. To be excommunicated is not to be "thrown out," but rather to be told that we already "outside." Excommunication is a call to come home by helping us locate how we have alienated ourselves from God and those that gather to worship God. Christian punishment only makes sense against the background of the practice of holiness commensurate with the Christian desire to be a people called to witness to the One who alone is able to forgive sins.[33]

32. Milbank, *Theology and Social Theory*, p. 421.

33. That Christians punish means we must also have practices that make it possible to recognize sins. In other words we need to know how to name actions such as lying, stealing, rape, adultery, killing. A fascinating question that needs exploration is the relation between what Christians call sin and what is understood as crime. Christians who commit crimes may sin; but criminals who are not Christians may not be sinners. Yet Christians no doubt have contributed to current understanding of crime that rightly makes it difficult to distinguish between sin and crime. In social orders as fragile as those in the so-called first world, one of the few places the language of the common good works is in agreements about what constitutes crime. But to recognize a crime requires an account of the positive goods the crime injures. It is not clear that liberal social orders can confidently name such goods, which makes their presumed arguments about crime increasingly arbitrary.

The Christian practice of punishment cannot help but resist being confined by the various theories of punishment. What Christians have to offer our non-Christian brothers and sisters is not a better theory, but a practice of punishment that can be imitated. There is always the question, however, whether what we do as Christians can be done abstracted from our worship of God, from which all that we do gains its intelligibility. Yoder, for example, reminds us that prisons were once called "penitentaries" because they were understood as places to repent.[34] Once the background practices that make repentance the *telos* of punishment were missing, prisons could not help but become the hell holes they are today.[35]

Christians are rightly concerned with prison reform. Christians rightly seek to live in societies that no longer use the death penalty. But Christians, particularly Christians committed to nonviolence, fail themselves and their non-Christian neighbors when they act as if punishment is a problem "out there." What Christians must first give to the world is to be a community that can punish. Only then will the world have an example of what it might mean to be a community that punishes in a manner appropriate for a people who believe that we have been freed by the cross of Christ from the terror of death. I believe that is the kind of community Duncan Forrester has always represented, and in so doing he became for the world the kind of "permeable boundary" God desires.[36]

---

34. Yoder, "Against the Death Penalty," p. 130.

35. Christians are not only rightly concerned with prison reform, but Christians have often been engaged in reform movements with disastrous results. See, for example, Andrew Skotnicki's comparison of the Quaker influence on the development of Pennsylvania's prisons to the more Calvinist influence in New York and Massachusetts in his *Religion and the Development of the American Penal System* (Washington, D.C.: University Press of America, 2000). Skotnicki helps us see how the Quaker practice of silence, when divorced from the practices that silence served, could have quite destructive results for prisoners. Skotnicki begins the last chapter of his book with the observation, "History suggests that the absence of a clearly defined moral organizational principle, one that articulates the justification and meaning of punishment, and to which each element of the penal environment is held accountable, is at the heart of the decisive problems in American correctional experience" (pp. 141–42). If religious language gave American penal institutions some purpose, no matter how inadequate, there is now no clear sense that we know what we do when we punish. Also relevant is Muriel Schmid, "The Eye of God: Religious Beliefs and Punishment in Early Nineteenth-Century Prison Reform," *Theology Today* 59/4 (January 2003): 529–45.

36. I am grateful to Alex Sider and Charlie Collier for their criticisms of an earlier draft of this essay.

9

SEPTEMBER 11, 2001

A Pacifist Response

I want to write honestly about September 11, 2001, but it is not easy. Even now I find it hard to know what can be said or, perhaps more difficult, what should be said. Even more difficult, I am not sure for what or how I should pray. I am a Christian. I am a Christian pacifist. Being Christian and being a pacifist are not two things for me. I would not be a pacifist if I were not a Christian, and I find it hard to understand how one can be a Christian without being a pacifist. But what does a pacifist have to say in the face of terror? Pray for peace? I have no use for sentimentality.

Indeed some have suggested pacifists have nothing to say in a time like the time after September 11, 2001. For example, the editors of the magazine *First Things* assert that "Those who in principle oppose the use of military force have no legitimate part in the discussion about how military force should be used."[1] They do so because according to them the only form of pacifism that is defensible requires the disavowal by the pacifist of any political relevance. That is not the kind of pacifism I represent. I am a pacifist because I think nonviolence is the necessary condition for a politics not based on death. A politics that is not determined by the fear of death means no strong distinction can be drawn

1. "In Time of War," *First Things* 118 (December 2001), p. 14.

between politics and military force—or, perhaps more accurately, I do not believe that the *esse* of politics is coercion or violence.

Yet I cannot deny that September 11, 2001, creates and requires a kind of silence. We desperately want to "explain" what happened. Explanation domesticates terror, making it part of "our" world. I believe attempts to explain must be resisted. Rather, we should learn to wait before what we know not, hoping to gain time and space sufficient to learning how to speak without lying. I should like to think that pacifism names the habits and community necessary to gain the time and place that is an alternative to revenge. But I do not pretend that I know how that is accomplished.

Yet I do know that much that has been said after September 11, 2001, has been false. In the first hours and days following the fall of the towers, there was a stunned silence. President Bush flew from one safe-haven to another, unsure what had or was still to happen. He was quite literally in the air, not quite sure where safety might be found on the ground. I wish he might have been able to maintain that posture, but he is the leader of the "free world."

Something must be done. Something must be said. We must be in control. The silence must be shattered. He knew the American people must be comforted. Life must return to normal.

So he said, "We are at war." Magic words necessary to reclaim the everyday.[2] War is such normalizing discourse. Americans know war. This is our Pearl Harbor. Life can return to normal. We are frightened, and ironically war makes us feel safe. The way to go on in the face of September 11, 2001, is to find someone to kill. Americans are, moreover, good at killing. We often fail to acknowledge how accomplished we are in the

---

2. In his wonderful response to September 11, 2001, *Writings in the Dust* (Grand Rapids: Eerdmans, 2002), Rowan Williams observes that things started to go wrong as soon as the fateful word "war" was invoked. As he puts it, "As soon as it was decided that the September atrocity was an act of war and that a 'war on terrorism' was to be undertaken, clarity disappeared" (p. 36). Chris Hedges echoes Williams, observing that "War makes the world understandable, a black and white tableau of them and us. It suspends thought, especially self-critical thought. All bow before the supreme effort. We are one. Most of us willingly accept war as long as we can fold it into a belief system that paints the ensuing suffering as necessary for a higher good, for human beings seek not only happiness but also meaning. And tragically war is sometimes the most powerful way in human society to achieve meaning" (*War Is a Force that Gives Meaning to Our Lives* [New York: Public Affairs, 2002], p. 10). Hedges observes that this is particularly true for societies like America just to the extent that war "reduces the headache and trivia of daily life. The communal march against an enemy generates a warm, unfamiliar bond with our neighbors, our community, our nation, wiping out unsettling undercurrents of alienation and dislocation. War in times of malaise and desperation is a potent distraction" (p. 9). I wrote this essay prior to reading Hedges' good book. His book, I believe, is a running commentary on what I have written in this chapter.

art of killing. Indeed we, the American people, have become masters of killing. We now conduct war in such a manner that only the enemy has to die. You can tell that our expertise in war-making embarrasses some in our military, but what can they do? They are but following orders.

So the silence created by destruction was soon shattered by the need for revenge—a revenge all the more unforgiving because we cannot forgive those who flew the planes for making us acknowledge our vulnerability. The flag that flew in mourning was soon transformed into a pride-filled thing; the blood-stained flag of victims transformed into the flag of the indomitable American spirit. We will prevail no matter how many people we must kill to rid ourselves of the knowledge that Americans died as victims. Americans do not get to die as victims. They have to be heroes. So the stock trader who happened to work on the seventy-second floor becomes as heroic as the police and firefighters who were doing their job. No one who died on September 11, 2001, gets to die a meaningless death. That is why their deaths must be avenged.

I am a pacifist, so the American "we" cannot be my "me," but to be alienated from the American "we" is not easy. I am a neophyte pacifist. I never really wanted to be a pacifist. I had learned from Reinhold Niebuhr that if you desire justice you had better be ready to kill someone along the way. But then John Howard Yoder and his extraordinary book, *The Politics of Jesus*, came along.[3] Yoder convinced me that if there is anything to this Christian "stuff," it must surely involve the conviction that the Son would rather die on the cross than have the world to be redeemed by violence. Moreover, the defeat of death through resurrection makes possible as well as necessary that Christians live nonviolently in a world of violence. Christian nonviolence is not a strategy to rid the world of violence, but rather the way Christians must live in a world of violence. In short, Christians are not nonviolent because we believe our nonviolence is a strategy to rid the world of war, but rather hopefully as faithful followers of Christ in a world of war we cannot imagine being anything other than nonviolent.

But what does a pacifist have to say in the face of the terror September 11, 2001, names? I vaguely knew when I first declared I was a pacifist that it might have some serious consequences. To be nonviolent might even change my life. But I do not really think I understood what that change might entail until September 11. For example, after I declared I was a pacifist, I quit singing "The Star-Spangled Banner." I will stand when it is sung, particularly at baseball games, but I do not sing. Not to sing "The Star-Spangled Banner" is a small thing that reminds me that my first loyalty is not to the United States but to God and God's church. I confess it never crossed

---

3. John Howard Yoder, *The Politics of Jesus: Vicit Agnus Noster* (2d ed. Grand Rapids: Eerdmans, 1995).

my mind that such small acts might over the years make my response to September 11 quite different from that of the good people who sing "God Bless America"—so different that I am left in saddened silence.

That difference, moreover, haunts me. My father was a bricklayer and a good American. He worked hard all his life and hoped his work would not only support his family but make some contribution to our common life. He held a critical job in World War II, so he was never drafted. Only one of his five bricklaying brothers was in that war, but he was never exposed to combat. My family was never militarized, but even as Texans they were good Americans. For most of my life I too was a good American, assuming that I owed much to the society that enabled me, the son of a bricklayer, to gain a Ph.D. at Yale—even if the Ph.D. was in theology.[4]

Of course there was Vietnam. For many of us Vietnam was extended training necessary for the development of a more critical attitude toward the government of the United States. Yet most of us critical of the war in Vietnam did not think our opposition to that war made us less loyal Americans. Indeed the criticisms of the war were based on appeal to the highest American ideals. Vietnam was a time of great tension, but the politics of the anti-war movement did not require those opposed to the war to think of themselves as fundamentally standing outside the American mainstream. Most critics of Vietnam (just as many that now criticize the war in Afghanistan) based their dissent on their adherence to American ideals, which they felt the war was betraying. That but indicates why I feel so isolated even among the critics of the war in Afghanistan. I do not even share their allegiance

---

4. I find it interesting how many essays written in response to September 11, 2001, invite the use of the first person plural as I have done in this essay. This is as true for those who support the "war on terrorism" as those who oppose it. The essays in *Dissent from the Homeland: Essays after September 11*, edited by Stanley Hauerwas and Frank Lentricchia (Durham: Duke University Press, 2002), essays critical of the American response, are unusual for the personal tone struck in so many of the essays. I take this to be an indication of how deeply the event of September 11, 2001, challenges us. I suspect that many who support the "war on terrorism" do so because it elicits deep and profound emotion shaped by World War II. I do not mean to belittle such emotion, but rather to observe that I often suspect that those who defend war on the basis of just war theory do so because they are emotionally disposed to support war on grounds other than just war. I suspect the same mechanism is in play for those like me who declare we are pacifist. I call attention to this presumption not to undercut argument about the morality of war, but rather to remind just warriors and pacifists alike that moral reflection on war entails, if we are to do it well, a disciplining of our emotions. I continue to think as I argued some time ago that we have war because we cannot break the habit of war that so determines our imaginations. See for example the chapter "Should War Be Eliminated?" in my *Against the Nations: War and Survival in Liberal Societies* (Notre Dame, Ind.: University of Notre Dame Press, 1992), pp. 169–208.

to American ideals, particularly when such "ideals" are nothing more than *ideological* abstractions.

So I simply did not share the reaction of most Americans to the destruction of the World Trade Center. Of course I recoil from murder on such a scale, but I hope I remember that one murder is too many. That Americans have hurried to call what happened "war" strikes me as self-defeating. If this is war, then bin Laden has won. He thinks he is a warrior, not a murderer. Just to the extent that the language of war is used, he is honored. But in their hurry to call this war, Americans have no time for careful discriminations.

But where does that leave me? Does it mean, as an estranged friend recently wrote me, that I disdain all "natural loyalties" that bind us together as human beings, even submitting such loyalties to a harsh and unforgiving standard? Does it mean that I speak as a "solitary individual," failing to acknowledge that our lives are interwoven with the lives of others, those who have gone before, those among whom we live, those with whom we identify, and those with whom we are in Christian communion? Do I refuse to acknowledge that my life is made possible by the gifts of others? Do I forsake all forms of patriotism, failing to acknowledge that we as a people are better off because of the sacrifices that were made in World War II? To this I can only answer, "Yes."[5] If you call patriotism "natural," I certainly do disavow that connection. Such a disavowal, I hope, does not mean that I am inattentive to the gifts I have received from past and present neighbors.

In response to my friend I pointed out that because he too is a Christian I assumed he also disdained some "natural loyalties." After all, he had his children baptized. The "natural love" between parents and children is surely reconfigured when children are baptized into the death and resurrection of Christ. Paul says:

> Do you not know that all of us who have been baptized into Christ Jesus were baptized into his death? Therefore we have been buried with him by baptism into death, so that, just as Christ was raised from the dead by the glory of the Father, so we too might walk in the newness of life. For if we have been united with him in a death like his, we will certainly be united with him in a resurrection like his. (Romans 6: 3–5)

5. I do not mean this "yes" to accept all the presuppositions behind this list of questions. I certainly do not speak as a "solitary individual," because the way I speak is possible only through what I have learned from others. I also do not think that a stance of nonviolence requires that we reject the gifts of sacrifice made by those who have fought in past wars. No account of nonviolence can be true that does not honor conscientious participation in war, which is a reminder that the way our lives are narrated is crucial for any perspective we take on war. Christian nonviolence names the narrative portrayal of our lives that helps us go on accepting our past without the need to repeat it.

Christians often tend to focus on being united with Christ in his resurrection, thereby forgetting that we are also united with him in his death. What could that mean if it does not mean that Christians must be ready to die, indeed have their children die, rather than betray the gospel? Any love not transformed by the love of God cannot help but be the source of the violence we perpetrate on one another in the name of justice. Such a love may appear harsh and dreadful from the perspective of the world, but Christians believe such a love is life-giving not life-denying.

Of course living a life of nonviolence may be harsh. Certainly you have to imagine, and perhaps even face, that you will have to watch the innocent suffer and even die for your convictions. But that is no different from those who claim they would fight a just war. After all, the just warrior is committed to avoiding any direct attack on noncombatants, which might well mean that more people will die because the just warrior refuses to do an evil that a good may come. For example, on just war grounds the bombings of Hiroshima and Nagasaki were clearly murder. If you are serious about just war, you must be ready to say that it would be better that more people died on the beaches of Japan than to have committed one murder, much less the bombing of civilian populations.

I need to be very clear. I hope the kind of criticisms I am making of the American response as a pacifist will not be heard as just one more version of the anti-American sentiments expressed by what many consider to be the American Left. I say "what many consider" because it is very unclear if there is a Left left in America. Nowhere is that more apparent than in the support given to the war on terrorism by those who identify as the "left." Yet much has been made by some of the injustice of American foreign policy that gives a kind of intelligibility to the hatred given form on September 11. I am no defender of American foreign policy, but the problem with such lines of criticism is that no matter how immoral what the American government may have done in the world, such immorality cannot explain or justify the attack on the World Trade Center.

American imperialism, often celebrated as the new globalism, is a frightening power. It is frightening not only because of the harm such power inflicts on the innocent, but because it is difficult to imagine alternatives. For example, pacifists are often challenged after an event like September 11 with the question: "Well, what alternative do you have to bombing Afghanistan?" Such questions assume that pacifists must have an alternative foreign policy. My only response is that I do not have a foreign policy. I have something better—a church constituted by people who would rather die than kill.

Indeed I fear that absent a countercommunity to challenge America, bin Laden has given Americans what they so desperately needed—a war without end. America is a country that lives off the moral capital of our wars. War names the time we send the youth to kill and die (maybe) in an effort to assure ourselves that the lives we lead are worthy of such sacrifices. They kill and die to protect our "freedom." But what can freedom mean if the prime instance of the exercise of such freedom is to shop? The very fact that we can and do go to war is a moral necessity for a nation of consumers. War makes clear that we must believe in something even if we are not sure what that something is, except that we are sure it has something to do with "the American way of life."

What a gift bin Laden has therefore given America. Americans were in despair because we won the Cold War. Americans won by outspending the USSR, proving that we can waste more money on guns than they were able to waste. But what do Americans do after they have won a war? The war was necessary to give moral coherence. They had to cooperate with one another because we were at war. How can America make sense of what it means for us to be "a people" if we have no common enemy? We were in a dangerous funk having nothing better to do than entertain ourselves with the soap opera named Bill Clinton. Now we have something better to do. We can fight the war against terrorism—a description that only further degrades the description "war" by making the war on terrorism on par with the war on drugs or the war on crime.

The good thing, moreover, about the war on terrorism is that it has no end. That it has no end makes it very doubtful that this war can be considered just. If a war is to be just, your enemy must know before the war begins what specifiable political purpose the war is to serve. In other words, they need to know from the beginning what the conditions are if they choose to surrender. So you cannot fight a just war if it is "a war to end all wars" (WWI) or for "unconditional surrender" (WWII). But a "war on terrorism" is a war without limit. Americans want to wipe this enemy off the face of the earth. Moreover, America even gets to decide who counts and does not count as a terrorist, which means Americans get to have it any way they want it. For example, some are captured as prisoners of war; some are detainees. No problem. When you are the biggest kid on the block, you can say whatever you want to say, even if what you say is nonsense. No problem. We all know the first casualty in war is truth. So the conservatives who have fought the war against "postmodernism" in the name of "objective truth," the same conservatives who now rule us, assume they can use language any way they please.

That Americans get to decide who is and who is not a terrorist means not only that this is a war without clear purpose, but that it is also a war without end. From now on we can be in a perpetual state of war. America is always at her best when we are on permanent war footing. Moreover, when you are at war you have no time for the poor, you have no space to worry about the extraordinary inequities that constitute this society, you cannot worry about those parts of the world that are ravaged by hunger and genocide. Everything—civil liberties, due process, the protection of the law—must be subordinated to the one great moral enterprise of winning the unending war against terrorism.

At the heart of the American desire to wage endless war is the American fear of death. The American love of high-tech medicine is but the other side of the war against terrorism. Americans are determined to be safe, to be able to get out of this life alive. On September 11, Americans were confronted with their worst fear—a people ready to die as an expression of their profound moral commitments. Some speculate that such people must have chosen death because they were desperate or, at least, they were so desperate that death was preferable to life. Yet their willingness to die stands in stark contrast to a politics that asks of its members in response to September 11 to shop.

Ian Buruma and Vishai Margalit observe in an article, "Occidentalism," that lack of heroism is the hallmark of a bourgeois ethos.[6] Heroes court death. The bourgeois is addicted to personal safety. They concede that much in an affluent, market-driven society is mediocre, "but when contempt for bourgeois creature comforts becomes contempt for life itself you know the West is under attack." According to Buruma and Margalit, the West (which they point out is not just the geographical West) should oppose the full force of calculating anti-bourgeois heroism, of which Al-Qaeda is but one representative, through the means we know best—for example, by cutting off their money supply. Of course, Buruma and Margalit do not tell us how that can be done, given the need for oil to sustain the bourgeois society they favor.

Christians are not called to be heroes or shoppers. We are called to be holy. We do not that think holiness is an individual achievement, but rather a set of practices to sustain a people who refuse to have their lives determined by the fear and denial of death. We believe that by so living we offer our non-Christian brothers and sisters an alternative to all politics based on the denial of death. Christians are acutely aware that we seldom are faithful to the gifts God has given us, but we hope the confession of our sins is a sign of hope in a world without hope.

6. Ian Buruma and Vishai Margalit, "Occidentalism," *New York Review of Books* (January 17, 2002), pp. 4–7.

This means that pacifists do have a response to September 11, 2001. Our response is to continue living in a manner that witnesses to our belief that the world was not changed on September 11, 2001. The world was changed during the celebration of a Passover in 33 A.D.

Mark and Louise Zwick, founders of the Houston Catholic Worker House of Hospitality, embody the life made possible by the death and resurrection of Jesus. They know, moreover, that Christian non-violence cannot and must not be understood as a position that is no more than being "against violence." If pacifism is no more than "not violence," it betrays the form of life to which Christians believe they have been called by Christ. Drawing on Nicholay Berdyayev, the Zwicks rightly observe that "the split between the Gospel and our culture is the drama of our times," but they also remind us that "one does not free persons by detaching them from the bonds that paralyze them: one frees persons by attaching them to their destiny." Christian non-violence is but another name for the friendship that we believe God has made possible and that constitutes the alternative to the violence that grips our lives.

I began by noting that I am not sure for what I should pray. But prayer often is a form of silence. The following prayer I hope does not drown out silence. I wrote the prayer as a devotion to begin a Duke Divinity School general meeting. I was able to write the prayer because of a short article I had just read in the *Houston Catholic Worker* (November 16, 2001) by Jean Vanier. Vanier is the founder of the La Arche movement—a movement that believes God's salvation has given us the time to live and learn to be friends with those the world calls "retarded." I end with this prayer because it is all I have to give.

Great God of surprise, our lives continue to be haunted by the spectre of September 11, 2001. Life must go on and we go on keeping on—even meeting again as the Divinity School Council. Is this what Barth meant in 1933 when he said we must go on "as though nothing has happened"? To go on as though nothing has happened can sound like a counsel of despair, of helplessness, of hopelessness. We want to act, to do something to reclaim the way things were, which, I guess, is but a reminder that one of the reasons we are so shocked, so violated, by September 11 is the challenge presented to our prideful presumption that we are in control, that we are going to get out of life alive. To go on "as though nothing has happened" surely requires us to acknowledge that you are God and we are not. It is hard to remember that Jesus did not come to make us safe, but rather he came to make us disciples, citizens of your new age, a kingdom of surprise. That we live in the end times is surely the basis for our conviction that you have given us all the time we need to respond to September 11 with "small acts of beauty and tenderness," which Jean

Vanier tells us, if done with humility and confidence, "will bring unity to the world and break the chain of violence." So we pray, give us humility that we may remember that the work we do today, the work we do every day, is false and pretentious if it fails to serve those who day in and day out are your small gestures of beauty and tenderness.

10

SEPTEMBER 11, 2001

A Sermon a Year Later

MICAH 4:1–5
EPHESIANS 2:13–18
MATTHEW 5:43–48

September 11, 2001, a day of terror. September 11, 2001, "a day of infamy" for those who remember Pearl Harbor. September 11, 2001, a day when I remember where I was and what I was doing, not unlike when I heard that Kennedy had been shot. September 11, 2001, a day that changed the world for those who long to live in the world without change. September 11, 2001, a day in which Americans discovered senseless violence can be quite effective particularly because it is senseless. September 11, 2001, a day when Christians, long accommodated to the sentimentalities of American culture, discovered that they had nothing of use to say.

A year later we find we are still silence-wrapped—a silence that could be redemptive if it were an expression of patient sadness. But such a silence is hard. The images are too strong. We try to resist, to forget, but such forgetting seems too much like a betrayal of those who died. We remember the beautiful arc the second plane made before erupting into the brilliant fireball that burned away any hope that all might not be lost. The terror those in the upper floors must have felt knowing they were doomed. Bodies, desperate bodies, choosing to float briefly on air rather than be trapped and incinerated. It was as if the whole world was caught in slow motion as the great towers imploded leaving barren sky. New York, New York, no longer a wonderful town. We divert our gaze, not wanting to be reminded of what is missing.

An apocalyptic moment Christians in America cannot ignore. Surely something like how we felt as we survived the days after September 11, 2001, is how the followers of Jesus felt after the crucifixion. Pure terror. The one on whom all hope was placed, the one we gave up all to follow, the one we had hoped was the one to redeem Israel, dead. It is not even clear who killed him or why he was killed. Another meaningless death against the blackness of a meaningless cosmos. Best to face the fact that it is kill or be killed. In such a world meaning is determined by those with the largest swords. They are the ones who will write the histories making it possible for us to know what "really happened."

Thank God, for the time being we are on the winning side. We get to call the violently secured order that makes our lives possible—peace. Only terrorists refuse to accept the peace our order names. The only way, moreover, to deal with the terrorist is vengeance. Justice demands vengeance. We cannot let the innocent die meaningless deaths. They were not victims. No American gets to die a victim. Sacrificially they died that we might live. They are freedom's martyrs. Lives made more significant by how they died than could have ever been imagined by how they lived. Their deaths will not be in vain.

But wait: some say he has been raised from the dead. He appeared to the disciples showing them his nail-marked hands and feet. He even ate a broiled fish. He ascended to heaven and they worshiped him. Worshiped him? You can only worship God. Yet it says clearly, Luke 24:52, that they worshiped him. What are we to make of that? We confess we are not quite sure. We have been at it for two thousand years and we are still "not quite sure." We often think we must find some way to explain the meaning of his death. We call such efforts "atonement theories." But the Scripture makes clear that we do not get to vindicate Christ. We do not need to avenge his death. His ascension to the Father is the only vindication needed.

In his book *He Came Preaching Peace*,[1] John Howard Yoder observes that in the New Testament the death of Christ is sometimes described as a sacrifice, sometimes as a ransom, descriptions we normally assume

1. John H. Yoder, *He Came Preaching Peace* (Scottdale, Pa.; Kitchener, Ontario: Herald Press, 1965.

name our reconciliation with God over the barrier of our sins. But Yoder observes that the barrier between people, a barrier as real as the wall of masonry in Jerusalem that separated the outer court for Gentiles from the temple proper, is not anybody's sins. Rather,

> the barrier is the historical fact of separate stories. It is not a barrier of guilt, but of culture and communication. It is not a barrier between each person and God but between one group and another. It is not the case that inner or personal peace comes first, with the hope that once the inward condition is set right then the restored person will do some social good. In this text it is the other way around. Two estranged *histories* are made into one. Two hostile *communities* are reconciled. (Pp. 111–12)

Note the breaking of this barrier is not something we must try to do. The breaking has been done. What was hidden from the ages is now revealed. We live in a new time. We live in an apocalyptic time. So it is only now that the rulers and authorities, the principalities and powers, can learn through the church what the rich variety of God's wisdom has always been (Eph. 3:10–11). God has judged between the peoples, God has beat the swords of the nations into plowshares. God has abolished war. We need no longer to learn of war.

But who are the "we" who no longer learn of war? Why are they those who were taught by the One raised that we must love our enemies? How can we possibly be told to love enemies—enemies who think nothing of wanton murder? A good question, but one those who live in the new age inaugurated by Christ need not ask. We know it is possible to love our enemies. Otherwise why would Christ in the Sermon on the Mount ask that we so love? Are we to make Christ a liar? If we do not think it possible to love our enemies, then we should plainly say Jesus is not the Messiah. But Jesus is the Messiah, not dead but alive, indeed present to us in this meal of the new age.

So we find ourselves living in the aftermath of two apocalyptic events. Those events produce two peoples with two quite different stories. The one fears and worships death as their only lord; the other fears and worships the Lord of death. The people of the September 11 apocalypse, the people who worship death, do not believe that God has removed the barrier between Jew and Gentile. The people of the September 11 apocalypse do not believe that Jesus has been raised from death. So these people of the September 11 apocalypse are determined to have vengeance. They are determined to make their world safe no matter what cost others must bear to ensure their safety. The people of the September 11 apocalypse rage against death, believing through the memory of their accomplishments that they do not have to die.

Jesus people are also an apocalyptic people. They are so because they worship the Lord of death. Like the people of the September 11 apocalypse, the Jesus people are also a storied people. But they do not think that they get to make their story up. Their story, moreover, is certainly not a story of their accomplishments. It is a story of their sinful unfaithfulness. It is the story of their living as if the work God accomplished in Christ is somehow not sufficient for our salvation. It is the story of the impatience of the Jesus people, desperate to convince ourselves and those outside the church that our God exists and on the whole is a pretty good guy. It is the story of our unwillingness to acknowledge to ourselves and others that we live in a dangerous world, a world of death, made all the more dangerous by our unbridled desire for safety.

If that is the story of the Jesus people, why, we must ask, would anyone want to be part of that story? The world is terrible enough. Why cannot we recognize that when all is said and done, we are pretty much the same, so let's just try to get along? Tempted though they may be by that story, the Jesus people know that it cannot be their story. It cannot be their story because their story is not really about them. The story that makes the Jesus people a storied people is the story of God and God's unfailing love for us. How extraordinary. How wonderful. It really is not all about "us." It is about God. A God not rendered powerless by events like September 11, 2001, but the God who has made his church, the Jesus people, the alternative to those who would rule the world in the name of putting right the terror of September 11, 2001.

But are we Jesus people? We think we might like to be Jesus people, but we know we are those storied by September 11, 2001. We may not want "to kill the bastards," but the images and the feelings we felt that day cannot be denied. I am not suggesting that we simply try harder to be Jesus people. Such trying I fear too often only increases our narcissism, underwriting the presumption that it is all about us. Perhaps a beginning is to recognize that we are an apocalyptic people, a new age people, who have been given all we need not to be captured by the powers fueled by our fear of death. Such a people do not need to try to be better, but rather only to receive the gifts we have been given.

Gifts as simple as bread and wine made by the Spirit the body and blood of the One whose sacrifice is the end of all sacrifice. At this table we find God's justice. We deserve death, but God refuses our refusal, making us his storied people, his Jesus people, so that the world may know that there is an alternative to terror. That alternative, at once terrible and wonderful, is us. Here at this table God lifts us up so that we become for the world the end of all sacrifices.

How extraordinary. How frightening. How wonderful. Amen.

POSTSCRIPT

A *Response to Jeff Stout's* Democracy and Tradition

1. WHY THIS POSTSCRIPT

If, as I argue in *Performing the Faith*, all life is contingency, it is a happy accident that Jeff Stout's new book, *Democracy and Tradition*, recently became available.[1] I hope that *Performing the Faith* will be read in the light of the criticisms Stout makes of my work in *Democracy and Tradition*. Stout has made a fresh conversation possible between those who support democratic aspirations and those, like myself, who have worried that the justifications often given for liberal democracies render strong Christian convictions politically irrelevant and imply that such convictions have no purchase on the way things are. In *Democracy and Tradition* Stout distances himself from Rawls and Rorty, who (each for different reasons but with the same effect) deny that religious convictions can play a role in democratic deliberations.[2] As a result, I hope Stout's new book will inaugurate the kind of discussion that is so desperately needed in America.

1. Jeff Stout, *Democracy and Tradition* (Princeton, N.J.: Princeton University Press, 2004). Page references to *Democracy and Tradition* will appear in the text.

2. Rorty, it seems, now grants Stout's point. See Rorty, "Religion in the Public Square: A Reconsideration," *Journal of Religious Ethics* 31 (spring 2003): 141–49. He reconsiders, however, only on the condition that "ecclesiastical organizations" stay sequestered. Rorty thinks religion at best must limit itself to "pastoral care." He has little to fear because that has become the function for most churches in America.

My enthusiasm for Stout's book may seem odd because Stout develops his argument for democracy through an extensive criticism of my work. According to Stout, I—along with John Milbank and Alasdair MacIntyre—represent a position he calls the "new traditionalist." Stout believes we are right to argue "that ethical and political reasoning are creatures of tradition and crucially depend on the acquisition of such virtues as practical wisdom and justice" (p. 11). But because we mistakenly think modern democracy is an expression of secularism, we encourage Christians to abandon the democratic project. Though Stout is extremely critical of Milbank, I think it is fair to say that MacIntyre and I are the subject of Stout's most thorough critique. I suspect this is the case because Stout thinks we are close enough to being right that we are more dangerous than Milbank. Yet what makes Stout's criticism of my work so important is that Stout and I now seem to agree more than we disagree, which means our disagreements are all the more interesting.

However, Stout is concerned about my influence. Indeed, I am taken aback by Stout's assessment of my work's effect. According to Stout "no theologian has done more to inflame Christian resentment of secular political culture" than I (p. 140). I have no idea whether he is right to suggest that I now have an audience "larger than any other theological ethicist in the world" (p. 157), but even if that is true, it cannot mean I am as much a threat to democracy as Stout thinks I am. How large could the audience be that reads theological ethics? "Theological ethicists" are not exactly intellectual icons among the cultural elites of our day. Moreover, as far as I can tell the influence I have had on Christians or even those in the ministry is not widespread. I cannot deny that over the past few years I have received a kind of notoriety that I neither sought nor desired. It would be stupid to say I found the attention without benefit, but it is also a very mixed blessing.[3] Given what I think about the work God

3. When I was told by David Reid, the director of communications in the Divinity School at Duke, that I was to be named "America's Best Theologian" by *TIME* magazine, I responded, " 'Best' is not a theological category. We are judged by whether we are faithful or unfaithful." I report this response not to indicate I have an appropriate humility about such recognition. (How would anyone know if they were appropriately "humble"?) But at least my response indicates that I have some sense that I recognize the irony that the secular media cannot quite get a fix on me. As far as I am concerned such recognition is a form of secular power that I certainly will try to exploit in the hope more Christians and non-Christians alike may think again about Christianity and in particular Christian nonviolence. Of course, you have to be very careful about such "exploitation" because what you think you are "using" can become who you are.

I have no explanation for the attention my work has been receiving, but if I have any positive account it is quite simply that I have something to say. It is not that I have something to say because of who I am, but that I have something to say because Christians have something to say that is not just what everyone already knows. If that is the case, then I am extremely grateful that God has so used me.

has given Christians, I am not interested in being "noticed." Christians are called to endure, not to win.[4] Yet Stout seems to believe that almost alone I have persuaded Christians to give up on democracy.[5]

Why should I, therefore, be so enthusiastic about a book that is so critical of me? The reason is very simple. Jeff Stout thinks theology matters. That he does so is not only a great gift to me, but to all Christians. That he has taken the time to read my work—to take what I say seriously, to criticize what I have said—is an act of charity I gratefully accept. Moreover, that he has taken the time to read and criticize me is not simply an act of friendship, though I am honored that he claims me as a friend, but is at the heart of the position he develops in *Democracy and Tradition*. For, contrary to the intellectual culture of our day, Stout argues that pragmatic rationality, what he calls "expressive rationality" (p. 12), does not entail the exclusion of strong theological claims being considered true.[6] He even suggests that democracy will suffer "if orthodox

4. This is not the place to explore the differences between Milbank's work and my way of doing theology, but I think the most profound difference has to do with why I think enduring is so important for how Christians are to learn to live in the world as we find it. Milbank wants Christians to win. (That John wants to win, of course, is a correlative of his defense of Christendom. Milbank may be right to claim that "Once there was no secular," but I think the Christianity for which there was no secular had its own problems. So the secular for me is a gift to humble the prideful pretensions of a church that needed humbling.) I think at best we should want as Christians to endure. There is an impatience—what some take to be an arrogance—to John's work that I admire, but I cannot follow. Such a difference, I suspect, is most clearly apparent in our different understandings of violence and the Christian use of violence. Of course one of the major differences between Milbank and me is that I do not have John's intellectual ambitions. Milbank is not only able but thinks it's desirable to take on, so to speak, "the world" more than I can or think necessary. As I suggested in an earlier article about him, what John wants to do at the highest level of abstraction, I must try to do much closer to the ground. See my "Creation, Contingency, and Truthful Nonviolence: A Milbankian Reflection," in *Wilderness Wanderings: Probing Twentieth-Century Theology and Philosophy* (Boulder, Colo.: Westview, 1997), pp. 188–98.

5. Stout also makes this claim in his "Postscript: A Response to Donagan and Hauerwas" in the Princeton edition of *Ethics after Babel: The Languages of Morals and Their Discontents* (Princeton, N.J.: Princeton University Press, 2001), p. 343.

6. In an extremely important footnote, Stout acknowledges he once did argue that the rationality of religious convictions could not pass muster in the kind of world in which we now live. He observes such a position was mistaken in at least two ways: (1) it wrongly attributed more uniformity to modernity than is justified and (2) such a view "employed an implausible rigorist standard of justification, which did in effect stack the deck against the possibility that a modern individual could be epistemically responsible in holding religious beliefs" (p. 317). In the same footnote Stout criticizes Phil Kenneson and me for not recognizing in a review article of the first edition of *Ethics after Babel* that he had explicitly rejected his earlier position. There he observes that "some version of theology could be true and the theologian's position at the margins of modern intellectual culture could be evidence of the decadence of that culture" (p. 187). That seems

Christians are unable to find a way to maintain their own convictions while also taking up their responsibilities as citizens" (p. 116).[7]

That is why I think it appropriate to attach this "Postscript" at the end of *Performing the Faith*. Stout sees clearly that questions of the rationality of Christian convictions cannot be separated from politics. Stout's understanding of practical reason and his defense of democracy are of a piece. Like the good pragmatist he is, Stout argues that democracy is not the rejection of tradition but

> a culture, a tradition, in its own right. It has an ethical life of its own, which philosophers would do well to articulate. Pragmatism is best viewed as an attempt to bring the notions of democratic deliberation and tradition together in a single philosophical vision. To put the point aphoristically and paradoxically, *pragmatism is democratic traditionalism*. Less paradoxically, one could say that pragmatism is the philosophical space in which democratic rebellion against hierarchy combines with traditionalist love of virtue to form a new intellectual tradition that is indebted to both. (P. 13)

---

right to me, but it also means that Stout should at least credit those of us who try to point out what such a "decadence" looks like. See *Wilderness Wanderings*, pp. 97–110.

Stout makes the important observation that "what makes some people religious is that the vocabularies in which they tell the story of their lives—including the stories of our common religious life—have religious content. Like Rorty, they tend to be speechless when pressed for linear reasons for adopting their final vocabularies. But unless those vocabularies become severely problematical, what reason would they have for abandoning them?" (p. 89). Stout is right to direct attention to "vocabularies," but there are indications in his book that he assumes that certain words, e.g., "justice," in our different vocabularies mean the same thing. I will try to show below that, without ruling out family resemblances, I think certain words—and in particular "justice"—may work very differently for Christians than for those who do not share Christian practices. I owe this point to Brad Kallenberg.

7. In the sentence just prior to the one quoted here, Stout observes that theologically most of the theologians he welcomes to the democratic conversation are "moving in the direction of heresies that I embrace, so I welcome their company" (p. 116). That is a fascinating comment, which makes me want to know more about the heresies with which Stout identifies. Heretics are blessed for Christians because we often do not know what we believe until someone claims to believe what we discover we do not believe. Stout is obviously an extraordinarily sympathetic reader of Christian theology though he does not count himself a Christian. In a lovely autobiographical paragraph in *Democracy and Tradition* (p. 91), Stout notes in college he "moved rapidly down the path that leads from Schleiermacher to Feuerbach, Emerson, and beyond." But if that is the case, I must ask why Stout thinks Emerson can be counted as a heretic. Did Emerson himself think he was heretical? My impression is that Emerson thought he had left Christianity behind. So he did not share enough in common with the Christian tradition to be counted a heretic. I am fascinated, therefore, that Stout thinks Emerson's "beyond" is "heretical"—a high status that makes me want to know more. I particularly want to know more given the passages in *Democracy and Tradition* in which Stout expresses admiration for Karl Barth and, in particular, for George Hunsinger's Barthian social criticism.

Put bluntly, this is a position with which we Christians not only can, but should want to, do business.[8] Stout does try to give an account of democratic life that is not in the first place state theory. I am extremely sympathetic with that project. Stout's understanding of practical reason, the centrality of the virtues, as well as the democratic tradition not only makes it possible for us to have a conversation, but makes such a conversation imperative. That does not mean, however, that I am ready to concede every point he makes in criticism of me. Rather, it makes it all the more important for me to respond to such criticisms in the same spirit they were made, that is, in the hope that we each might come to a better understanding of what is at stake in the differences we represent.

Before I respond to Stout's criticisms, I want to make one more general observation about why I think what Stout has done in *Democracy and Tradition* is so important. That observation is quite simple: Stout has something to say, and he cares passionately about what he writes. That may seem a given, but in the academic culture Stout and I inhabit, too often criticism by academics of one another is but a game or, worse, a "career move." In contrast, Stout obviously cares about the community he describes in the "Conclusion" of *Democracy and Tradition* (pp. 300–307). I should like to think I care as deeply as Stout does for the communities, and in particular the churches, that sustain my life, which is but a way to say why I find Stout's challenge to me so important. Neither of us is merely trying to score points.[9] Rather we are trying to understand

8. However, I do have to register my unease with Stout's dislike of hierarchy. I realize he thinks he is following Emerson and Whitman in this respect, but I do not see why he thinks Whitman's understanding of the priest as one who declares an imaginative work to be an account of the priesthood we ought to accept (p. 30). Stout celebrates the demise of the authority of the priest in Catholicism, which is odd, given his commitment to respect other traditions (p. 31). The authority of the bishop, in which the priest shares, is necessary to keep the process of interpretation open, not to shut it down. Of course such authority has been abused, but that does not make it illegitimate. That Stout seems to think what has happened to the priesthood in America a "good thing" betrays just a bit his willingness to respect religious traditions. I wrote this "Postscript" as well as this footnote prior to reading John Milbank's *Being Reconciled: Ontology and Pardon* (London: Routledge, 2003), in which Milbank provides an account of the role of the bishop quite similar to the one I try to suggest (pp. 124–26). Milbank notes: that the theologian is answerable to the bishop is not a spatial hierarchy but "rather a hierarchical, educative *manductio* of the faith down the ages. Equally the theologian is answerable to a specific location, or even multiple specific localities, such that his or her sense of perpetuating a history must be combined with a sense of carrying out an archaeology and mapping a geography. Finally, s/he is also answerable to the mode of the reception of sacrament and word by the congregation, even if this is now in the early twenty-first century frequently impossible and the theologian must exercise what is an excessive critical function by ideal standards" (p. 126). I confess I find this last sentence worrisome. About the last thing we need is for theologians to try to be heroes.

9. Stout, however, cannot resist taking a potshot now and again. For example, he suggests that many of my readers take consolation from my idea that strengthening their

and defend the convictions that constitute the lives of people whom we believe make our lives possible.

2. LIBERALISM, DEMOCRACY, THE VIRTUES

Stout develops his criticism of my position in chapter 6 of *Democracy and Tradition*. In order to understand his criticism of me, however, it is first important to attend to his critique of Milbank and MacIntyre in chapters 4 and 5. Just as important for understanding his criticisms of the three of us is the very interesting account of the importance of the virtue of piety for democratic life Stout develops in the first chapter. Drawing on Emerson and Whitman, Stout argues that democratic tradition requires a respect for the past that rightly appreciates the importance of history for any display of practical reason. Accordingly, he distances himself from liberal justifications of democracy, justifications that put proceduralism at the heart of democracy with the result that

---

identification with the church rather than the nation is the most important step one can take toward membership in a community of true virtue. As a result the "primary beneficiaries" of my revival of virtue ethics are not Dorothy Day but John Paul II and William Bennett (p. 296). I think Stout is simply having fun when he tries to make me responsible for Bennett. I can recognize someone having fun because I make similar rhetorical moves from time to time. Stout knows very well, however, that I wrote what I hope is a withering critique of Bennett in *After Christendom?* (Nashville: Abingdon, 1996), pp. 74–92. Charlie Pinches and I also briefly criticize Bennett's understanding of the virtues in *Christians among the Virtues: Theological Conversations with Ancient and Modern Ethics* (Notre Dame, Ind.: University of Notre Dame Press, 1997), p. 55. Bennett's recently disclosed addiction to gambling wonderfully exposes his failure to understand that the virtues, like the vices, are habits, not "value recommendations." (Of course, Aquinas rightly argues that the virtuous habits confer dispositional coherence; whereas the habits that are vicious are "disordered.") If the revival of virtue ethics has benefited John Paul II, then I think (as I am sure Dorothy Day would have thought) that is a very good thing.

Stout also suggests in the same paragraph (p. 296) that I have not seen fit to remind American Christians that as a majority in a wealthy world power they display the character of their community by discharging their responsibilities well or poorly as citizens. I take this to be a suggestion that I have not shown appropriate sympathy with liberation theology. I am not sure if anything I could say to these charges would be adequate, but I do want to call attention to the "Preface" I wrote to the 1996 edition of *After Christendom?* There I provide a quite appreciative reading of Gustavo Gutiérrez's *Las Casas: In Search of the Poor of Jesus*. I doubt this "Preface" would change Stout's dislike of *After Christendom?* but I have sometimes thought he hates the title more than what I actually say in the book. The subtitle (*How the Church Is to Behave If Freedom, Justice, and a Christian Nation Are Bad Ideas*) was not mine but suggested by an editor at Abingdon Press. This does not mean I should not be held responsible for the impression the title gives that I think justice is a bad idea. What I think are bad ideas are abstract accounts of justice divorced from the practices through which people discover the goods they have in common.

managers rule in a manner that squelches the conversation constitutive of democracy.

Stout rightly notes that Augustine maintained that true virtue is impossible without true piety, which for Augustine is the right worship of the true God. This means the piety that characterizes democracies is not the same as Augustinian piety. Yet Stout calls attention to those Augustinians (Reinhold Niebuhr, Paul Ramsey, and Jean Elshtain) whom he thinks rightly judge democracy to be the best form of rule for which Christians can hope because of the ambivalence that is at the heart of democratic piety. So from Stout's perspective Milbank's position is a particularly perverse form of Augustinianism, because he turns Augustinian ambivalence toward any political order into a traditionalist rejection of secular society (pp. 26–27).

Stout's strategy in his chapter on Milbank, therefore, is to develop an alternative account of secularization to challenge Milbank's account of "the secular" as determinatively anti-Christian and violent. According to Stout, Milbank wrongly underwrites the narrative that makes secularization the inevitable outcome of modernity. Such narratives not only oversimplify the complex character of modernity, but fail to see that secularization primarily concerns "what can be taken for granted when exchanging reasons in public settings" (p. 97).[10] Stout does not deny that

10. Stout may be right to try to defend this much more chastened sense of secularization, but surely more needs to be said concerning why the "sources," in Charles Taylor's sense, now seem to make strong Christian convictions unintelligible. I find it interesting, for example, that Stout never discusses the significance of the distinction between the public and the private—a distinction, I believe, that has had deleterious effects for the good order of the church. I am aware that the distinction may not have been intended to apply to the church itself; but too often Christians uncritically assume the distinction between the private and the public should govern the politics of the church. Of course, that is a Christian problem, which means some account of the distinction may make sense for "secular" political life. But even in the workings of the politics about which Stout cares so deeply, the distinction between the public and the private often invites arbitrary judgments.

I have always been rather careful not to "buy into" any one account of the development of "the secular." One reason for my hesitancy is because there are too many "seculars" to assume any one cause. Stout may be right, however, that my appeals to Milbank commit me to Milbank's views about the development of the secular. I remain unconvinced, however, that Milbank's account in *Theology and Social Theory* (Oxford, U.K.: Basil Blackwell, 1990) is as misguided as Stout thinks. I think it is increasingly clear that one of the sources of secularization is the characterizations Christians have used against one another. See, for example, Ephraim Radner, *The End of the Church: A Pneumatology of Christian Division in the West* (Grand Rapids: Eerdmans, 1998). I do not, however, accept the narrative that says secular regimes were required because of the "religious wars." Stout's narrative sometimes seems to suggest he assumes just that view of the so-called wars of religion (p. 100). If he does so, he has to respond to William Cavanaugh's "A Fire Strong Enough to Consume the House: The Wars of Religion and the Rise of the State," *Modern Theology* 11 (1995): 397–420. What Cavanaugh helps us see is that "secularization," at least in some of its modes,

some defenders of democracy clearly have more robust understandings of secularization that in principle do preclude strong religious convictions in the so-called public arena. But Stout thinks such accounts are mistaken. According to Stout, Milbank's resentment against a world that does not privilege Christianity results in an authoritarian dismissal of "the secular" and as a result he fails to appreciate the achievement of democracy. In opposition to Milbank, Stout recommends the Barthian politics of a George Hunsinger as an alternative that is appropriate in a democratic culture, or at least in the kind of democratic society that Stout is willing to defend (pp. 112–17).[11]

Stout's criticism of MacIntyre—like his criticism of me—is that MacIntyre's critiques of liberalism and/or modernity have effectively convinced many to give up their support for democracy. Stout agrees with MacIntyre's contention that liberalism is a tradition, but contrary to MacIntyre, Stout argues that liberalism can acknowledge it is so without contradiction (p. 129).[12] Stout, however, recommends that a better alternative than reconceiving liberalism would be quite simply to quit talking about "the liberal project." We should do so because, like the description "modernity," liberalism turns out to be too various to be given any singular identity. If, as MacIntyre argues, a society is to be judged by the kind of people it produces, then, according to Stout, that MacIntyre's dislike of the social arrangements of "liberalism" is overly

---

was not inevitable but a project that was intended by determined political and economic actors. Stout discusses Cavanaugh's article "The City: Beyond Secular Parodies," which appeared in *Radical Orthodoxy* (London: Routledge, 1999), pp. 188–200, but dismisses Cavanaugh's account in that essay for assuming ideas matter. I suspect Stout thinks such a dismissal warranted because Cavanaugh is one of the advocates of "radical orthodoxy." However, Cavanaugh is not a card-carrying member of the "Radical Orthodoxy Movement." For a fuller account of Cavanaugh's arguments, see his book, *Theopolitical Imagination: Discovering the Liturgy as a Political Act in an Age of Global Consumerism* (London: T & T Clark, 2002). For an account of secularization that argues quite effectively that secularization was not an inevitable result of certain historical movements, but rather the result of a determined effort of a cultural elite, see *The Secular Revolution: Power, Interests, and Conflict in the Secularization of American Public Life*, ed. Christian Smith (Berkeley: University of California Press, 2003).

11. "The kind of democratic society that Stout is willing to defend" is a very important qualification that makes Stout's regard for Hunsinger's position, an admiration I share, a good deal more complex. George Hunsinger has long argued that we may well be living in a "confessing church" situation in America. At the very least that means Stout owes us some account of how he differs from Hunsinger's apocalyptic description of the challenges facing us in America. See Hunsinger's *Disruptive Grace: Studies in the Theology of Karl Barth* (Grand Rapids: Eerdmans, 2000), pp. 89–113.

12. MacIntyre has explicitly discussed this criticism of his work in "A Partial Response to My Critics," in *After MacIntyre: Critical Perspectives on the Work of Alasdair MacIntyre*, ed. John Horton and Susan Mendus (Notre Dame, Ind.: University of Notre Dame Press, 1994), pp. 292–93.

generalized is evident just to the extent that people buy his books, debate his ideas, and offer him distinguished professorships. So, contrary to MacIntyre's complaint, debate and genuine argument are possible in America (pp. 138–39).

Stout's arguments against Milbank and MacIntyre are more detailed than I have indicated. He challenges their reading of particular thinkers (Burke) and also calls attention to figures (Emerson) they overlook or ignore whose importance would make the story they tell more complex. I think, however, it is fair to say that Stout's primary argumentative strategy against Milbank and MacIntyre is to change the subject. Stout simply denies that the kind of democracy he is willing to defend reflects Milbank's or MacIntyre's understanding or criticisms of modernity or secularism.

Stout's criticisms of Milbank and MacIntyre serve to introduce his critique of my position. Stout alleges my criticism of modernity and secularity, like the work of Milbank and MacIntyre, fails to acknowledge the complex character of the world in which we find ourselves. Stout's criticism of my work, however, is more developed than his criticisms of Milbank and MacIntyre. Indeed, Stout provides a fascinating account of my intellectual development. He notes that at the heart of my work has always been the Methodist stress on sanctification, which I developed through a recovery of the virtues and, in particular, Aquinas's account of the virtues.[13] Stout even suggests that my emphasis on the virtues was the reason Notre Dame hired me to teach theological ethics.[14] In general I think Stout more or less approves of my work as long as I stuck to the virtues.

Things started to go wrong, however, as soon as I came under the influence of John Howard Yoder and Alasdair MacIntyre. Drawing on this unholy alliance, I combined Yoder's emphasis on the church/world distinction with MacIntyre's critique of liberal modernity to call Christians from their efforts to work for a more nearly just social order. As a result I have used the boundary between church and world to create "a rigid and static line between Christian virtue and liberal vice" (p. 154). I have been

---

13. Stout is certainly correct that my understanding of sanctification—and in particular, Aquinas's understanding of participation—has been at the heart of my work. For example, Aquinas observes that "no man has grace unless he be virtuous" (*Summa Theologica*, 2.2.47.14, trans. Fathers of the English Dominican Province [Westminster, Md.: Christian Classics, 1981]). That simple claim turns out to be anything but simple, but I believe when Christian theology denies or forgets what Thomas here maintains, we become something other than Christian. A. N. Williams has provided a wonderful account of Aquinas's understanding of participation in *The Ground of Union: Deification in Aquinas and Palamas* (New York: Oxford University Press, 1999).

14. I can understand how retrospectively Stout may think Notre Dame hired me because I was a Protestant saying Catholic things, but I do not think the considerations that led to my hiring at the time were that coherent.

able to do this because, following MacIntyre, I have failed to distinguish liberalism from democracy (p. 155). As a result I have shown insufficient attention to the demands for justice by minorities and women.[15]

I think Stout is wrong to think my worries about liberalism only began with MacIntyre's *After Virtue*. My first criticism of (certain) liberalism(s)—and I know of no better label to use—was the result of what I learned from Aristotle and, in particular, Aristotle's moral psychology. What I learned from Aristotle was reinforced by reading Wittgenstein as well as Anscombe's *Intention*. I became convinced that any attempt to recover the significance of the virtues required a moral psychology that displayed how our actions are constituted by our agency. It seemed to me at the time that most accounts of moral action, accounts I think that reflected a moral psychology thought necessary to sustain liberal regimes, made it almost impossible to recover Aristotle's understanding of activity. This is because most liberal theory, both political and ethical, depended on being able to separate action from the agent.[16] That separation, moreover, had everything to do with the liberal attempt to form a politics and ethics without memory. Rawls's "original position"

---

15. I have always tried to avoid the tiresome response to criticism that goes something like this: "If my critic had read X or Y that I have written, they would see I have already answered that criticism." I hate that response. Moreover, when you have written as much as I have, you have no right to ask anyone to read all of it. (Stout has read more of me than most and I am grateful for that. I also take delight in publishing in obscure places, which makes it difficult even for those who want to read what I have written.) I do feel bound, however, to call attention to my response to a book of essays done in my honor in England in which I respond to the complaint that I have not constructively engaged feminist thinkers. The book is *Faithfulness and Fortitude: In Conversation with the Theological Ethics of Stanley Hauerwas*, ed. Mark Thiessen Nation and Samuel Wells (Edinburgh: T & T Clark, 2000). My response is called "Where Would I Be without Friends?" I have also responded to Gloria Albrecht's critique in an essay called "Failure of Communication or A Case of Uncomprehending Feminism," *Scottish Journal of Theology* 20/2 (1997): 228–39. My problem with some forms of feminism has never been the just claims I believe women have made, but that too often the idiom of religious feminisms has been Protestant liberalism.

16. Stout gets this just right in his observations about Barth and the *Barmen Declaration*. He observes, "Christians must always be prepared to enter a broader discussion in which various words will be spoken. Their utterances in that domain should display the courage of their convictions. They must speak the truth as they see it, which means affirming Jesus Christ as the truth, and be ready to pay the price for saying what they believe. They should resist any form of pluralism or relativism that would be incompatible with the practice of making truth-claims or with their own commitment to this particular truth-claim" (p. 111). Stout criticizes secularists for rigging the rules in advance to exclude religious voices and Christians for treating the church as the only source of truth (p. 112). I certainly think Stout is right about secularists, but I cannot think of any Christians (at least any Christians before modernism shaped certain forms of Christianity) who thought the church is the only source of truth. The very use I make of Aristotle should indicate I do not think truth is only to be found in the church.

has seemed to me the perfect metaphor for the presumption that a morally defensible politics is possible without the people who make up that politics being virtuous.

This is not to say that liberalism cannot give some account of the virtues. In fact, attempts to show that liberalism is compatible with an emphasis on the virtues has over the last few years become something of a cottage industry.[17] The problem was not whether liberalism could give some account of the importance of the virtues but rather what virtues were recommended. I long ago suggested, for example, that one of the primary intellectual virtues for liberalism is cynicism. I thought such a virtue to be correlative of the demand for autonomy that assumes I must always be able to "step back" from my engagements.[18] What I "do" is, therefore, not "who I am." As a result my body is only secondarily "me" because my body is primarily something I use. To be habituated to be "free" in this sense makes it difficult for those so formed to recommend how they have learned to live to others. We each have to become the managers of our lives.

Stout thinks that my criticism of liberal theory for its failure to develop an account of the virtues, however, paid far too much attention to academic philosophers and failed to attend to the obvious virtues recommended in literary and popular contexts.[19] He is certainly correct that I did not and have not tried to incorporate figures like Emerson and Whitman into the account I have tried to give of "the way we live now," but I certainly knew and called attention to the fact that there were richer moral resources in American life than found expression in American ethical and political theory.[20] I also maintained, however,

17. There are numerous books that have been recently written that argue that liberalism is compatible with an emphasis on the virtues. See, for example, Peter Berkowitz, *Virtue and the Making of Modern Liberalism* (Princeton, N.J.: Princeton University Press, 1999). I think Berkowitz, however, is quite right to suggest that liberalism is the victim of its own success just to the extent that "liberal principles work to weaken the extraliberal or nongovernmental sources of virtue in liberal orders" (p. 174). Berkowitz's account of John Stuart Mill is quite interesting in this respect. According to Berkowitz, Mill saw that modern democracy promotes "a collective mediocrity but depends on excellence in its legislatures" so the "state has an interest in adopting special measures to insure the presence in government of the voice of the 'instructed minority' " (p. 165). In other words, Mill certainly saw the necessity of privileging cultural elites.

18. Under the influence of Stuart Hampshire's *Thought and Action* (New York: Viking, 1959), I used the metaphor of "stepping back" in *Character and the Christian Life*. But I soon realized that while the metaphor may be appropriate for certain engagements, the very idea of always being able to "step back" was a mistake.

19. Stout quite rightly refuses to identify democracy with the mythical "the people." Yet I wonder—and it is only a question—if Stout finally has a more optimistic view about people "working things out" than his admiration for Reinhold Niebuhr should allow.

20. I remain agnostic as to whether I need to appreciate Emerson for rethinking the moral possibilities found in the American tradition. I confess I have never really liked

that liberal practices often were parasitical on habits and institutions for which such practices could not account in liberal theory, and often the richer resources were destroyed by liberal practice. The having and rearing of children always seems to me a critical test case.

This is to say the following: I think Stout is mistaken that the work I have done on the virtues can be separated from my criticism of liberal political theory, ethics, and practice.[21] But what do I have to say to Stout's further claim that I let MacIntyre overdetermine my understanding of liberalism? Stout is certainly right that I am and continue to be indebted to MacIntyre's work, but my indebtedness began earlier than *After Virtue.* When I was a graduate student I had begun to read MacIntyre's work in the philosophy of action and the social sciences. MacIntyre helped me

---

Emerson, but having finished Robert Richardson's *Emerson: The Mind on Fire* (Berkeley: University of California Press, 1995), I have gained a grudging admiration for Emerson. Stanley Cavell says, "I don't imagine that anyone can have thought less well of Emerson's pretenses to philosophy than I did, coming to him after my immersion in Thoreau's *Walden.* I found Emerson's sentences preposterous in their self-inflation and in the evident vagueness with which they treated philosophical ideas. So I was floored when its idea started to dawn on me. There came a time, as with any text I feel I know, when every word seemed to have found its place." *Philosophical Passages: Wittgenstein, Emerson, Austin, Derrida* (Oxford, U.K.: Blackwell, 1995), pp. 98–99. I am afraid my attitude toward Emerson remains closer to Cavell's first impressions.

21. Nor can how I have thought about the virtues be separated from the account of rationality I have tried to develop in *With the Grain of the Universe: The Church's Witness and Natural Theology* (Grand Rapids: Brazos, 2001). I think Stout and I hold quite similar views of many of these issues. I at least know I found his account of "modest pragmatism" (p. 251) extremely interesting. His views, I think, are quite similar to those of William James. Indeed Stout seems to have done what I suggested (in *With the Grain of the Universe*) James had no reason to do on pragmatic grounds, that is, rule out of court strong Christian convictions such as those about the Trinity. I should like to think, moreover, the defense Stout provides, drawing on Emerson, Whitman, and Thoreau, of "inspired speech" as necessary to democratic pragmatism (p. 167), is not dissimilar to my argument in *With the Grain of the Universe* for the necessity of witness. I take Stout to be making a somewhat similar point when he calls attention to how Beckenbauer changed the standards of what it means to defend in soccer (p. 274). I quite appreciate Stout's primary conversation partners on these matters to be Robert Brandom and Bas C. van Frassen, but I would have been very interested to see what Stout makes of MacIntyre's notion of an "epistemological crisis" and whether MacIntyre's realism is more robust than Stout thinks defensible.

I am largely sympathetic with Stout's account of "common morality," but I am not sure I agree that "all moralities" are "about roughly the same topics" (p. 228). If description is everything, and if act and agency are constitutive of one another, then it is not at all clear to me that we can be confident about the "same topics." I am not denying some commonalities may be found, but you have to look. I would press this same set of issues in relation to Stout's thought experiment concerning the atheist who does the same act in two possible worlds with the only difference being that in one of the worlds God exists. I am not at all convinced that in such worlds we can be confident it would be the *same* act. Charles Pinches provides the best exploration of these questions in his *Theology and Action: After Theory in Christian Ethics* (Grand Rapids: Eerdmans, 2002).

see quite early the significance of Aristotle for contemporary political theory and practice, as well as how some aspects of Marx could be interpreted in the Aristotelian tradition. It is not surprising, therefore, that I was also deeply influenced by the work of political theorists such as C. B. Macpherson and Sheldon Wolin.

Few books have shaped how I think about politics more than Wolin's *Politics and Vision*. In particular Wolin's last chapter, "The Age of Organization and the Sublimation of Politics," convinced me that liberal political theory ironically too often legitimates the substitution of organizational manipulation for genuine politics.[22] Wolin taught me to read Rawls not as the exemplification of democracy, but rather as an attempt to deny the necessity of politics. I read Wolin, moreover, against the background of debates at Yale during my graduate training generated by the work of Robert Dahl. I became convinced that critics of Dahl's defense of interest-group liberalism—such as William Connolly, Robert Paul Wolff, Ted Lowi—were right to see that there is a "bias of pluralism."[23] When I read and began to understand Yoder, I thought I was beginning to see how the church could make a genuine contribution to American political life by being "itself," that is, a community that refuses to come to judgment without hearing the voice of the "weakest member."[24]

There is, of course, the question of whether the political arrangement we call America is liberal. Should we as Stout suggests quit talking about liberalism? I simply am not convinced that Stout is right to argue liberalism has lost all of its descriptive power. At the very least, if Stout is to make his case then he needs to argue against

22. Sheldon Wolin, *Politics and Vision: Continuity and Innovation in Western Political Thought* (Boston: Little, Brown, 1960), pp. 352–434.

23. William Connolly edited a book of essays called *The Bias of Pluralism* (New York: Atherton, 1969).

24. Yoder developed his case for democracy as the polity that has the time to hear from the weakest member in his essay "The Christian Case for Democracy," which appears in *The Priestly Kingdom: Social Ethics as Gospel* (Notre Dame, Ind.: University of Notre Dame Press, 2001), pp. 151–71. I have discovered I do have a vocation in life—I write "Forewords" and "Introductions" for books that bring to print Yoder's unpublished work or works about Yoder. This new edition of *The Priestly Kingdom* has one of those "Forewords." I am not complaining, but rather stating a fact.

That Yoder has been noticed by political theorists (well, at least by Rom Coles and Thomas Heilke) I think suggests that there are some interesting ways to explore Yoder's understanding of the politics of the church and those political theorists who are beginning to think of themselves as "radical democrats." I am thinking of political theorists like William Connolly and Peter Euben. I have found Peter Euben's *Corrupting Youth: Political Education, Democratic Culture, and Political Theory* (Princeton, N.J.: Princeton University Press, 1997) particularly interesting. I am happy to say that Coles and Euben are my colleagues.

C. B. Macpherson's contention that the "liberal-democratic society is a capitalist market society, and the latter by its very nature compels a continual net transfer of part of the power of some men to others, thus diminishing rather than maximizing the equal freedom to use and develop one's natural capacities which is claimed."[25] Stout suggests that I have more or less ignored the economic inequities in American society. But under the influence of Macpherson I have always assumed my criticisms of liberalism were criticisms of the dominance of capitalist modes of life.

Stout may well think this response is a day late and a dollar short. Why have I not said these things before? Well, I have. In particular I would call attention to my essays "Politics, Vision, and the Common Good," in *Vision and Virtue*, and "The Church and Liberal Democracy: The Moral Limits of a Secular Polity," in *A Community of Character*.[26] I realize these are very early essays. *Vision and Virtue* was originally published by Fides Press in 1974, but I do not think Yoder's or MacIntyre's influence has led me to reject the position I tried to work out there concerning how Christians should think about the social order we confront in America.[27] Particularly important is my claim that liberal social orders do not have the means to acknowledge

25. C. B. Macpherson, *Democratic Theory: Essays in Retrieval* (Oxford, U.K.: Clarendon, 1973), p. 10. I am aware that Macpherson's argument that Locke's self is the capitalist "possessive self" is disputed. I continue to think the case Macpherson made in *The Political Theory of Possessive Individualism: Hobbes to Locke* (Oxford, U.K.: Oxford University Press, 1962) is a good one, but I do not think the power of Macpherson's argument depends on showing that Locke assumed an incipient capitalist self. Whether Macpherson's historical case can be sustained is almost beside the point, given that he is surely right about the self that is assumed in modern political theory. The current dominance of rational choice methods in political science witnesses how politics in America has become both in theory and in practice dominated by economic models.

26. See my *Vision and Virtue: Essays in Christian Ethical Reflection* (Notre Dame, Ind.: University of Notre Dame Press, 1981), pp. 222–40; and *A Community of Character: Toward a Constructive Christian Social Ethic* (Notre Dame, Ind.: University of Notre Dame Press, 1981), pp. 72–88. More recently I have addressed economic issues in "Christian Schooling or Making Students Dysfunctional," in *Sanctify Them in the Truth: Holiness Exemplified* (Nashville: Abingdon, 1998), pp. 219–26.

27. I am grateful to Stout for making me return to some of my early work. I seldom refer back to what I have done in the past, but that may mean I forget what I need to say again in order to appropriately contextualize what I am now saying. By forcing me to think about what I once said, Stout helpfully makes me make connections that may help readers better understand what I have been trying to do. I do not mean to imply, however, that I always find myself in agreement with what I once thought. Often it is not a matter that this or that I once said I think is now outright wrong, though sometimes it is, but rather it's a question of emphasis. For those interested in an assessment of some of my past work, see the "Postscript: Twenty Years Later," in *The Peaceable Kingdom: A Primer in Christian Ethics* (London: SCM, 2003).

goods in common. Such goods in liberal theory are at best confused with common interest.

Stout praises my early criticism of Yoder for not considering that there are forms of justice open to unbelief that can have a positive relationship to the life of faith (p. 144). He suggests, however, I abandoned this commitment to justice—indeed justice "became a bad idea"—because I was overly influenced by Yoder's pacifism and MacIntyre's antiliberalism. Stout notes that I do say that Christians should not give up working for justice, but claims that I never say what I mean by that (p. 149). Stout, however, is just wrong that the increasing influence of Yoder and MacIntyre chastened my use of appeals to justice. How could that be if, as Stout observes, there is nothing in Yoder that would make Christians give up the language of justice (p. 149)?

It is extremely important to understand that Yoder understood that nonviolence requires the kind of conversation Stout associates with democracy. If you cannot kill those with whom you may disagree, it becomes all the more important to learn to listen to what they have to say. At times the commitment to nonviolence may mean you can only listen from a distance, but you still need to listen. Moreover, by listening you may well discover you have something to say in response.[28]

What I began to understand, however, is that abstract appeals to justice could underwrite social arrangements that are detrimental for the development of good people. For example, in a footnote in *A Community of Character* commenting on Macpherson, I observed that "many who seek to secure a more equitable distribution of goods in our society often fail to see that a 'justice' so secured may well only reinforce a more fundamentally unjust view of ourselves. The problem with American egalitarianism, as Michael Walzer has argued, is that egalitarians fail

---

28. I have tried to explore such an understanding of the politics of nonviolence in *Sanctify Them in the Truth*, in the chapter entitled "The Nonviolent Terrorist: In Defense of Christian Fanaticism." For the best account I know of how I have tried to think about these matters, see Mark Thiessen Nation, "On Following the 'Narrow Way' of Jesus Christ Today When 'Freedom', 'Justice', and 'A Christian Nation' Are Bad Ideas: Learnings from Stanley Hauerwas" in *Balanceren Op De Smalle Weg* (Uitgeverij, Netherlands: Boekencentrum-Zoetermeer, 2002), pp. 86–99. Nation rightly calls attention to a quotation from Will Willimon and me in *Resident Aliens* (Nashville: Abingdon, 1989) that I wish Stout might have noticed. We say, "Big words like 'peace' and 'justice,' slogans the church adopts under the presumption that even if people do not know what 'Jesus Christ is Lord' means, they will know what peace and justice mean, are words awaiting content. The church really does not know what these words mean apart from the life and death of Jesus of Nazareth. . . . It is Jesus' story that gives content to our faith, and teaches us to be suspicious of any political slogan that does not need God to make itself intelligible" (p. 38). Such a view does not mean, of course, that Christians cannot work with non-Christians to try to make our world less violent and more just.

to see that different goods should be distributed to different people for different reasons."[29]

There are also theological reasons I refrain from general appeals to justice. After Reinhold Niebuhr, liberal Protestants thought the way to be "politically responsible" was to leave talk about Jesus behind and instead talk about love and justice. So, the problem of something called "social ethics" became how to understand the relation between love, that is, disinterested regard for each person, and justice, dealing fairly with conditions of scarcity. Justice named the arrangements necessary to secure more equitable forms of life when love could not be achieved. At least one of the problems with putting the issue that way is that love and justice become abstractions divorced from concrete practices necessary for Christians and non-Christians alike to know what we mean when we say "justice." We should not be surprised such abstractions began to dominate ethical theory because that is exactly the result Niebuhr wanted. Good Barthian (and Yoderian) that I am, I had to resist those who thought that justice qua justice was more important than the justice God has shown us in the cross and resurrection of Jesus.

Connected to this theological problem were my continuing reflections on the virtues. As Stout well knows, in Aquinas the virtues are connected. I, therefore, resisted the attempt to make justice the overriding virtue if that meant that justice is intelligible separate from faith, hope, charity, and, in particular, patience. I acknowledge that justice is an extraordinarily important virtue for Aquinas. Indeed Aquinas makes a remark about justice he makes about no other virtue:

> A thing is said to be just, as having the rectitude of justice, when it is the term of an act of justice, *without taking into account the way in which it is done by the agent:* whereas in the other virtues nothing is declared to be right unless it is done in a certain way by the agent. For this reason

---

29. Hauerwas, *A Community of Character*, p. 249. I note that one of Stout's favorite political theorists, Michael Walzer, I have always read with interest. I have always found Walzer's commentary on American economy particularly helpful.

Stout praises what I have written on the mentally handicapped as well as my reflections on medicine and suffering (p. 157). I am gratified he finds what I have to say useful, but I wish he might also see that to talk about the mentally handicapped *is* one of the ways I learned to talk about justice without talking about justice. When people use the language of justice in the abstract in relation to the mentally handicapped, it turns out the mentally handicapped are judged not to have the characteristics to be treated justly. I deeply believe that due regard for the mentally handicapped is a question of justice, but I am also aware that I think that to be the case on theological grounds. For a defense of my refusal to separate appeals to justice from a substantive account of a "relatively thick notion of the good," see Fritz Oehlschlaeger, *Love and Good Reason: Postliberal Approaches to Christian Ethics and Literature* (Durham, N.C.: Duke University Press, 2003), pp. 251-70.

justice has its own special proper object over and above the other virtues, and this object is called the just, which is the same as *right*.[30]

With Aquinas I am quite prepared to acknowledge that justice can and should name appropriate actions that are correlative to social practices that should be done or not done irrespective of whether the agent is made virtuous by the doing of them. Aquinas's lengthy discussion of justice in the *Summa* is the direct result of his understanding of how justice differs from the other virtues. Accordingly, he had to specify the practices that make the language of justice work.[31] What has concerned me about liberal accounts of justice is their unwillingness to describe the practices that make the language of justice concrete. The ahistorical character Stout criticizes in much of liberal theory is exactly what has bothered me about appeals to justice qua justice. Put differently, liberal accounts of justice have tried to make justice an end in itself abstracted from the constitutive goods named through the practices necessary for the achievement of those goods.

I do not think justice is a "bad idea." (I am, however, unsure what it means to call justice an "idea.") I do not even think democracy is a "bad idea," though I am even less sure I know what I am talking about when I say "democracy" than when I say "justice." I hope, however, it is now clear that my worries about justice do not come from any sectarian withdrawal from the world. The call for the church to be the church is meant as a reminder that the church is in the world to serve the world. But such service is rendered less than it should be when the church no longer is able to maintain the politics of Jesus. As I hope is clear from *Performing the Faith*, neither Yoder nor I have assumed the boundary between church and world is impermeable.[32] Not only is it permeable,

30. Aquinas, *Summa Theologica*, 2.2.57, 1. The first emphasis is my addition.

31. I do not think, however, that Aquinas thought that justice could become an independent virtue separate from the other virtues. For some aspects of life he clearly thought you could specify actions that were just or unjust without the necessity of those acting justly becoming just in the doing of justice. But given his understanding of the interconnection of the virtues, he could not have thought a person could be just without being, for example, courageous, much less without charity.

32. Stout fails to see, or at least there is nothing in his text that indicates he understands, the significance of Yoder's (and my) insistence that the difference between church and world is a difference about agents. See Yoder's *Christian Witness to the State* (Scottdale, Pa.: Herald Press, 2003; originally published by the Institute of Mennonite Studies in Newton, Kansas, in 1964), pp. 28–32. That the difference between church and world is a difference in agency is why Yoder insists this is a "duality without dualism," with the further implication that the duality can only be displayed historically, that is, the grounds of the duality constantly require discernment. Such discernment is made possible by the practices of the church acquired by faithful performance.

but something has gone wrong when the church is not learning from the world how to live faithfully to God.[33]

I appreciate that Stout has read and taken the time to criticize my work, but I also need to say that I have not written for Stout. My criticism of liberalism is not even directed at liberals. (But one of the confusing issues is that prominent "liberals"—e.g., John Locke, Ralph Waldo Emerson, and Reinhold Niebuhr—have claimed to be Christians or at least have been associated with Christianity.) Indeed I think liberals are doing about the best they can with what they have. My ire is not against liberalism, but against Christians who have confused Christianity with liberalism. As a result Christians have little to offer to a world dying for examples. Stout observes that church councils became a resource for Christians to develop a more collegial exercise of authority in the church and that Protestant radicals helped move England toward a more egalitarian society (pp. 204–5).[34] All I have tried to do is remind Christians that few things are more important than how we learn to govern our relations to one another as a people constituted by the worship of God. What, for instance, could be more important for the world than Christians refusing to kill one another? Of course that is only a start, but you have to begin somewhere.

3. ON MACINTYRE AND YODER

The most interesting criticism Stout makes of me, I think, is his suggestion I cannot have Yoder and MacIntyre too. He says, "One cannot stand in a church conceived in Yoder's terms, while describing the world surrounding it in the way MacIntyre describes liberal society, without implicitly adopting a stance that is rigidly dualistic in the same respects that rightly worried Hauerwas in 1974" (p. 149). What I find interesting

33. I wonder what Stout makes of sentences like these from *The Peaceable Kingdom* (Notre Dame, Ind.: University of Notre Dame Press, 1983), a book written long after I had "gone bad," in which I say: "The church can never abandon the world to the hopelessness deriving from its rejection of God, but must be a people with a hope sufficiently fervid to sustain the world as well as itself. That is why as Christians not only do we find that people who are not Christian manifest God's peace better than we ourselves, but we must demand they exist. It is to be hoped that such people may provide the conditions for our ability to cooperate with others for securing justice in the world" (p. 101).

I wish those who constantly accuse me of "sectarianism" might from time to time ask themselves why they are so angry about what I say. If I have "withdrawn" from "public" debates surely I am not worth the time they spend in attacking me.

34. I have long thought A. D. Lindsay's *The Modern Democratic State* (New York: Galaxy, 1962) is one of the more important books for helping us understand how the experience of the Puritan congregations was more important for the actual political process in England than Hobbes or Locke.

is not that such a move (whether "I intend it or not") is "rigidly dualistic," but whether there is not a deeper tension between Yoder and MacIntyre than Stout names. I worry that the kind of grand narrative MacIntyre develops, particularly a grand narrative that is a narrative of declension, entails assumptions about history that betray the eschatological character of the gospel.

Stout observes that in responding to those who charge me with sectarianism, I say almost nothing about my debt to MacIntyre. As Stout puts it:

> If Yoder's outlook, taken separately, were the real issue, then the critics would have been writing mainly about him, and Hauerwas would be viewed as a relatively minor figure—a herald preparing the way for the master. But in fact it is Hauerwas's amalgam of themes from Yoder and MacIntyre that generates the controversy. It is therefore crucial to determine what MacIntyre adds to the mix. (P. 148)

I am not a modest person, but I do think I am a minor figure compared to Yoder. Indeed I have said so several times.[35] More important, however, I think the very notions of "major" or "minor" betray what I have learned from Yoder (and Barth). That lesson is quite simply that theologians are not "thinkers." We betray the very gospel we are to serve if we have "positions" that become substitutes for what the church is about. Put in Catholic terms that Yoder would not have liked (though John often said his only problem with bishops is that they did and do not act like bishops), the bishop remains the theological heart of the church. That is why theologians are subordinate to the bishop and should be disciplined by the bishop if our work threatens the unity and holiness of the church.[36]

Contrary to Stout, MacIntyre's influence on me has not pushed me toward "sectarianism." The problem is just the opposite. My use of MacIntyre threatens to make me Constantinian. The grand narrative that MacIntyre develops is, as Stout denotes, at least in the ballpark of

---

35. See, for example, my "Foreword" to Craig Carter's *The Politics of the Cross: The Theology and Social Ethics of John Howard Yoder* (Grand Rapids: Brazos, 2001), pp. 9–11; and my "Introduction" to *Patient Conversation as (the) Christian Practice (of Peace): The Theological Legacy of John Howard Yoder*, ed. Gayle Gerber Koontz and Ben Ollenburger (Philadelphia: Cascadia, 2003). Koontz and Ollenburger's book contains invaluable essays on Yoder from the Believer's Church Conference at Notre Dame (2002), which was dedicated to Yoder's work. Several of the essays explore the similarities and differences between Yoder and me. I confess I remain a bemused spectator when such comparisons are made.

36. This sentence of course betrays one of the besetting problems of my work—namely my ambiguous ecclesial position. My best attempt to be as coherent as I can be is my book *In Good Company: The Church as Polis* (Notre Dame, Ind.: University of Notre Dame Press, 1995).

Hegel.[37] That it is so I do not take to be a criticism. Moreover MacIntyre is clearly not Hegelian (at least the Hegel that is alleged to assume the dialectic ended with himself) just to the extent he argues, following the form of the *Summa,* another objection can always be made. Yet MacIntyre's work can be interpreted as Constantinian if in fact he is committed to the view that our history suffered a decisive declension. Declension narratives can imply that at one time Christians got it right but then "something happened" and as a result Christians lost control of their world.

Yet I am not convinced that MacIntyre, even in *After Virtue,* implies that "what happened" suggests that history, or even his account of our history, has suffered such a disaster. To be sure, he thinks that we have diminished intellectual resources to sustain the practices necessary for forming virtuous lives, but he does not think that those who live after the Enlightenment are devoid of virtue. Our problem is we lack the ability to articulate the resources that make it possible for us to live morally worthy lives.

So I do not think there is an inherent contradiction between Mac-Intyre's account of tradition qua tradition and Yoder's understanding of the church/world dialectic.[38] MacIntyre's understanding of the contingent character of rationality means he, like Yoder, assumes that how we tell the story of our lives and the life of our communities is always open to challenge and the necessity of retrospective renarrations. MacIntyre's account of our history may appear to mimic the grand narratives correlative to Constantinian presumptions, that is, to give us the illusion we are in control. But MacIntyre, like Yoder, knows that we are not "in control" of our own lives, much less in control of history.[39]

Yoder, however, does not only think historically, but he thinks of history apocalyptically. I have tried to follow Yoder's lead, but that I have done so may make me even more problematic from Stout's perspective. For example, Stout complains that postmodernism is apocalyptic in tone, forcing a choice between the radically new or nostalgic

37. I do not know if Stout is right to suggest that MacIntyre has failed to acknowledge his debt to Hegel. I do know that I remember MacIntyre discussing Hegel in many of his essays. According to Stout, I also am remiss in not acknowledging Hegel's influence. I read Hegel, or at least the *Phenomenology,* years ago. I have also read Charles Taylor on Hegel. However I have no idea how I may or may not have been influenced by Hegel. I am happy to report I shall soon teach the *Phenomenology* for the first time.

38. Greg Jones has made the interesting observation that I seldom discuss Yoder and MacIntyre in the same essay or chapter of a book. This may indicate a failure to integrate them into a common project. Jones notes that such an integration is best found in *With the Grain of the Universe.*

39. I am indebted to Alex Sider for helping me make these connections.

traditionalism (p. 289).[40] I take it from this comment that Stout does not have a favorable account of apocalyptic. But the way I have tried to do theology, the way Yoder (and Barth) has taught me to think, is from beginning to end apocalyptic. Doug Harink has illumined what it means to think apocalyptically by reading Yoder's and my work through Pauline theology and in my case through Paul's letter to the Galatians. According to Harink, Paul is a determinatively apocalyptic thinker because Paul

> sees in Christ nothing less than the whole of creation and all of humanity under God's final judgment. There is something profoundly illiberal and intolerant about Galatians in this reading. Paul is uncompromisingly focused on a single, incomparable, final, and exclusive theological reality which constitutes, includes, and determines all other reality: Jesus Christ.[41]

This apocalyptic perspective I think helps illumine how I have tried to use MacIntyre to help and defend Yoder's perspective. First and foremost from an apocalyptic perspective, as far as the church is concerned one time is just that, another time. The challenge before the church is always the same challenge to be faithful to God's apocalyptic redemption. Ironically, such an apocalyptic view means movements and figures so often self-identified or described as apocalyptic—that is, those that claim that the "crisis" is imminent and that we must cease all normal activity—betray the apocalyptic character of the gospel. The apocalyptic character of what Christians believe has happened in Christ, which means that Christians must carry on with the small acts of kindness and mercy that are made

40. Stout observes that is the kind of choice MacIntyre presents in his chapter in *After Virtue:* "Nietzsche or Aristotle?" I am not sure Stout is right about MacIntyre in this respect. As David McCarthy pointed out to me, you have to take the question mark seriously. Surely on MacIntyre's grounds you never have a clear choice between Nietzsche or Aristotle. Of course such a comment is but an indication of the difficulty that has always confronted MacIntyre. That difficulty is not unlike the challenge before Wittgenstein in the *Tractatus.* The very terms of the analysis can betray your argument. For example, you probably only discover the importance of tradition when yours is no longer in good working order. It is never a question of tradition qua tradition, but what kind of tradition. MacIntyre confronts the same problem with the title, *After Virtue.* MacIntyre is well aware that some virtues have to exist even in liberal societies, so it is never a question of being devoid of resources for reclaiming some account of the virtues. So the "after" does not mean that some virtues are not still present, but that we no longer have the philosophical means to articulate their importance. I must admit I find rather funny Stout's suggestion that MacIntyre's as well as my own favorable appeal to figures that clearly are "modern" contradicts our criticism of modernity. Trollope as well as the novel itself only make sense as a modern form in which Trollope excelled.

41. Douglas Harink, *Paul among the Postliberals: Pauline Theology beyond Christendom and Modernity* (Grand Rapids: Brazos, 2003), p. 81. For Harink's more developed account of apocalyptic, see pp. 68–69.

possible by our conviction that God has redeemed the world.[42] Such a conviction is the background of my oft-made claim that Christians are called to nonviolence not because we think nonviolence is a strategy to rid the world of war, but rather in a world of war, as faithful followers of Christ, we cannot imagine being anything other than nonviolent.

In a letter to Doug Harink praising Harink's account of my work, Rusty Reno makes a criticism of me that I think is much closer to the mark than Stout's worries. Reno observes:

> I think Stanley's work is overdetermined by a reaction against "American-ism." This leads to distortions in his analysis of the present age. For example, you accurately report that he thinks that American Christians treat American liberal democracy as the One Great Thing for which they will die (as soldiers?). This strikes me as false. Most Americans have no particular thoughts about liberal democracy. Their loyalties are more primitive and atavistic (and more typical of the human condition for centuries). Currently, most "support the troops" out of the same patriotism that makes the ordinary Iraqi resent the occupation of his country by U.S. forces, regardless of his views about the Baathist party. Sometimes I think Hauerwas is overwrought by a fear of the attractions of American power and wealth—as if our society were unique and sui generis. This gives America and Americans too much credit. Though I am not a pacifist, I agree with Hauerwas that the church is a counter-cultural form of life. Yet I think this should give one a measure of freedom from contemporary American life, both a freedom from an undue love, but also a freedom from an undue fear.[43]

42. See, for example, my chapter "Taking Time for Peace: The Ethical Significance of the Trivial," in *Christian Existence Today: Essays on Church, World, and Living in Between* (Grand Rapids: Brazos, 2001), pp. 253–66. *Christian Existence Today* was originally published in 1988. In a recent essay Leszek Kolakowski observes the problem that what Christians have to say, our traditional teachings, has become "incomprehensible" for contemporary people. "There is no ground for the opinion that we have suddenly become dumb, that something that was understandable for the people of the Middle Ages has become inaccessible for us. What matters most is simply the distance between the daily life of our experience and the inherited theological idiom." "God in a Godless Time," *First Things* 134 (June/July 2003): 17. I believe Kolakowski's remark is just right. I should like to think everything I have tried to do is an attempt to respond to that challenge.

43. I am extremely grateful to Professor Reno for allowing me to reproduce these comments. Let me say that Rusty has earned any views he has of my work, having written a very good article on my work for the *Blackwell Companion to Political Theology* (Oxford, U.K.: Blackwell, forthcoming). I think I agree with most of what Rusty says about me, but I remain unconvinced he is right to suggest most Americans have no thoughts about liberal democracy. The problem is not "thoughts," but clichés such as "everyone has a right to their own opinion," which are then used to say why the terrorists hate us is because of our "freedom." I am also a bit suspicious about general appeals to "human nature." Reno does qualify his appeal to human nature by "for centuries," but I am not sure if that is adequate. Any account of "human nature" requires concrete display. For example, I think

When I said in *A Better Hope*[44] that I wanted to write a more positive book, I was trying to avoid what Reno says I have not avoided in most of my work. Yet ironically, at least ironically from Stout's point of view, my use of MacIntyre has been my attempt to resist the tendency to make the character of "American liberalism" assume more importance than it should. The insistence that the distinction between church and world is required by an apocalyptic eschatology can too easily take the form of a complete rejection of "the world." My use of MacIntyre (as well as Wolin and Macpherson) has been my attempt to develop immanent critiques commensurate with the way Christians have discovered God would have us live in that politics we call church.[45] In this respect I see nothing that prohibits Christians from using anything they find helpful—such as the kind of democratic conversation Stout desires—to engage in the work of living in a more peaceable and just society.[46]

---

it possible to say that because of our sinful condition you can presume most of us will be greedy, but such an observation is not very helpful if we are to diagnose our current situation. Humans may usually be greedy, but I believe that capitalist orders make greed a duty. So greed assumes a quite different form in a table of the vices in our time than in the past.

44. Stanley Hauerwas, *A Better Hope: Resources for a Church Confronting Capitalism, Democracy, and Postmodernity* (Grand Rapids: Brazos, 2000), p. 9.

45. I share Barth's (and Yoder's) assumption that the governing authorities have been redeemed. Accordingly I try to avoid all the Lutheran dualisms. For example, Barth argued that had Pilate taken himself absolutely seriously as a representative of the state, he would not have condemned Jesus to death. Barth observes, "we cannot say that the legal administration of the State 'has nothing to do with the order of Redemption'; that here we have been moving in the realm of the first and not of the second article of the Creed. No, Pontius Pilate now belongs not only to the Creed but to its second article in particular." Karl Barth, *Community, State, and Church* (New York: Anchor, 1960), p. 114. This conviction is what grounds Barth's attempt to develop analogies, quite arbitrary analogies, between Christian doctrine and the form of the governing authorities. Yoder may be understood as differing from Barth in this respect by concentrating not on doctrine, but on the life and practices of the church for providing resources for constructive Christian witness for political life beyond the church. See, for example, Yoder's *The Christian Witness to the State*. Also soon to appear from Herald Press is Yoder's important and earlier work in German, *Discipleship as Political Responsibility*. I have written a brief "Foreword" to this important early essay that I think helps us understand better what Yoder was about.

46. Jeff Stout was kind enough to send me *Democracy and Tradition* in manuscript. On first reading I called Jeff asking where I could possibly find his account of democracy materially instantiated. He replied I could find his democracy instantiated in the same place you could find my account of the church—a clever response, but one that I think may be a bit misleading. The very existence of the church makes her internal critique possible. I am not convinced that the logic of the kind of democracy Stout desires can work in the same way. That said, I am more than happy to work to make the kind of modest state (p. 40) Stout wants a reality. I do think, however, that Stout needs to tell us a good deal more about what he means by a "civic nation" (p. 297) and how that "nation" is or is not related to the modern nation-state. I believe Stout and I share many similar worries about the latter. For example, I think he is right to suggest that social contract

I do not find the language of Constantinianism helpful for exploration of the Christian commitment to seek the peace of the city in which we find ourselves. I do think Constantinianism names a temptation that besets Christians. That temptation is to make ourselves at home in the world by using alien power to make ourselves safe. So to be at home betrays the apocalyptic character of the faith. But I think anyone will search in vain to find in my work the attempt to pinpoint a moment that constitutes the "fall of the church." Yoder never assumed that even in the most compromised forms of Christianity there were not faithful people developing faithful ways of being in the world.[47] My use of MacIntyre has been my attempt to serve my neighbor both in and out of the church by saying what I take to be true given what I have learned from the church.

For example, I think MacIntyre's historicized account of rationality to be at the very heart of how Christians must think about the way we must think. For me the fundamental problem with liberalism, and I suppose by liberalism I mean primarily liberal theory, has been the attempt to suppress memory in the interest of eliminating conflict. Yet I believe it impossible not to be what we were made to be, whether we are Christian or not, which means we cannot live without memory. Indeed I think there is a kind of "natural law" effect—that is, there will be negative results—when people attempt to suppress the wrongs of the past in the interest of cooperation.[48] I do believe, after all, that the cross is the grain of the universe.

But finally what about "pacifism"?[49] Stout suggests the core of my anti-Constantinianism is my commitment to "absolute pacifism" (p. 158). He notes my pacifism is justified on biblical grounds as a vocation of discipleship to Christ. That is not quite right, because I do not use the language of

---

theories in their practical expression become a form of control (p. 81). This makes me all the more puzzled by Stout's worries about my criticisms of democracy because those criticisms are directed as his are to the nation-state that we both believe is anything but "democratic." For example, I have distanced myself (just as Stout says we must) from the communitarians who believe the subject of that description can be the nation-state. See my "Communitarians and Medical Ethicists: Or, Why I Am None of the Above," in *Dispatches from the Front: Theological Engagements with the Secular* (Durham, N.C.: Duke University Press, 1994), pp. 156–63.

47. Particularly important is Yoder's *Preface to Theology: Christology and Theological Method*, ed. with an "Introduction" by Stanley Hauerwas and Alex Sider (Grand Rapids: Brazos, 2002). See also the important articles by Alex Sider, "Constantinianism before and after Nicea: Issues in Restitutionist Historiography," and Gerald Schlabach, "The Christian Witness in the Earthly City: John H. Yoder as Augustinian Interlocutor," in *Patient Conversation as (the) Christian Practice (of Peace)*.

48. See, for example, my chapter "Why Time Cannot and Should Not Heal the Wounds of History, But Time Has Been and Can Be Redeemed," in *A Better Hope*, pp. 139–54.

49. This is obviously one of the points of disagreement between MacIntyre and me. It is moreover a disagreement that goes all the way down. As I try to argue in "The Nonviolent Terrorist: In Defense of Christian Fanaticism," in *Sanctify Them in the Truth*

vocation, but it is close enough.[50] What is important, however, is to see that christological pacifism is not adequately understood as "absolute." "Absolute" suggests something more like a position rather than an ongoing way of life of a people dedicated to the worship of God. I hope what I have written about pacifism in the past makes clear I do not think nonviolence is a position that can be justified apart from discipleship; but if not, hopefully the chapters in *Performing the Faith* will throw some light on the kind of nonviolence I am willing to defend. At the very least these essays should make clear I do not believe pacifists are any less implicated in the violence that grips our lives than those who believe that violence is a "necessary evil."

If, as Stout suggests, I have not made clear the demands that pacifism entails, that is because I think we can never anticipate what we will be called on to be or do because we have disavowed the use of violence. I am not sure what to make of Stout's criticism that I do not recommend that people join Pax Christi or World Peacemakers. I would, if asked. I am a member of the Baptist Peace Fellowship, the Catholic Peace Fellowship, and the Ekklesia Project.[51] Those in the Ekklesia Project are committed to having our lives challenged by each other to discover ways we may not be living appropriately to our commitments. Stout is not a member of the Ekklesia Project, but I think I must be open to his suggestion that I may read the Bible selectively. He may, moreover, be right that I do not live as if I believe that wealth is a problem. I certainly

---

(pp. 177–90), MacIntyre's position commits him to the necessity of war. War is necessary when peoples share so little that they cannot put one another into an epistemological crisis. Charlie Pinches and I tried to explore whether MacIntyre's account of the virtues presupposes an agonistic mode of life in "The Renewal of Virtue and the Peace of Christ," in *Christians among the Virtues*, pp. 55–69. I remain unclear whether MacIntyre's account of the virtues explains the significance of Aquinas's claim that charity is the form of the virtues.

50. I suspect Stout picks up the language of "vocation" from Scott Davis's account of Yoder in his book *Warcraft and the Fragility of Virtue: An Essay in Aristotelian Ethics* (Moscow: University of Idaho Press, 1992), pp. 27–52. Davis's account of Yoder's nonviolence remains one of the best we have, but his use of the language of vocation to describe Yoder's overall position derives more from Davis's presuppositions than Yoder's own self-understanding.

51. Information about the Ekklesia Project can be found at www.ekklesiaproject.org. I have written a pamphlet with Mike Budde called "The Ekklesia Project: A School for Subversive Friendships," which tries to describe what has led some of us to be part of the project. A copy can be obtained from Wipf and Stock Publishers in Eugene, Oregon.

I confess I am not sure what to make of Stout's pleasant surprise that I participated in a panel about the impending war against Iraq in Washington, D.C. I have never thought my theological commitments required me not to be "public." Given my arguments against the sequestering of theological claims, I have thought it my duty as an advocate of nonviolence to accept opportunities to speak when asked in any context. I would like to think this might give pause to those who accuse me of "withdrawing," but if the past is any indication I am sure that will not be the case.

believe, as Dorothy Day argued, that there is a close connection between poverty and pacifism.[52] At the very least that means as a full professor at a major American university, I can never assume that my life may not underwrite forms of violence that put my salvation in jeopardy.

Stout may be right about me, but I do not think he is right about the unpersuasive character of Yoder's "biblical scholarship" (p. 323). Stout makes this assessment of Yoder in a footnote that calls attention to the portrayal of Yahweh in the Old Testament, who seems to fight on behalf of his people. It is not clear to me if this is the biblical evidence with which Stout thinks Yoder has not adequately dealt. Stout does not credit Yoder's refusal to make the supersessionist moves that would have shown that "God becomes nonviolent" only in the cross. Indeed that is one of the reasons Yoder's reading of Scripture has become so interesting for Jews. Here is a Christian who believes the Jews have more nearly lived the way God meant for all of us to live through the cross and resurrection of Christ.[53] At the very least Stout owes us a much fuller account why he thinks Yoder's "biblical scholarship" is so deficient.[54]

I am an eclectic thinker. My work is not self-generated, but I find out what I think by thinking with others. Stout suggests I lack "interpretative charity" (p. 157), particularly toward those with whom I disagree. I am sure I sometimes use the term "liberal" in a dismissive way, but I usually do so in a context in which I hope it is clear I am not pretending to provide a close analysis of, for example, Rawls or Nozick. Moreover, when I so use a term like "liberal," I do so because I have in other places taken the time to analyze the work of a Rawls or a Reinhold Niebuhr. I write for quite different audiences, which means, particularly when I am writing for Christians who do not have the disadvantage of being associated with the university, I make generalizations that in other contexts might need qualification. However, I do not pretend that I have gotten it all right, but I am sure what I have learned from MacIntyre and Yoder has made what I have to say closer to being right than I could have ever hoped without them.

4. ON BEGGING AND DOROTHY DAY

In his discussion of rights-talk, a discussion which I think is filled with good sense, Stout makes an offhand observation that I think is extremely important. He underwrites Annette Baier's observation that modern rights-

52. Dorothy Day, "Poverty and Pacifism," *The Catholic Worker* (May 2003), p. 1.

53. See Yoder's *The Jewish Christian Schism Revisited*, edited by Michael Cartwright and Peter Ochs (Grand Rapids: Eerdmans, 2003).

54. For example, Stout makes no reference to Richard Hays's extremely appreciative account of Yoder's "biblical scholarship" in *The Moral Vision of the New Testament* (San Francisco: Harper, 1996), pp. 239–53.

talk should be associated with "an unwillingness to beg" (p. 205). If that is the case, then I think it to be the locus of the most profound disagreement between what I think Christians believe and what Stout wants. Christians think we are creatures that beg. Prayer is the activity that most defines who we are. Through prayer we learn the patience to take the time to beg, to beg to the One alone who is the worthy subject of such prayer. Through prayer Christians learn how to beg from each other. Christians, therefore, can never be at peace with a politics or economic arrangements built on the assumption that we are fundamentally not beggars.[55]

Begging is, moreover, the heart of Dorothy Day's understanding of the work of the Catholic Worker. The Worker lives by begging in order to help those that have no choice but to beg. As a result a politics and economy are created that help us see that there are alternatives to our feverish desire to live as if we are not beggars. That the Worker is so constituted no doubt helps explain why Dorothy Day saw no tension between what might be thought to be her quite conservative Catholic piety and theology and her radical politics. I should like to think I have in some small ways tried to say in my work what Dorothy Day lived. If that means that the limits of my own life are exposed, so be it. Better to have the limits of my life exposed than to say what I know is less than the truth.[56]

---

55. I am indebted to Kelly Johnson of the University of Dayton for her extraordinary reflections on these matters in her dissertation, "Beggars and Stewards: The Contest of Humility in Christian Economic Ethics" (Ph.D. diss., Duke University, 2001). I am happy to say that a revised version of this dissertation will soon be published by the University of Notre Dame Press as the inaugural volume in the Scholarly Book Series of the Ekklesia Project. Dan Bell's *Liberation Theology after the End of History: The Refusal to Cease Suffering* (London: Routledge, 2001) is also an extremely important critique of capitalist formations. I hope in the future I will be judged not only on what I have written but also on what my students have written.

56. I am in debt to Peter Dula, Jonathan Tran, and Charlie Collier for their critical reactions to this "Postscript." Alex Sider was particularly helpful by forcing me to rethink some of my initial modes of response.

After I had written this postscript, I read Russell Hittinger's chapter on Christopher Dawson in Hittinger's, *The First Grace: Rediscovering the Natural in a Post-Christian World* (Wilmington, Del.: ISI Books, 2003), pp. 243–64. According to Hittinger, Dawson did *not* think liberalism was a theory of democracy because liberals feared the leveling effects of democratic egalitarianism. Nor did Dawson equate liberalism with Enlightenment rationalism because such rationalism threatened spontaneous genius. From Dawson's perspective John Stuart Mill articulated the central tenet of liberalism, that is, the need of civilization for people capable of discovering new truths and who are also able to show when what were once truths are no longer. Such people must also be capable to begin new practices and set examples of more enlightened conduct and better taste for human life. So if Dawson is right, Emerson and Mill share much in common. Even though I think liberals often do claim what Dawson says they disavow, he is right to argue further that liberalism is incapable of sustaining itself or a cultural project because the commitment to individual liberty cannot resist the rise of technology that it necessarily fosters.

INDEX